THE COMPANY OF TREES

THE COMPANY OF TREES

A Year in a Lifetime's Quest

THOMAS PAKENHAM

WEIDENFELD & NICOLSON

First published in Great Britain in 2015
by Weidenfeld & Nicolson

1 3 5 7 9 10 8 6 4 2

A CIP catalogue record for this book
is available from the British Library.

HB ISBN-13   978 0 297 866624 4

Printed in Italy
Map on p.vii by Hemesh Alles

Weidenfeld & Nicolson

The Orion Publishing Group Ltd
Carmelite House
50 Victoria Embankment
London, EC4Y 0DZ
An Hachette UK Company
www.orionbooks.co.uk

CONTENTS

Map   vii

Introduction   1

1   Two White Goddesses (15 December 2012-1 January 2013)   7

2   A Tour of the Demesne (2 January)   17

3   Murdering Your Friends (4 January)   23

4   Monkeys' Despair (8 January-1 February)   31

5   Plagues from the East (6-27 February)   41

6   Knicker-Pink (18 March-15 April)   49

7   Sharawadgi (30 April)   63

8   To the Rescue (1 May)   73

9   Pity the Poor Sycamore (10 May)   85

10   Lost Horizon (20 June)   93

11   How Old Is an Old Yew? (1-16 July)   105

12   Flames at My Heels (21 July-14 August)   117

13   Lake of the Oaks (10 September)   127

14   Dancing at Knockeyon (11 September)   137

15   On the Track of the Green Man (12 September-10 October)   145

16   'But Where Is His Lordship?' (10 October)   155

17   Coolattin: the Forlorn Hope (15 October)   165

18   Fireworks (31 October-5 November)   173

19   The Trees That Lost Their Heads (8 November)   181

20   Hunting for Dr Falconer's Rhodo (25 November-25 December)   189

21   Epilogue (15 February 2014)   197

List of chapter illustrations   201

Bibliography   202

Index   206

For my ten remarkable grandchildren
and the ten remarkable trees planted in their honour

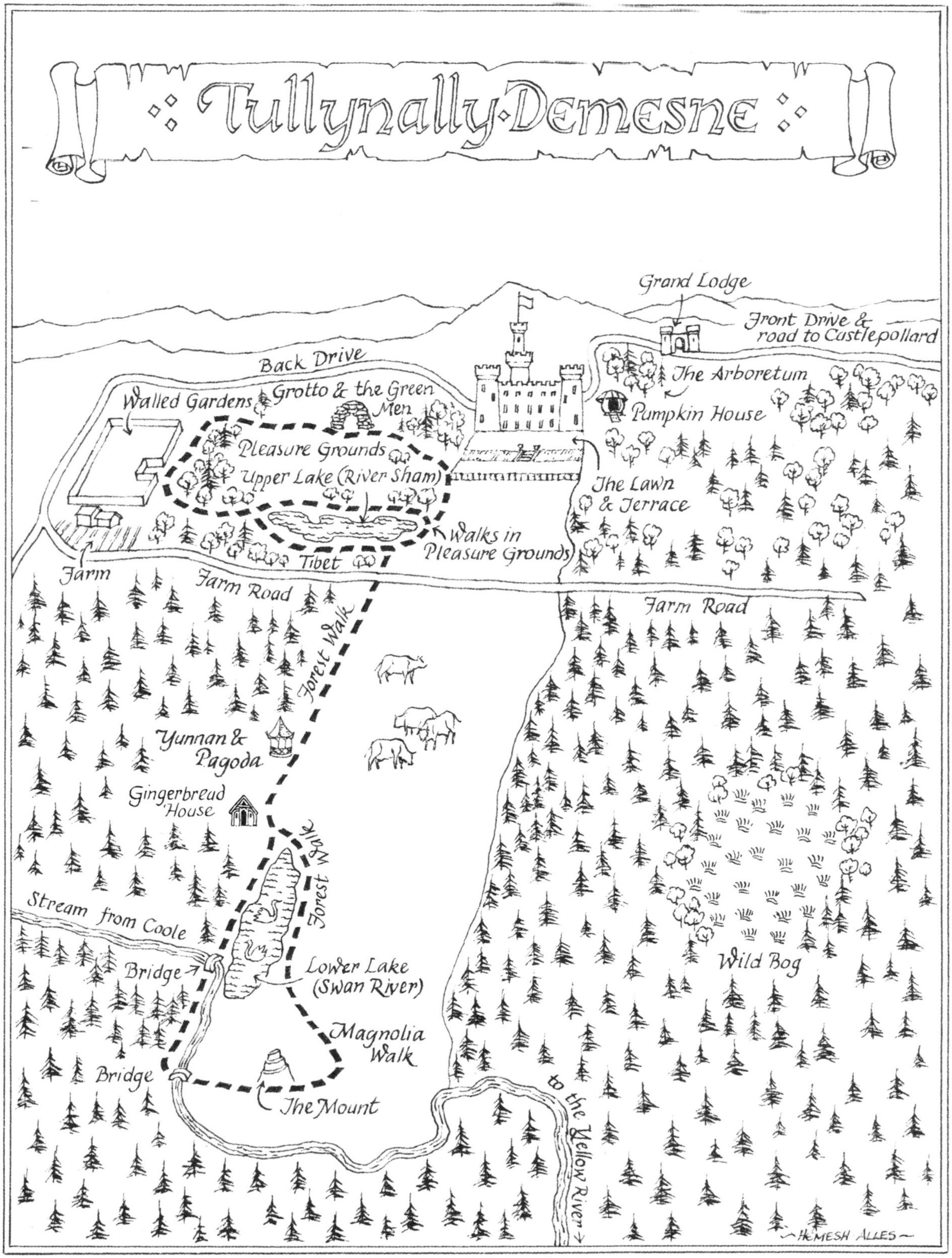

Tullynally Demesne

Grand Lodge

Front Drive & road to Castlepollard

Back Drive

The Arboretum

Walled Gardens

Grotto & the Green Men

Pumpkin House

Pleasure Grounds

Upper Lake (River Sham)

The Lawn & Terrace

Tibet

Walks in Pleasure Grounds

Farm

Farm Road

Farm Road

Forest Walk

Yunnan & Pagoda

Gingerbread House

Forest Walk

Wild Bog

Stream from Coole

Bridge

Lower Lake (Swan River)

Magnolia Walk

Bridge

The Mount

to the Yellow River

~ HeMESH ALLES ~

INTRODUCTION

I have been remarkably fortunate. I developed a passion for trees and the trees responded. At any rate, most of my trees seem happy where I planted them. Many will, I fondly believe, outlive the youngest of my grandchildren. And, unless they fall victim to global warming (which, sad to say, is quite possible), these trees will give comfort and pleasure to children yet unborn.

To tell this story I have used the framework of one year at Tullynally, our family estate in Ireland. I chose the year 2013 more or less at random. It was a year of unusually fine weather, but we had our ration of disasters: storms from the Atlantic, plagues from the East, flames from the bog. There were lessons to be learnt and opportunities, too.

Why did I develop this passion for trees? Like most sensible people I find them irresistible. And in my case I believe that the roots of my passion for trees lie deep in my childhood. My sister Antonia and I were 'Irish twins': we were born within eleven and a half months of each other. In 1936, when I was three, the centre of our world was a large, airy nursery on the upper floor of a large, plain house at Rose Hill, in the unfashionable suburbs of south Oxford. Our garden was somewhat bleak. The house, appropriately, was called Singletree.

For most of the day, our lives were ruled by Jean, our young and energetic nurse. But at six o'clock, if we were lucky, we would be brought down, in pyjamas and dressing gowns, to meet our mother in the drawing room. Here she would be seated, shining like a goddess, ready to read us a book of our choice. And we would sit, dazzled by this privilege, snuggling up on either side of her on the green sofa. My favourite book was called *The Wood That Came Back*.

When my younger daughter Eliza was three, she explained what made a good children's story: 'Make it horrible, Daddy, with a happy ending.' I suppose most of the stories our mother read to Antonia and me followed the same formula - especially *The Wood That Came Back*. It was written and illustrated (I later discovered) by an accomplished British artist called Clare Leighton. The theme would be topical today but, I now realise, had a special resonance at Singletree.

A married couple buy a site to build a house. But the site is already occupied by a clump of beech trees, and a community of squirrels, rabbits, foxes, jackdaws and other birds. The husband, in plus fours, cuts down the trees with an axe, one by one. The animals and birds are driven away, and a new house is built where the trees once stood. But the foolish couple have left the stumps intact. Imperceptibly the trees re-grow from the stumps, eager to get their revenge. Meanwhile the birds and animals have joined forces to drive out the newcomers. The story ends with nature and the trees triumphant, as the foolish couple run screaming down the hill, desperate to escape their tormentors.

There's a later, more prosaic explanation for my passion for trees. In the first week of February 1961, I was twenty-seven and had just got a job as a cub reporter in London on the diary of the new-born *Sunday Telegraph*. That week, as the new paper rolled from the presses, I heard news that was to change the direction of my life. My father's elder brother Edward, the 6th Earl of Longford, was then fifty-eight and a remarkable man in many different ways. He was a passionate Irish nationalist, who had devoted his life to the rescue and running of the Gate Theatre in Dublin; he owned our 1,500-acre family estate in Westmeath; and he seemed in perfect health, although he was believed to weigh twenty-four stone. On 4 February he died suddenly of a stroke. My father Frank inherited the Longford title. But under a family settlement, originating before my uncle was born, the bulk of his fortune passed directly to me. I felt like someone who has won a prize in the lottery, and in a sense I had: the anachronistic lottery of birth. Antonia was the eldest child, but the nineteenth-century settlement had no time for girls. All that mattered to the lawyers was that I was the eldest son.

The family estate at Pakenham Hall (a name I quickly abolished by restoring the original Irish name, Tullynally) seemed to me magnificent, perhaps because I knew nothing about farming. There were 1,000 acres of boggy farmland, grazed by half-bred heifers and bullocks, two small Ferguson tractors and 500 acres of gardens and woods. The house was a crumbling neo-Gothic castle. But there was a snag. In those days death duties in Ireland seemed to be designed to crush the life out of an old estate. In my case they would run to 62 per cent. So I would start my new career as a farmer up to my ears in debt. But how could I resist those boggy acres, the crumbling castle – and those noble beech trees and oak trees that studded the demesne?

It was the ancient trees in the parkland that from the beginning grabbed my imagination and excited my senses. This was my treasure trove. Most of my eighteenth- and nineteenth-century predecessors made their careers serving (and sometimes dying) as generals in the army or as captains in the navy. Men like that would have felt no need, even if they could afford it, to impress their neighbours by buying Chippendale sideboards or landscapes by Richard Wilson and Claude Lorrain. But they loved the family estate and planted many parkland trees to make it beautiful. Now these were in my care: individual oak and beech and sweet chestnut as fine as you could observe in any great park in Britain or Ireland. These were the treasures I had inherited – living landscapes by Wilson and Claude. And with the joy of possession went the duty of looking after them.

I say, looking after them. In practice, like most ancient trees, my towering beech and oak asked for little more than benign neglect. My job was to protect them from timber dealers and other threats. In this negative role I was encouraged by our forestry adviser, Professor Clear of University College, Dublin. Planting rows of Sitka spruce in the commercial woodland was his professional responsibility. Those bread-and-butter trees would be harvested one day without mercy. But Professor Clear had a romantic soul, and solemnly warned me not to touch any of the great trees in the parkland, if I wanted him to continue as my adviser.

What new trees was I planting myself? The strange thing, I now realise, is that during the 1960s and 1970s – the first twenty years of my life at Tullynally – I hardly planted a single tree. I can only offer various excuses. True, the demesne and the pleasure ground were well stocked with giant beech until battered by a series of storms in the 1970s. But the main reason was that I was engaged in a tormenting struggle to pay off my debts to the government and the bank. To create a 300-cow dairy farm and make it a commercial success was the main imperative. At the same time I was committed to writing a series of history books – *The Year of Liberty* (a history of the Irish rebellion of 1798), *The Boer War* and *The Scramble for Africa* – which took the rest of my energy. It was not until 1987 that I finally broke free from my debts, and leased the farm, by then a successful business, to an accomplished neighbour.

By 1990 I could at last indulge my passion for trees. That year I founded the Irish Tree Society, with the help of some friends, and began the research for my first tree book, *Meetings with Remarkable Trees*. It's a personal selection of monumental trees. I chose, whimsically enough, sixty individual trees in Britain and Ireland and portrayed them with pen and camera. Many were very large and some were very ancient. What they all shared was a photogenic face or figure, and a strong personality.

What was the main theme? Writing history books had brought me face to face with great trees in many remote regions, especially the wilder parts of South Africa. I began to realise that our own great trees in Britain and Ireland were exceptional by the standards of the world. In fact they were the biggest living things in these islands: heavier than any land animal, taller than most buildings, older than many ancient monuments. And yet they could only too easily be taken for granted. This was the inspiration for that first tree book.

For my second tree book, *Remarkable Trees of the World* (2002), I chose another sixty monumental trees with strong personalities. This time the portraits were culled from many parts of the globe. And by now I was becoming aware of the alarming number of threats that face the world's population of trees. I listed some of them in the section called 'Trees in Peril': predatory loggers and complacent governments in Australia and western North America, impoverished farmers all over the world.

In 2007 I completed the third book in my trilogy (dare I say treelogy?), *In Search of Remarkable Trees: On Safari in Southern Africa* (2007). By then it was obvious that threats of all kinds were intensifying. Global warming and climate change, ideas considered alarmist in the 1980s and 1990s, were now part of the conventional wisdom. Yet how many governments were listening to the climate scientists?

In this volume I have tried to focus on some of the alarming new threats. As forecast by scientists, our weather seems to be becoming more extreme. Storms from the Atlantic appear to be more frequent, and our long-suffering trees pay the price. In the last two years we have lost about a quarter of our oldest and tallest beech which once screened the house.

At the same time Europe's common trees - sweet chestnut, ash and horse chestnut - are being assailed by a cohort of new diseases. Perhaps these, too, are a product of rising temperatures. They are certainly lethal to more than a dozen specific trees. The most damaging of these invaders would seem to be four new diseases which I shall call the Four Horsemen: Acute Oak Death, Sudden Oak Death (lethal to American oaks and many other plants including Japanese larch), *Chalara fraxinea* (ash die-back) and *Pseudomonas syringae* (lethal canker of horse chestnuts).

At Tullynally this fourth horseman has already taken five of our largest and oldest horse chestnuts. A recent survey reported that 49 per cent of *all* horse chestnuts in England showed signs of the lethal infection. It seems to have been inadvertently introduced from the East more than a decade ago. Like the elms in the 1960s, our

European horse chestnuts may now be facing extinction. And we are, once again, helpless to save them.

Of course science may come to the rescue. But I doubt it. So far no treatments for the new diseases have proved effective. All we can do is to keep planting the trees that seem relatively safe from disease. Here at Tullynally I have done what I could, but of course it was not enough. I have replanted parts of the demesne with beech and oak, filled the pleasure ground with exotics like maples and magnolias, stocked the Forest Walk with plants I had brought as seed from the Himalayas and created a new arboretum.

I felt I owed it to my grandchildren. And I owed it to the trees.

*   *   *

In the last four years I have incurred numerous debts of gratitude to my friends and family and those who worked at Tullynally.

First of all I should thank the staff at Tullynally. For thirty years Jimmy Dalton and Brendan Burke helped me remodel the garden and woodland. I did some of the more enjoyable work. But most of the digging and planting and mulching and watering of the trees was done by Jimmy and Brendan. Without their enthusiasm and energy nothing would have been achieved. Both have now retired, and their successors, Colm O'Shea and Peter McEvoy, are equally dedicated. I should also like to thank our garden consultant, Octavia Tulloch. She devised many of the best ideas for the garden and woodland - and vetoed all the worst ones.

To the generous friends and relations who read all or part of the first draft of the book I shall always feel grateful. I have gladly accepted most of their criticisms and acted on them. They include my wife Valerie, my daughter Eliza and her husband Alex, my sisters Antonia and Rachel, and six friends - Mark Girouard, Jacky Thompson, Aidan Walsh, Liam O'Flanagan, Neil Porteous and Martyn Rix.

I owe a great debt to the staff of my publishers, Weidenfeld & Nicolson, especially to Alan Samson, Lucinda McNeile and Helen Ewing. I am also most grateful to Michael Dover, my former editor at Weidenfeld, and Jonathan Lloyd at Curtis Brown for all they have done to inspire this book.

I must also thank the large number of people who gave me advice or hospitality and those who supported me (sometimes quite literally) on the slopes of the Himalayas.

In Ireland: Antoine Pierson, David Davies, Robert Wilson-Wright, Marie-Alice Dunsany, Michael Scott, Meryl and Christopher Gaisford St Lawrence,

Grania Langrishe, Jan Ravensberg, Paddy and Julie Mackie, Tracy Hamilton, Dina and Michael Murphy, John Fairleigh, Allen and Lorena Krause, Daphne and Jonathan Shackleton, Paddy and Nicky Bowe, Bruce Johnson, Kristin Jameson, Adam Whitbourne, Margie Phillips, Helen Dillon, Maureen and Liam O'Flanagan, Penelope and Tim Mahon, Philip Harvey, Charles Horton, Caroline Elliott, Adam Whitbourne, Seamus O'Brien, Matthew Jebb, Brendan and Ali Rosse, Desmond and Penny Guinness, Anthea Forde, Lindy Dufferin, Barbara FitzGerald, Olda and the late Desmond FitzGerald, Geraldine Critchley and the late Ambrose Congreve.

In Britain: Rosemary FitzGerald, Neiti Gowrie, Colin Hall, Tony Kirkham, Roy Lancaster, Tamsin and Teddy Clive, John Berkeley, Alice and Simon Boyd, Jane Martineau, Arabella Lennox-Boyd, Patricia and Timothy Daunt, Nella Opperman, Maurice and the late Rosemary Foster, Patrick and Kate Kavanagh.

In Belgium: Ghislaine de Spoelberch and Philippe de Spoelberch.

In South Africa: Barbara Bailey and all her family.

In the USA: Mark Duntemann and Peter Crane.

1

Two White Goddesses

Tullynally, 15 December 2012 – 1 January 2013

It's nearly midnight. Outside the uncurtained window there's a warm Atlantic wind blowing us here in Ireland a premature spring. (Of course the idea of spring sounds crazy. We've still got a week to wait before we decorate the hall with holly for Christmas.) Inside the kitchen I've just finished sowing the last of the Sikkimese seeds which I collected in the Sikkim Himalaya less than three weeks ago.

The six green plastic seed-trays, bulging with brown peat mould, straddle the kitchen table like baking tins awaiting the oven. Tomorrow I'll soak the trays in pale blue liquid fertiliser (half-strength will be quite enough for these delicate infants) and drop them into the hotbox down in the greenhouse. Forty-eight other trays, with yesterday's sowings, are down there waiting for their companions.

Sowing seeds sounds easy. Actually it can be as delicate as mending a watch. Most species of conifers need heat to extract the seeds from the tight layers of fir cone - if you collect the cones, as I do, fresh in the autumn. Our kitchen range does the job, but you have to be careful. Other seeds, from giant rhododendrons for example, are even more elusive. When you shake out the seed-pod onto a sheet of white paper, the seeds are barely visible. Like the grains of mustard seed in the Gospels, these rhododendron seeds are so many flecks of powder. But that's the point of Jesus' parable. A giant tree can grow from these humble beginnings. Or the opposite can happen. The seeds can fall on stony ground.

Snug above the Aga, my Internet radio switches ominously from the calm of Beethoven's *Pastoral* to the thunder of the *Emperor*. Will my seeds fall on stony ground? I skim the white plastic labels tucked into the sides of the trays. Each tray is carefully named and numbered and each name and number represents a heady experience for me. This is where, on our third day in Sikkim, I slipped down a rocky bank and was lucky to escape without breaking a leg or an ankle. This is where I first saw Kanchenjunga, the 28,000-foot White Goddess of Sikkim, rise at dawn from the mist above Darjeeling. And of course each botanical name, *Rhododendron thomsonii* or *Magnolia campbellii*, represents a triumph for the plant hunter who first discovered the species and first sent back the seeds to Europe to have them propagated. But will my seeds be equally fortunate? Will they flourish here in my garden in Ireland as the plant hunters' seeds flourished in Kew Gardens 150 years ago?

Tomorrow, before I take these last six trays down to the greenhouse, I'll invite my family to share this exciting moment. Our younger son, Fred, who lives in one of our flats with his partner Claire (and two boisterous Jack Russell terriers), is a keen gardener. So is our son-in-law, Alex, who used to run a business selling bulbs; he and our daughter Eliza, and their three teenage boys, drive down from Dublin most weekends. I'm sure my wife Valerie will come, too - although, sad to say, she's less addicted to plant-hunting than I am. And I'll add a touch of swagger to the occasion. I shall invite a few of my neighbours - Octavia, Charles, Aidan and others who plant exotic trees in their gardens - to a modest ceremony. I'll give a small party to celebrate the fifty-four seed-trays, a celebration lit by candlelight. I'll drink the party's health in prosecco (and in the delicious green tea I have brought back from Darjeeling). And I'll invoke the blessing of my hero, the great Victorian plant hunter, Sir Joseph Hooker. It was to walk in Hooker's footsteps in the Himalayas that I set out for Sikkim. And many of the rare seeds I collected were originally discovered by Hooker at the risk of his own life.

*   *   *

Less than a month ago, with eight other plant hunters, including four intrepid middle-aged ladies, I flew north from Calcutta to the borders of Sikkim. At nearly eighty, I was much the oldest. But I had sworn I was in good shape for the mountains, never suffered from altitude sickness, had spent a fortune on boots and jabs and visas and thermal underwear and all the rest of it. Sikkim is the small Indian state squeezed between Nepal on the west and Bhutan on the east. It sticks up like a prong - like a sore thumb, is no doubt what its neighbours feel - pointing towards Tibet and the heart of the Himalayas.

Our plan was to follow more or less the same route that was taken by the first two European plant hunters to explore this area, Joseph Hooker and his friend Archibald Campbell. When Hooker arrived, in the spring of 1848, Sikkim was a wayward independent kingdom just beyond the borders - and the grasp - of British India. Campbell was the British agent, that is, a kind of ambassador, accredited to the Rajah of Sikkim; Hooker a shy, bespectacled, brilliant, boyish naturalist, artist, geologist, cartographer and explorer.

At thirty-one Hooker had already enjoyed more than his fair share of adventures in pursuit of rare plants, shells and fossils. He had spent four years as the surgeon-naturalist on board HMS *Erebus*, one of two converted bomb-ships (the other was HMS *Terror*), under the command of Captain James Ross. The bomb-ships, specially reinforced to withstand the pressure of ice, had been sent to explore Antarctica and determine the position of the South Magnetic Pole. It did Hooker no harm that his father was Sir William Hooker, Professor of Botany at Glasgow University, and later the masterful first Director of the Royal Botanic Gardens at Kew. In fact it was Sir William who had wangled the place on the boat for young Joseph and arranged for him to do a short course in medicine and map-making in addition to his botanical studies. But what a credit to the old man young Joseph proved.

On his return, the navy was persuaded to sponsor a princely two-volume *Flora Antarctica*. It was written by Joseph, illustrated with coloured plates worked up from his sketches, and based on the astonishing number of plant specimens he had collected during the long and dangerous voyage. The book made him an instant celebrity. The Prince Consort was shown the delightful sketches - shown by Sir William, of course. The great and the good of the scientific world rallied to congratulate him. Charles Darwin became his friend and confidant.

Hooker left for the Himalayas in 1847, sponsored by the Admiralty, who agreed to send him there on half-pay. As usual his father had fixed it. Joseph travelled out to Calcutta in style: as a guest in the retinue of Lord Dalhousie, the new Governor-General. From Calcutta Hooker travelled by boat, elephant and pony and reached Darjeeling on the southern border of Sikkim in April 1848. He had excellent contacts which he exploited with his usual energy.

A year earlier a distinguished Scottish naturalist and geologist, Hugh Falconer, had been appointed Director of the botanical garden at Calcutta. Like Darwin, he was a man of subversive ideas. In fact he had been taught geology by the same Edinburgh tutor as taught Darwin. And he had found in India new evidence to shake the scientific establishment to its foundations: the fossilised bones of not only creatures long extinct but of man's predecessor – and ancestor – a primeval ape. He had made his botanical garden the centre for what we would now call economic botany and conservation: promoting research for the tea industry, fighting malaria with quinine, defending the teak forests against reckless loggers. It was Falconer who encouraged Hooker to hire a pony (or elephant) and head for Sikkim. His own health was precarious. High time for someone young and energetic to explore that botanical treasure house. But was Hooker just a shade *too* energetic?

For two centuries, Sikkim had been a hermit state, effectively closed to Europeans. In 1835, after part of his territory had been invaded and occupied by Nepal, the Rajah had agreed to rent out to the British a small slice of the southern borderland around Darjeeling. The British would expel the Nepalese and pay him a good rent for the use of Darjeeling as a healthy summer retreat. But the rest of the country remained closed to them. Now, under pressure from the Governor in Calcutta, the Rajah had reluctantly given Hooker and Campbell permission to explore his kingdom. In fact Campbell had given a kind of personal guarantee that Hooker could be trusted to behave himself. 'Dr Hooker's temper', as he told his boss, 'and his disposition towards the natives are worthy of entire confidence.' But permission to enter Sikkim carried a solemn warning to both Hooker and Campbell. Not a step across the northern border of Sikkim, not a single step. This was the border with Tibet, a vassal state on the wild fringe of the Chinese empire. And a border incident in Tibet could only imperil the delicate relations between the mighty Emperor of China and the impoverished Rajah of Sikkim.

In the event Hooker behaved like a crazy sixteen-year-old. He crossed the 16,000-foot pass into Tibet one afternoon and galloped off to hunt for Tibetan plants, disregarding both the shouts of the border guards and the reproaches of the unfortunate Campbell. Hooker's Tibetan foray nearly brought disaster to both men. They were arrested immediately on their return by orders of the Dewan, the ruler's brother-in-law and chief vizier. Campbell was beaten and tortured (a bamboo twisted round his thumb to make him confess), and both men were locked up for two months in a windowless wooden hut in the grounds of the Dewan's palace.

It's possible both would have been killed if they had been ordinary plant hunters. Or perhaps they would never have been arrested. The Dewan had naïvely imagined he could blackmail the British government by locking up the two men. But back in Darjeeling and Calcutta the affair was regarded with some seriousness. The Viceroy had taken young Hooker under his wing when Hooker first sailed up the Hooghly to Calcutta. And poor Campbell was one of the Raj's best men, known as a safe pair of hands in handling touchy native rulers. There was huffing and puffing – and talk of a punitive expedition. So the Rajah took fright and told the Dewan to back down. And Hooker and Campbell were released from the windowless hut and returned safely to Darjeeling and British India. (Later Hooker had himself painted in a clearing in the jungle attended by Sikkimese maidens. I think he had earned it.)

* * *

Our first step, after crossing the border from Darjeeling, would be to track down the hut in the grounds of the Dewan's palace, if there was anything left to see. We would then drive north towards the Tibetan border. I hoped to collect many of the rare plants that Hooker and Campbell had discovered in the north of Sikkim. But there was a snag. You could say that the ghost of the Dewan still haunts relations between Sikkim and China. At any rate in 1962 India and China fought a border war here in the north-east, and India was forced back, with a bloody nose. So this part of Sikkim is now a closely guarded military area, and our group had only permission for a fleeting visit. Five days and nights at the most. That was all we were allowed. How many botanical treasures could we see in five days?

We started, as every tourist starts, from Darjeeling. The town of 300,000 Sikkimese, Nepalis and Bengalis is what the travel brochures call 'vibrant', meaning it's something of a mess. True, there's a ridge above the town with a snow leopard in a zoo and an elegant Anglican church and a school called St Paul's, a famous British-style, Anglican public school (whose headmaster generously entertained us in the bungalow where Hooker had stayed). But you will see little else to remind you that this was once the summer capital of the Raj. In Kipling's day, starchy British memsahibs spent the monsoon months up here, 6,000 feet above the steaming plains of Bengal, just as their counterparts from Delhi spent months at Simla, refugees from the burning plains of the Punjab. But today the heart of the town is all confusion. The bazaar has swallowed the town centre, and anyway the centre is only a mass of wooden shacks, concrete bungalows and half-decayed flats flung up against the mountainside. The main road to the North runs through the town and it's hardly wider than an Irish boreen, a country lane. To make sure it's blocked most of the day, there's a railway line on the upper side with five ancient trains a day steaming down the road. Of course there's no room for a pavement. The world and his wife have to fight it out with the trains and the cars and the rickshaws and the cows in the same narrow lane.

To escape from Darjeeling into the crystal air of the mountains nearby: what could be more delightful? And this is precisely what Hooker did in May 1848 as he waited for Campbell to get permission for them to cross into Sikkim. Hooker decided to explore Mount Tonglu on the border with Nepal, three days' tramp through a rain-soaked bamboo forest to the north-west. For us it was all rather easier. We aimed to be there and back in a long day – to drive in our three white Toyota taxis to the foot of the mountain and then scramble up to the summit.

My main target was one of the most spectacular of all Hooker's discoveries, a species he named after his friend Archibald Campbell. He had found a new Himalayan magnolia which deserved a place among the people of Brobdingnag. It grew to a prodigious size – as big as a full-sized beech in Europe, and its flowers were the size of soup plates. Usually these gigantic flowers were as white as whipped cream, although inferior versions of the same species were found later in other parts of the Himalayas; these trees regularly produced smaller, garish-coloured flowers. Oddly enough, it was the seeds of these coloured versions, often as pink as a shrimp (or a Gaiety Girl's pair of knickers) that were later introduced to Europe by plant hunters. So this was my first task: to conquer Mount Tonglu and return to dazzle the world with the seeds of the white form of Hooker's species, *Magnolia campbellii alba*, that had remained a rarity so long.

Mount Tonglu is over 10,000 feet above sea level, but no more than 3,000 feet from the green valleys directly below. Its ascent, if I can call it an ascent, took four hours; I was glad to find a regular path with stone steps for much of the way. Like many Himalayan mountains it was sacred to Buddhists. We were greeted by flower-decked shrines on the way up, among groves of imported Japanese cedars and forests of tree rhododendrons and evergreen oaks. I scrambled up to the summit with nothing worse than a blistered toe. The rewards were even more delightful than expected: a packed lunch of chapattis in a kiosk built for pilgrims, and a view that would knock the breath out of you – if you were not already breathless.

The face of the Great White Goddess, Kanchenjunga, 28,000 feet high (that is, only 800 feet short of Mount Everest) stared at us imperiously across the void. I can understand now why Buddhists feel the need to worship (and try to propitiate) their mountains. Even an agnostic like me can feel uncomfortable faced with these regal creatures from the edge of space. I calmed myself by taking a cheeky digital photograph of the Goddess on my small Sony. Despite the forty-five miles between us, the lens caught the twist of her icy lips, her long, bony forehead, and the mane of snow.

But where was the other White Goddess, Hooker's white magnolia I had come so far to find? I had stopped to scoop up various seeds on the way to the summit: winged seeds of Sikkimese maples, fluttering like grey butterflies; fat green seed-pods of Falconer's rhododendron, hidden among the rusty underleaves; blue Sikkimese asters - the local Michaelmas daisies - still flowering in the November sunlight. But where, oh where were the magnolias?

It was not till we had been climbing down for an hour, picking our way over the rocks and past a Nepali border post with a single guard, that I saw my prey. Three large trees, leafless, but laden with pink seed-pods, crowned a knoll beside the track. We were still over 8,000 feet above sea level - high enough to ensure that any future plants would be able to cope with the 15 degrees of frost we expect in the coldest Irish winters. But how to reach up to those clusters of luscious pink seed-pods? Luckily for me the ladies in our party were as nimble as lemurs. Vanessa leapt up among the branches. And soon one of my brown envelopes was overflowing with the seeds of *Magnolia campbellii alba* - more than enough to fill a new Sikkimese garden at Tullynally.

Two days later our three white Toyotas sped north across the Teesta River and into Sikkim. My first aim was to collect seeds in the grounds of the Dewan's palace - seeds that could have sprung from the trees beside the hut where Hooker and Campbell had been imprisoned. Unfortunately the oak trees were stunted and barren, and anyway the altitude was too low for any of their progeny to be able to survive an Irish winter. The Dewan's palace was a heap of stones, decorated with bright green bushes of *Edgeworthia* (a plant that I was delighted to hear had first been discovered by Pakenham Edgeworth, Maria Edgeworth's half-brother and one of my own very distant relations). Otherwise little had changed since the days Hooker had sketched the scene for publication in his best-selling travel book, *Himalayan Journals*. The large, bulbous Buddhist shrines had survived almost intact on the terrace below the ruined palace. You could see where the hut had once stood, commanding a magnificent prospect of orchards and paddy fields in the valley far below. No doubt a clear sign of the Dewan's admirable taste in landscape. But not a place where I would choose to be incarcerated in a windowless wooden hut.

We had now to decide how to spend our meagre ration of five nights and days allowed for north Sikkim. We all agreed to go for the northern frontier. No one, I think, was planning to gallop, like Hooker, up the road to Tibet. But we would go as far as we could, scooping up the seeds of the great rhododendrons on the way, the magenta-flowered *R. hodgsonii* and the scarlet-flowered *R. thomsonii*, two of Hooker's most famous discoveries that were christened after two of his closest friends in British India. In fact we found the seed of ten kinds of rhododendron in all, including a purple-flowered rarity called *Rhododendron niveum*. We also hunted down dozens of other rare plants, including a laburnum-like creature called *Piptanthus nepalensis* and a homicidal rose with huge thorns, *Rosa macrophylla*. Many rhododendrons were mere bushes, others the size of trees, and we could well understand how the local Sikkimese used the wood to make ladles for their porridge and saddles for their yaks. But the highlight of our journey north was the tantalising glimpse of Tibet. At 15,000 feet, with the temperature well below zero, we reached the pass five miles from the place where Hooker had suddenly gone crazy and crossed the forbidden frontier.

I think I know what came over him. For my own friends – respectable middle-aged men and women – suddenly went mad that afternoon. I watched in amazement as they tore off their clothes and plunged into a hot spring close to the road. Fortunately none of them were arrested and imprisoned by the authorities (which would have had the Dewan laughing in his grave). But I still don't know why the spirit that seized them didn't seize me. I suppose I was too old, or too cold, for such high-jinks. Next day the three white Toyotas started the long drive back to the plains of Bengal.

Tullynally, 1 January 2013

The New Year has brought me heady prospects of a new expedition. Last month I flew back from the Himalayas laden with seeds. Next week I fly to the Argentine bound for the Andes. Perhaps I am going mad after all. Why not a few weeks at home in Ireland? And why the Argentine? January is high summer south of the Equator. So it will be too early in the year to collect any seeds. But I've never been south of

Mexico and this is the chance of a lifetime. I'll go tree-hunting with a half-Argentine friend who has a ranch in the Andes. She says that over there the forests of wild beech fill the mountains up to the snowline and monkey puzzles grow on the ranch like weeds.

In the afternoon I go down to the hotbox in the greenhouse to take a look at the seeds – my guests from Sikkim. Have any yet woken from sleep? Not a murmur so far from most of the seeds that are closest to my heart. But some of the others are stirring in their trays. There's a pair of rounded green heads showing in tray number 19; they must belong to the willow-like Asiatic buckthorn, *Hippophae salicifolia*. Trays number 10 (Sikkimese daisies), number 16 (Capitata primulas) and number 40 (Colvile's buddleia) all look promising. And, unless I'm mistaken, there's a green fuzz on the surface of trays number 13 and 38. This is where I sowed two of Hooker's most important discoveries, the tree rhododendrons named after his friends Hodgson and Thomson.

But tray number 17, the largest, is the one that grabs my attention. It's the tray with Hooker's White Goddess, *Magnolia campbellii alba*. Last month I sowed over a hundred of her small black seeds, squeezed out of the pink seed-pods, in that double-sized tray. But nothing stirs. Are those seeds taking a nice, long holiday in my hotbox, relaxing after the hurly-burly of life in my backpack, and the shock of being dragged by me halfway round the world? Or is this quite simply the sleep of the dead? I shall know by the spring – or at least by the summer. Of course I may have to make a second journey to Sikkim, later this year, to risk my life once again in a quest for the White Goddess. I think my hero, Sir Joseph, would have expected it of me.

2

A Tour of the Demesne

2 January 2013

It's clear and calm and sunny, with remnants of glaucous hoar frost fading fast under the tallest beech trees. Next week I will be in high summer south of the Equator – in Patagonia. But today let me take you on a brief tour of the demesne, the Irish name for a park.

We should begin at the Swan River (or lower lake) at the southern end of the demesne. The Swan River dominates the view. But it's nearly 80 feet lower than the house and a regular frost pocket. Last night there must have been a hard frost down here, and ice has sealed off the ebony-black water beside the self-sown alders and willows.

No sign of our pair of swans this morning. I expect they've flown back to their winter quarters on Lough Derravaragh. (This is the big lake a mile away, the lake made famous by the legend of the Children of Lir who were turned into swans.) Our own wild swans were no doubt protesting at the weather. But they've been lucky this year. We've only had about a dozen frosty nights and part of the Swan River has always remained open. Most mornings, when I'm at home, I go down the Forest Walk with a bag of crushed barley or oats to feed to them. I cross the slippery wooden bridge to the small island where spotted orchids grow in summer.

Then, steadying myself by a solitary oak, I throw three handfuls of meal to them, shouting words of encouragement. Of course I get little thanks. Often they repay my generosity with a savage hiss, the nearest a swan can get to a snarl.

Thirty-four years ago I found an earlier pair of swans locked into the ice. The temperature was so low (about zero Fahrenheit, I believe) and the frost had struck so fast that they had had no time to make their getaway. I was shocked by the sight, and ran back up the Forest Walk to get help. But how do you help a hissing, snarling swan to extricate itself from such a trap? In the end I brought down a large thermos of hot water and a small ladder. But my mission of mercy took too long. By the time I returned, the swans had somehow freed themselves and flown off to the open water on Lough Derravaragh, and you could have safely walked across the ice where they had been trapped.

How different it all looks when the oaks and the willows and alders break into leaf in early spring. Every April the pair of swans disappear behind the alders at the far end, scooping out tussock grass for the conical nest, and by May they have hatched half a dozen cygnets. If all goes well, and the mink (or otters) are hunting for food elsewhere, the cygnets grow with amazing speed. By September their wings are strong enough for their parents to make a start with flying lessons. Up and down the Swan River the cygnets go, thrashing the water in desperation. Then somehow they learn the trick. And before the first frost has rolled down the hill to the Swan River, the cygnets are off, beating the air with musical strokes, the Children of Lir in V-shaped formation, winging their way to meet new friends and relations on Derravaragh. Later the parents return to the Swan River if the rest of the winter is mild.

This Swan River, hardly more than an acre of water, is the only large relic of the early-eighteenth-century landscape that once graced our demesne. Geometry, with formal avenues and circular basins, was then all the rage. This solemn style was borrowed from Italy and France, and may have looked somewhat incongruous in the wilds of Ireland. But that missed the point. Fashion demanded at least a whiff of Tivoli and Versailles. There was no shortage of do-it-yourself books on the subject. (One of them, by John James, translated from the original French edition of Alexandre Le Blond, remains in our library. It shows a pair of swans beside a topiary hedge of yew.) You planted your trees in radial avenues, often with a canal and a waterworks to add an extra dimension. Here at Pakenham Hall (as Tullynally was then called) the squire, young Thomas Pakenham, could not afford anything very elaborate like classical statues or temples. But trees cost little, and wages in Ireland were only a few shillings a week. Best of all, water was free, once the squire had tapped a powerful spring below the terrace on which the family's house was built. So he laid out a basin below the terrace, leading to a canal and an avenue, with a second basin beyond it. And there it was for all his neighbours to see: a demesne on the cusp – one might almost say, watershed – of high fashion.

I often wonder about these early-eighteenth-century ancestors of ours. What are we to make of them? And what, for that matter, would they have made of *us*? At least they would have approved of my passion for trees. But we know so little about them. True, their portraits were painted by one of the best Irish painters of this period, James Latham, an artist trained in the Low Countries. So we know that both the Pakenham brothers, Thomas and George Edward, wore lace around their blue and yellow waistcoats, and powdered their wigs, and faced the canvas in excellent humour the day they were painted.

But what kind of people were these two brothers? None of their letters have turned up in our archives - or indeed other people's, as far as I know. Fortunately one diary has survived, a jewel of a diary by contemporary standards. It was written by the younger brother, George Edward, in 1737-8, a couple of years before the elder brother, Thomas, had the good fortune to find a Longford heiress and marry her. So the diary gives us a snapshot of the two bachelors and their lives at an exciting moment. And what makes the snapshot especially vivid is that the two brothers had lived apart for a number of years. Their father had died young, and Thomas had inherited the family estate. Their mother had remarried and lived in England with George Edward. Now he was back, but feeling almost like a foreigner, wide-eyed at the life of his brother and the Irish gentry.

Which brings us back to the upper basin, the canal and the Swan River. 'My brother's house,' he writes on his arrival, 'is situated on the declivity of a Hill to the South; from whence descending by variety of Slopeworks you come to a Bason of 300 foot wide. From this is a Cascade, falling into another Bason at the Head of a Canal 150 foot wide and 1200 foot long. On Each Side a large Grass walk planted with trees. From this Canal there runs in a direct line another near a mile in length, equal in breadth to the first and terminates in a large bason at the foot of 3 or 4 beautifull hills.'

*   *   *

If you climb back up the slope to the upper part of the demesne, you will find that here, too, the ghost of the old formal landscape peers from underneath the sweeping clumps and shelter belts of the late eighteenth century. In fact you need to look at our earliest estate map, dating from 1835, to get a clearer idea of that ghost. But fragments of the radial avenues remain obvious today. Most of those trees seem to have been common lime trees, *Tilia x europea*, and I'm not surprised. This was the preferred species for the formal landscape in all parts of northern Europe. It was tough and long-lived – indeed almost indestructible. Best of all, it produced trees far more uniform than other species. As a natural hybrid between two European species (the small-leaved lime and the large-leaved lime) it was easy to grow from cuttings. Each of these would be genetically identical. By contrast, other trees like oak and beech had to be propagated by seed. So the same batch of acorns or beech mast could produce a crop of giants and a crop of dwarfs.

As I said above, this hybrid lime is almost indestructible. Let me explain. I once behaved very badly to one of these ancient limes. It happened more than forty years ago, but it still makes me blush with shame. Remnants of a long-vanished avenue, two old limes stood in the way of our plans to seed a paddock with rye-grass for the cows. In those days the farm was losing money hand over fist. At least one of the magnificent old limes had to go. I chose one of them to sacrifice and grimly watched the chainsaws at work. Then came the bulldozers, gouging out the roots and stacking the wreckage ready for a bonfire. The fire was lit and re-lit, and a bulldozer returned to stack the heap a second time. Yet another bonfire. I assumed that this was the last I would see of the unfortunate lime.

Thirty years later I was walking in the demesne when a vixen and her cubs emerged from a small copse. I peered inside and shrank back, incredulous. The ancient lime had come back from the dead. It was now reincarnated as a small grove of limes with trunks several feet thick. The foxes lived happily underneath. But what had brought the tree back to life? Part of the huge root ball must have survived the bonfire, and then produced a series of cuttings. I wonder if a nuclear bomb would finish off a hybrid lime. But I rather doubt it. Like the ginkgo which survived the bomb at Hiroshima, our European lime is the Lazarus of the world of trees.

In the demesne, beyond the site of the murdered lime tree, are clumps of unusually tall beech and oak, planted, it seems, more or less at random. These would be typical of the new fashion for a 'natural' landscape, ultimately based on the romantic landscapes of Claude, a fashion that swept Britain and Ireland in the second half of the eighteenth century. Clumps and winding paths and curving rivers were now all the rage. Geometry and radial avenues and canals were hopelessly out of date. In England the leading exponent of the style was Lancelot Brown, who had risen from the ranks of ordinary gardeners by spotting the 'capability' of each estate. (Hence his nickname.) In Ireland the new style seemed particularly apt. Radial avenues had always seemed to run against the grain of the country. Better to adapt the rolling hills and marshy fields to the new fashion. Many gentlemen in Ireland picked up tripods and surveying tools and looked at the 'capability' of their own fields. Why waste money on landscape architects if you could do it yourself? Among these enthusiasts, I'm sure, were my Pakenham ancestors.

By 1756 that marriage with the Longford heiress had borne a bumper crop of fruit – in every sense. Plain Thomas Pakenham was no more. Now he was the 1st Baron Longford of a new creation. His elegant wife Elizabeth, née Cuffe, came of intellectual stock; her family house in Dublin was a kind of salon for the great and the good. She was also rich by the standards of the time. Her father's great-uncle, Francis Aungier, had been a seventeenth-century building tycoon, created Master of the Ordnance and Earl of Longford by Charles II. So the new Lord Longford had married brains, money, land, honours and power all together.

How delighted he must have been at his choice of a wife. Now he had a promising family of six children, with two boys destined for the navy. His landed income had increased to over £2,000 a year. And he controlled the 'closed' (that is, rotten) borough of Longford. This gave him two seats in the Dublin Parliament. He had also one for himself in the Lords. No wonder he felt free to add a third storey to the family house in Westmeath, roofing over the inner yard to form a new hall where he could entertain the tenants. And of course he planted trees by the thousand. Inside the demesne he put clump after clump in the new style. But he left the old shelter belts much as they were in his father's day. They framed the rolling hills and the rectangular fields of grass and ploughland let on long leases to local farmers.

Today, when I walk around the demesne, I try to imagine that I'm that enthusiastic Lord Longford back in the mid-eighteenth century. I picture myself on horseback, wearing brocade waistcoat and tricorne hat, surrounded by labourers. I'm carefully supervising the work as each acorn is plopped into the heavy clay soil. Plant it too deep and it will die, too shallow and the crows will take it for breakfast. The future clump is surrounded by a wooden paling made of posts and rails. Without that protection the cattle will make short work of my young plants, even if they are brought from our nursery as saplings. Secure behind a paling, acorns can put their tap-roots straight down into the soil – and never need to be disturbed again. (Of course there's a catch. You need plenty of labour to weed the young oaks. But that's no problem for me back in the eighteenth century.) Beside the acorns I plant a few tough seedlings to act as temporary nurses: evergreens like Scots pine and silver fir, deciduous conifers like larch. Most of them will have to be removed in due course. Meanwhile they'll give shelter to the oaks as well as adding spice to the clump.

Enough of this daydream. More relevant to try to identify which trees planted in the mid-eighteenth century are still alive and well today. In my book *Meetings with Remarkable Trees* I described the tallest and straightest of a group of oaks as 'the Squire's Walking Stick'. This was a whimsical name, but I like it. It was based on John Loudon's account in 1838 of a young giant of a tree on our estate, a tree then ninety years old – that is, planted in 1748 (I now believe the tree in question was a bit younger than that. In other words it may have been 'the Baron's Walking Stick'. No matter.) What's important is that this is one of the most remarkable oaks in Ireland. It rises straight as a column for the first 40 feet, and then spreads out its branches like a delightful green umbrella. I have long been its passionate admirer.

We had a bumper year for acorns in 1980, so I planted a hundred in the nursery frames, collecting them from the grass under the Squire's Walking Stick. Many of these have grown unusually tall and broad. Good acorn years have followed at roughly five-yearly intervals: 1990, 1995, 2000, and so on. I grab at every chance to breed from my champion, like a racehorse owner with a champion mare. And I am filling the estate with its progeny. Most of these, I think, will be better than average: taller, broader, faster-growing. But will any of them ever rival their mother-tree? No doubt this will be obvious enough in a couple of centuries.

But meanwhile I must clear the ground – no, I mean, clear my mind – ready for the planting season. In two months we shall start the new planting in the arboretum. Some kind of overall plan is recommended by experts, and they're right. Of course you can muddle along and simply put selected trees in any space that's free. I admit I sometimes do. But it must be better, before you plant trees in the ground, to plant them first in your head.

3

Murdering Your Friends

4 January 2013

Today, the day before I leave for Patagonia, I was confronted with a crisis in the new arboretum. This is sad but not unexpected. One of the ten ancient beech trees, the towering green and silver pillars that give it structure, has collapsed in a storm. It broke through the southern boundary fence, deluging the field with pieces of trunk and limbs, the poor creature's body parts.

I've just been down in my scarlet woolly hat and green wellies to see the scene of the disaster. I call these huge, ancient beech trees collectively 'the Ents', but they all have very different personalities. Several are uncannily like the Ents in Tolkien, big-boled and splay-footed, and apparently benevolent. I'm glad to say that these splay-footed beech look good for a few more decades. But two of the more elegant ones have bracket fungi growing from their feet and an unhealthy lean to the east, no doubt the relic of previous storms. It was the larger of these that was felled by the storm last Thursday.

I talked to Martin Mulvey, the local farmer who has bought the remains for a healthy sum, €450 I think. (The firewood market's going like a steam engine this year because of the unholy rise in the price of oil.) I reckon he'll get nearly fifteen tractor loads of firewood, weighing about 20 tons, when he and his friends have finished sawing it up. There was nothing you could sell for planking. The huge trunk has snapped off 10 feet from the ground and landed yards away. (I wonder if anyone heard the crash. Probably not; the storm would have drowned it.) I'm amazed to find the tree's hollow for the first 50 feet – half its total length – and festering with sponge-like fungi. The wonder is that it has stood so long, stoically facing the gales year after year.

How old is an old beech tree? I once counted 220 annual rings on a slice from a huge beech – surely some kind of record. It was felled here, in this same wood, by a storm in the 1990s. That tree must have been planted by my great-great-great-grandfather in about the mid-1780s. Martin has now cut me a slice from the middle of the newly felled beech, choosing the first place where the trunk's intact enough for us to count the annual rings. The result is hard to interpret – these rings could only represent about half the tree's life – but they seem to confirm the earlier figures. This gouty old Ent, and probably all the other nine Ents, were planted just after the end of the American War of Independence. (My ancestor, the Lord Longford of the day, had returned understandably crestfallen from the wars. I suppose he planted these trees to celebrate the peace.)

It will only take Martin a few days to clear the large void left in the south-east corner of the arboretum. How should I fill the space? And that raises bigger questions. What was my plan when I started the arboretum? And what *is* the current long-term plan? I find it hard to give myself straight answers. But I can dig up the old files and notebooks, and scan the screen for early photographs. I'm not even certain when the project began. But I'm fairly sure that it was eleven years ago, in 2002, that I started the first holes for what began as the 'New Grove' and is now called the 'New Arboretum'.

Before that time – for the previous forty years – I had planted thousands of young trees in various parts of the estate. Most of them were designed, I must admit, purely to make money. I was up to my ears in debt, the result of that 62 per cent bill for death duties on this estate, left to me by my Uncle Edward, my father's elder brother. So I wooed my creditors with spiky, blue-green Sitka spruce, elegant Lodgepole pines and acrid-smelling thuyas. (These were once the trees of choice for the wigwam and the war canoe of the Quinault and other Native Americans of the Pacific north-west. Now they're the Irish bank manager's favourites.) A minority of my new plantations were belts of hardwoods. Most of these were designed, like the sphinxes in the garden, purely for ornament. I replanted the sinuous shelter belts – beech and oak and Scots pine and larch – laid out in the late eighteenth century, and painted in watercolours in the estate survey of 1835.

Of course I made beginners' mistakes. I had no idea, when I started planting, that breeding and bloodlines were so important in the world of trees. I restored a grove by the so-called Grand Gate, using wizened little beech self-seeded from an old wood. The new trees grew up as twisted as their parents. I was hardly more successful when I bought beech from a well-known nurseryman. I think he must have thought I wanted beech for hedging. At any rate the wretched things refused to be tall, aristocratic columns. Many continued to insist they were bushes.

By 1980 the penny had dropped. If you want a good tree you must grow it yourself. (I'm reminded of the advice given by Disraeli, a best-selling novelist before he climbed the political ladder. 'Read any good books lately, Prime Minister?' a colleague asked him one day. 'When I want to *read* a good book,' the great man replied, 'I *write* it myself.') And if you're daring enough to create your own trees, it makes sense to go for the best bloodline you can find. So I started to breed my own oaks from the most noble-looking oaks in the demesne. That year, 1980, was a year to make hungry jays and pigeons and grey squirrels rejoice. Many of our oldest oaks were bulging with green and brown acorns – an invitation for both me and the hungry birds and animals. I filled a bucket with acorns, harvesting them from the muddy ground underneath the tallest and straightest trees, and sowed a hundred in the greenhouse as a beginning. Fifteen of this first harvest grew up to be tall and strong like their parents, and are now the pride and joy of the garden. And in each good acorn year, which comes roughly once every five years, I compete once again with the jays and pigeons. (But not, any more, thank heavens, with the grey squirrels. Miraculously, these American pests disappeared about eight years ago, and have never returned.)

It was the same with my new groves of beech. By 1995 I had bred hundreds of saplings from our largest beech, a family retainer over 100 feet high and more than 23 feet round the waist. Raised in the greenhouse, the oaks and the beech became pushy adolescents within a few years. At first I added them to the existing shelter belts, mixing them with pine and larch.

By 2002 I had a bolder plan. I would create a new arboretum at Tullynally using as a foundation an old grove of oak and beech. This was the shelter belt designed to protect the house from the north-east wind. At first these two old retainers, native oak and naturalised beech, would dominate the place. But I would gradually introduce more exotic species – you could call them our guests from abroad. Red oaks from North America, southern beech from South America, Himalayan birch from China, cork trees from Japan – the world was my oyster. This was my plan for an arboretum, a simple one, but not a bad one, I think, except for two potentially fatal flaws.

The first flaw should have been obvious from the beginning. To her credit, my wife saw it long before I did – and I think she would have been happy if I had left this shelter belt to its own devices. But I refused to listen. Today I know that if you want a good planting site, you should choose a nice green field. Don't choose a piece of an old garden backed by ancient trees or, worse still, the remains of an ancient wood. It's true that your trees could do well, for the first decade or so, because old soil will be rich, and old trees will be kind to your saplings by giving them shelter. But wait till the old trees turn nasty, skittled over by storms, leaving your prize plants mutilated or dead. And just wait till the thin, black strands of honey fungus – ghosts of long-dead trees – rise up to haunt you. Nothing can exorcise these ghouls, which can lie for decades waiting for their next victims. By contrast an ordinary green field, once grazed by sheep or cattle, will be equally safe from falling trees and hidden fungi. Of course a grove of ancient beech and oak has more poetry than an ordinary green field. And, like a fool, I chose the old grove as the site for my new arboretum.

Predictably, the first big storm made a meal of my early plantings. At that time there were still twelve 'Ents' dominating the wood – ancient beeches planted, as I believe, in the 1780s. Two of these Ents, spanning half the arboretum, fell in a westerly gale that rampaged through Ireland on the night of 4 January 2004. Miraculously, most of my sapling beech and oak were so small that they survived, although some lost their leading shoots, and a few were blown out of the ground. (One small oak, squashed flat by the 20-ton corpse of the Ent, actually rose from the dead; a new tree sprang up from its original roots.) The most visible damage was to the surviving Ents themselves. One of the most beautiful was left with half its head shorn off. It took weeks with a digger to dispose of the two mangled corpses. But next year something happened that changed my perception of that storm. Malignant as it was, the storm had brought new life into the grove. Around the stumps of the two fallen Ents a crowd of young beech, mixed with bluebells, were seizing their chance. One day some of these trees, too, would take their turn as Ents. I felt less bitter about the disaster. Although I knew the grove was no place for an arboretum, its wounds were being healed and it was bubbling with life. Here was a real family, with old and young combined; a natural community, quite unlike an artificial plantation of trees all of the same age.

To return to my beginners' mistakes, the second flaw was less obvious. And none of our family, as far as I remember, pointed it out to me. Indeed I notice that most people who make a collection of trees large enough to call itself an arboretum make the same mistake as I did. I muddled along without a master-plan for the future.

It was heady work. I chose my favourite trees, dug large holes in the browny-yellow clay, added dollops of black compost and spread the delicate tree-roots with the care of a mother. Many of my babies reached adolescence with a speed that astonished me (and sometimes alarmed me). As I had planned, the young beech and oak, added to their elderly ancestors, proved a solid foundation. These two common species were first to provide the temporary framework – and then room for expansion. I would have plenty of young oak and beech to spare. I would give the poorer specimens the chop when I needed room. (I thought it would be rather like thinning radishes.)

But I gave little thought to planning in other ways. I had chosen my exotics as favourite individuals, and planted them more or less at random. I failed to ask myself how I should place them. Should I go for a botanical arrangement, as you might meet in a botanic garden: all the maples lumped together, the oaks and pines and silver firs and so on, lined out, genus by genus? Or was I to arrange them geographically, segregating the trees according to the map of the world: Chinese pines set apart from their Japanese neighbours, European oaks from North American, and so on? Or perhaps I should arrange the collection thematically? Would my trees play a part in a narrative – telling the story of, say, Joseph Hooker and other famous plant hunters? Or would they be living monuments, marking births, deaths, triumphs, disasters? But these were not, I have to admit, questions I ever considered when I began.

And I failed in other ways. How to design an arboretum that delights the eye? It took years for me to realise one truth that should have been obvious: designing an arboretum is like designing a garden. I mean, much the same artistic rules that apply to plants in the garden apply to trees in the arboretum.

My epiphany, if I can call it that, came on one of my regular visits to Westonbirt Arboretum in Gloucestershire. This astonishing place was created by two parvenu millionaires, Robert Holford and his son, Sir George Holford, who poured money and ideas into the 600-acre estate for more than eighty years. Their vast wealth is somewhat mysterious. Part of it came from the New River Company, a boon for

Londoners (its water was safe from typhoid), part of it from the currency speculations of a bachelor uncle who left a cool million to young Robert in 1839. Their arboretum followed the prevailing style of the period: the picturesque style. But it appears they designed it themselves without professional help. The range of trees and other plants was stunning. For this was the golden age of plant-hunting, and both father and son had the money to back expeditions going anywhere in the temperate world. But even more stunning than the range of trees was the artistry with which they were arranged. Sometimes it took weeks before Robert Holford was happy about the placing of a new acquisition. His trees meant as much to him as the works of art he had bought with his millions - the Rembrandts and Titians and Claudes.

How to describe the secrets of Westonbirt? The golden rule, I think, on which everything hangs, is the rule of contrast. Deciduous must contrast with evergreen, light with dark, dark with light. Apple-green maple leaves must contrast with spiky, dark green holly; creamy magnolias with coarse-textured yew; rough, pink sycamore bark with smooth, silver beech bark; trees like church spires with trees like lollipops - they are all chosen for contrast. And you can find that the same applies in gardens.

Of course I have learnt these lessons somewhat late in the day. My family - especially Valerie and my son-in-law, Alex - did not conceal their views, however critical. And this time, I think, I listened. Fortunately it was not too late to apply some of the most important lessons. Let me explain how my own arboretum has evolved - muddled through, if you like - in its first ten years of life.

I have certainly tried to exploit the Holfords' rule of contrast. Belatedly, I squeezed in among deciduous trees a loose semicircle of evergreens. At the back of the main clearing I planted half a dozen Caucasian silver firs (*Abies nordmanniana*). I also inserted fourteen different kinds of holly: plain and silver-variegated, coarse hybrids with one parent from Madeira (the Highclere hybrids) and elegant, cut-leaf forms from China. These evergreens in fact do more than provide a contrast with the deciduous trees around them. They give a framework to the core of the arboretum and dominate the place from autumn to spring, that is, from the moment the oaks and beech and maples drop their leaves.

At the same time I have arranged part of the arboretum to reflect a series of themes which caught my fancy. Now the Ents have divided the grove naturally into compartments, forming half a dozen separate glades and clearings. These are linked by winding paths cut through the grass. The theme in the first compartment is plant-hunting. In the 1990s I had travelled to China and Tibet to collect seed. But of course

I was only a late comer myself. The modest hero of this clearing is one of the first and greatest of all modern plant hunters, Augustine Henry. He was an Irish doctor who tramped the wilds of China searching for rare plants in the 1880s and 1890s. He hailed from County Tyrone, the son of a Catholic businessman who had gone out to Australia to hunt for gold - without much success. He himself qualified as a doctor in London and sailed for China to work for the Chinese Imperial Customs. Plant-collecting was merely his hobby. But in twenty years he discovered much more gold than his father - that is, a treasure trove of rare plants, many unknown to science. No one knows how many rarities he posted back to the botanic gardens of Europe. According to one estimate he parcelled up more than 15,000 dried specimens of Chinese plants, including 500 species and 20 genera that were his own personal discoveries. So the first compartment in my arboretum is now the Augustine Henry clearing. It's a modest place. You'll find Henry's lime and Henry's viburnum and half a dozen of his other favourites. They look happy enough for the moment. But there's an ancient copper beech a few yards away, worst luck, and he (and they) may not survive the next storm. I wouldn't bet on it.

The second compartment is reserved for some of our eight, boisterous grandchildren. I'm not sure that I've matched their trees very well with their own characters. But I've done my best. Two of them are elegant ten-year-old twins called Matilda and Anselm. I've planted an elegant pair of ginkgos for them, trees that I raised from the seed of an elderly female ginkgo in Mount Auburn, the neo-classical cemetery near Harvard in Cambridge, Mass. I've planted a more showy tree for their twelve-year-old brother Samuel: a liquidambar which colours a furious red and blue and orange in autumn. And I'll plant trees for the two latest additions, Julia and Tom, as soon as I hear which species would best suit their characters - a pushy young Turkey oak, a graceful Russian larch or a stunningly beautiful magnolia.

The third compartment has the whimsical name of Tesco Corner. This is because the two biggest-girthed trees started their lives as a pair of walnuts that I found, one Christmas, on the shelves of Tesco. You can try this trick yourself. The nuts are so oily that they can survive for years as viable seed. (Prehistoric travellers on the Silk Road are said to have brought the original seeds from China in the saddlebags of their camels.) And, much to my surprise, these Tesco walnuts are going for the sky as if they thought they were poplars.

The rest of the arboretum is arranged on more conventional lines. I have grouped most of the rare oaks together in a loose semicircle around the main clearing. But I have mixed them with the maples to contrast the sober greens of the oaks with the flaming reds of the maples in autumn. I have added other red-hot species like bushy Persian ironwoods and tall Katsura trees. Throw in a dozen more Japanese maples – 'Osakasuki' may sound like a motorbike but is as red as Red Ridinghood – and the main clearing, this autumn, will pulse like a ring of fire.

This clearing, now the centrepiece of the whole arboretum, was not part of my original design. In fact I believe that I owe its existence largely to my son-in-law, Alex. Six miles away to the south there's a 700-foot conical hill called Knockeyon ('Hill of St Eyon') that dominated our landscape. You saw it from the lawn. You saw it from most of our demesne. But not from the arboretum. Then one day Alex pointed out that, if I sacrificed a few scrubby beech, I could make a clearing with a vista focused on Knockeyon. The scrubby beech were duly dispatched and the vista created. The next step was to throw up a wooden hut in the clearing to command the same vista. Alex insisted the hut should be planted on a small mound, and he was obviously right. But should the hut be designed in the style of a Greek temple? Our local eccentric, a brilliant French cabinet-maker called Antoine, decided otherwise. He built the hut from curved sheets of oak so that it looked like an acorn upside down. (It was quickly nicknamed the 'Pumpkin House' alias the 'Womb with a View'.) And it's here, with the sun caressing Knockeyon, that I should be happy to end my days.

Later.

Today, cold but dry, is the day I've been dreading for months. I have marked with a can of red paint a group of sixteen sturdy oaks – about a third of those I planted ten years ago in the arboretum. The red paint means they are surplus and due for the chop. I hate the whole idea. I remember how I reared them in the greenhouse and moved them into the frames and how happy they looked. But the arboretum is becoming congested. And we need more room for newcomers. So these perfectly healthy trees, some over 30 feet high, have to be sacrificed.

I watched the small yellow digger brutally dispatching each oak in turn. The bigger ones fought back, determined to stay, their roots twisting round the steel claws until the roots snapped. The small ones died without a struggle.

I feel rather sick. I was wrong to have thought it would be like thinning radishes. It's more like murdering your friends.

But I must try to forget the butchery. Tomorrow I leave home for a fortnight in Patagonia skimming the flanks of the Andes. The idea still strikes me as a little crazy. But it was a chance not to be missed, a chance of a lifetime.

4

Monkeys' Despair

Eastern Patagonia, 8–20 January

About five in the evening we saw our first monkey puzzles and the sight was surreal. 'Look, Araucarias . . . monkey puzzles,' said Ghislaine, our generous Belgian host. She's half Argentine, too, and she wasn't all that impressed. The limousine didn't stop. 'You'll see better ones tomorrow on our *estancia.*' There were about a hundred of the trees here by the road, flat-topped and spiky and black against the dusty hills on our left, as the road climbed up a rocky canyon. There were no other trees in this part of the eastern foothills of the Andes, only sun-bleached tufts of grass on the bleak hillside. I'm not sure what I expected. But these wild, twisted creatures looked more like a thicket of thorn trees - or a thicket of spiders.

　　Later that evening we saw hundreds of them growing out of the rocks. Ghislaine had to admit she was impressed. She told her chauffeur, Roberto, to pull in to the side. The scrawny creatures crowded the line of cliffs with their bare trunks and spiky heads. Three of them crowned a cliff shaped like a gigantic hand. These were not at all like the pampered, upright monkey puzzles of my own experience.

Ever since childhood I had admired the prodigious, solitary monkey puzzle that grew on the lawn of my parents' house in Sussex. I realise now that many people in England find the shape of these trees outrageous. They mock the trees for their spiky symmetry: too incongruous even for the suburbs. Plant them in England and they're an insult to the native oak and beech – that's what some people think. But as a child I found the tree's spikiness intensely exciting. Unable to climb it, I had the perversity to love it. Almost 70 feet high, and 8 feet round the stomach, this was our largest family pet.

One day in the 1950s we were visited by my heroine, Vita Sackville-West, poet, novelist and arbiter of gardening good taste. (She and her husband, Harold Nicolson, had created a magical garden nearby at Sissinghurst.) Imagine my shock when I saw she did not share my feelings about the tree. In fact she looked down her long, thin Edwardian nose and said sternly to my mother: 'Elizabeth, I'm surprised you allow that thing on the lawn.' I'm glad to say the tree long outlived her and died full of honours in 2009.

I wonder if Vita would have relented if she'd seen the monkey puzzles that we encountered in the next few days. For me it was a journey of crazy enchantment. We had only a fortnight to spend in the Argentine, skimming the eastern flank of the Andes, and we began with these astonishing creatures. On this side of the Andes, the terrace they occupy is barely 200 miles long and 50 miles wide – a mere speck in this vast subcontinent. Most of it is bare, stony hillside, 2,000 to 3,000 feet above sea level, in sight of a zigzag string of snow-covered volcanoes. (These are dormant – or not so dormant, as it sometimes turns out. Last year the whole region was treated to a blizzard of grey, volcanic dust from an exuberant local volcano.) Across the Andes, in Chile, I believe the monkey puzzles have more room to stretch their feet, and they have spread from the western Andes to the sea. But here in the Argentine they are boxed in between the high forests of southern beech and the dry plains below.

Next day Ghislaine took us to see her family's own private forest of monkey puzzles. The *estancia* seemed to cover half the province – in fact about 200,000 acres, a sizeable slice of country even in the Argentine. It had been bought in the 1990s by her late husband, partner in a Belgian brewery fortune, and an ardent and hospitable sportsman. Herds of red deer had been imported from Scotland (where he had bought another estate) and the sport here in the wilds of the Argentine was apparently stunning. So, I soon found, were the monkey puzzles.

They grew thickest in a small canyon under the shadow of a rocky outcrop. A few were dead and many had broken limbs. The more exposed ones were twisted by wind and snow into grotesque shapes. There were dwarfs from Grimm, elves from Arthur Rackham, orcs from Tolkien. Nearly half were female and, if safe from the wind, prolific breeders. You could see the aggressive green cones of these females – cones the size and shape of cannon balls, jostling each other on the scaly tips of the branches.

The biggest tree was a galumphing male with four trunks and two immense spirals of branches. He was a natural pollard; presumably someone or something had removed his original trunk when he was young and he had grown four new trunks to compensate. I can't say he was beautiful, though I admired his enormous, elephantine feet. I measured his girth with my leather belt and he was 20 feet around at breast height – over twice the girth of that family pet on our lawn in Sussex.

Other trees had upper branches contorted like the blades of broken propellers or the spokes of smashed umbrellas. Of course any genuinely wild forest is a knacker's yard of dead and dying trees. The wreckage accumulates as there is no one to take it for firewood. But these monkey puzzles added to the wreckage a reckless geometry of their own, their twisted limbs covered with moss and ferns, their trunks bloated with carbuncles and their elephant feet splayed out drunkenly across the rocky hillside.

The genus *Araucaria* has a long and noble ancestry, and still consists of twenty-five species, all in the southern hemisphere. Palaeobotanists have traced the ancestors of the genus back as far as the Jurassic era. And Jurassic they certainly look. Common to all twenty-five of the species is the brutal geometry we associate with the time of the dinosaurs. The trees radiate whorls of branches stiffer and spikier than those of any other conifers. The scaly leaves are like armour, the trunks like rusticated columns of stone. The great majority of the genus are confined to the tropical jungles of New Caledonia, east of Australia. But four species (*A. excelsa, A. bidwillii, A. columnaris* and *A. cunninghamii*) originate from cooler lands further south, like the rainforests of Queensland and windswept Norfolk Island. Even these four species are still too delicate to be grown in the parks and gardens of northern Europe. But fortunately our monkey puzzle, *Araucaria araucana*, is a tree of the Andes and can take an icy winter in its stride.

There's a story of how the species was discovered by Archibald Menzies and brought to Europe at the end of the eighteenth century. Menzies was the surgeon-naturalist aboard *Discovery*, named after Cook's ship and now under the command of Captain Vancouver. In 1791 the British Admiralty had sent Vancouver to explore the Pacific coast of North and South America. The crew had no time, or indeed permission, to wander far inland in Chile, then part of the Spanish empire. But they put into the harbour of Valparaiso and were given a banquet by the Spanish authorities. One of the delicacies on the table was a plate of nuts which they heard were the staple diet of the local Araucano Indians. Unobserved, Menzies slipped a handful of these mysterious nuts into his pocket. After the ship sailed he planted them as an experiment. And before the *Discovery* docked in England the following year, Menzies had five little seedling trees, christened after the Araucano, growing in pots in his cabin.

It was these five that became the first monkey puzzles introduced into Europe. One of them was planted at Kew Gardens and helped launch the tree's career, although the species didn't become fashionable in England until the middle of the next century, when a large consignment of nuts was brought back by the plant explorer William Lobb. The name 'monkey puzzle' was coined in the 1840s. The French have a romantic version: *le désespoir des singes* – 'monkeys' despair'. I much prefer it to our own term, although I'm afraid it's too late to change. Anyway, the exotic creature now became all the rage. No one, I imagine, actually hugged its spiky trunk. But dukes were glad to give it precedence in their parks, and an avenue of fifty monkey puzzles became the status symbol of the age. It welcomed you to a great Victorian mansion like a green version of a red carpet. (I believe our family pet on the lawn dated from this glittering era.) But the see-saw came down, and the tree fell out of fashion, consigned to the suburbs and mocked by the great and the good.

* * *

Now our limousine was back on the road, heading south into the heart of Patagonia, leaving behind the dry, stony hills where the monkey puzzles are still honoured. Perhaps *tolerated* would be nearer the mark. The tree is supposed to be protected on both sides of the Andes. But, in the Argentine at least, the government encourages landowners to plant incongruous rows of pine trees in and around the wild groves of monkey puzzles. These boisterous timber trees, mainly *Pinus ponderosa* from North America, will rapidly outbreed the locals.

As we drove deeper into Patagonia, the landscape soon changed with a flourish. Wild yellow *alstroemeria* – as luscious as in a British florist's – splashed the side of the dusty roads. The thorn trees carried spirals of flowering creepers called *Mutisia*: one species eight-petalled and pink, the other eleven-petalled and orange. Strings of enormous lakes, sapphire-blue in the midsummer sun, carried the eye to the actual peaks of the Andes. Before this we had only glimpsed these snowy prongs from 50 or 60 miles to the east, and heard their romantic Indian and Spanish names: Laline, Cerro Tronador and so on. Now we were at their feet – suppliants for a few precious days. I would have liked to spend weeks exploring these sapphire lakes and the forests of southern beech that swept up several thousand feet from the water's edge to the edge of the glaciers themselves. Few sights are more astonishing than the melting and collapse of a glacier – an iceberg in the sky – thousands of feet above one's head. One day we drove out to Cerro Tronador (the 'Thunderer') and scrambled up the rocks beyond the treeline. We watched in awe as the chunks of melting snow and ice morphed into the necklace of waterfalls feeding the blue-green river beside us, which fed in turn the forests of southern beech.

There are six species of *Nothofagus*, the southern beech, on both sides of the Andes, and none of them would pass for a beech in Europe. In fact they lack the most beguiling qualities of our northern beech: bark smooth enough to be disfigured by lovers' names; trunks like columns of a temple, plated with silver; leaves that go scarlet and gold before they die in the autumn. But two of these six southerners – *N. alpina* (formerly *procera* or *nervosa*) and *N. obliqua* – grow much faster than our beech and can almost keep up with our poplars. And they are deciduous, too, which means they can better stand our icy northern winters. Thirty years ago I planted as an experiment a dozen of both species in my garden and woodlands at Tullynally. I wish I could say the experiment succeeded.

Three languished and died in the garden, where they were exposed to something worse than an icy wind: the rhizomes of honey fungus that find the roots of guests from abroad particularly inviting. Out in my plantations the trees did better at the beginning. They sprinted away from the local beech, and grew fat shiny-brown boles that looked as if they'd be ready for the sawmill in half the time needed to grow European beech. Then gradually they lost heart, and will soon be overtaken, I fear, by the local beech and oak. It's all very frustrating, but my friends tell me it was only to be expected. Why do the trees fail? I don't think the experts know. Dendrology, like most branches of science, is full of riddles and mysteries. All you could say is that these southern beech are not happy in Ireland – homesick, if you like, for the Andes.

Now we could see their homes for ourselves, reflected in those sapphire Patagonian lakes. It was high summer, and at this altitude the sun is your friend. For the next week we had the good fortune to explore by car and boat three lakes in particular: the lake centred at Bariloche, called Lago Nahuel Huapi, and two more to the south, Lago Menendez and Lago Futalaufquen. It turned out that we were too far south for the two deciduous species I already knew well, to my cost: *N. alpina* and *N. obliqua*. These mountainsides were dominated by an exciting evergreen species, *N. dombeyi*, known locally as the coihue. And this coihue was a revelation. For the first time I saw a southern beech that could compete in size and beauty with the great European beech I knew. In fact I was told that the coihue can grow to a height of 40 metres (about 130 feet), making it much the tallest of the genus – and taller than any of our beech at Tullynally. True, the bark was disappointing: as rough as an oak's or an ash's without the elegant patterning. But the scale was tremendous and the form wonderfully varied. We saw some gigantic examples at a private estate straddling the shore near Villa Angustura. The trunks rose like columns for 60 feet and then exploded in an umbrella of small, shiny leaves. The owner, a beautiful divorcee called Alicia, entertained us to an al fresco banquet that lacked only the nuts of the monkey puzzle. (It was high summer, and Menzies' nuts were out of season.) I must admit the sparkling white wine was delicious. Otherwise I would have sworn all the beech were at least 40 metres tall.

Time was now running short. We had bagged two of the most inspiring trees in the southern hemisphere: the monkey puzzle and the coihue. What of the third, much rarer prize, of which botanical enthusiasts never ceased to talk, the *Fitzroya cupressoides*, known here as the Alerce?

Today the tallest Alerce in the Argentine is believed to be just over 70 metres high (230 feet): a dizzy height for any tree. Experts estimate it's more than two thousand years old. But no one will ever know how tall these trees once grew, how long they lived – or indeed how common they once were in the rain-soaked forests either side of the Andes. Sad to say, the loggers had taken most of the giants by the end of the last century. The resinous red timber made exceptionally durable planking, perfect for building. And the lakes gave easy transport to the new towns in Patagonia, and beyond. The railway, later celebrated by Paul Theroux, could spirit the lumber to the cities of the Pampas to the east, including the capital, Buenos Aires.

Of course the rape of the old-growth forests was a fact of life wherever colonists needed timber for building. It was a story repeated in the Americas, Australia and New Zealand. By the 1890s, the loggers had chopped down and sawn up most of the giant sequoias of California – by volume the biggest trees in the world. The trackless sequoia forests of the Sierra Nevada were reduced to a mere seventy-five separate groves. Then by a miracle, or rather, by virtue of one of the first great environmental crusades, the loggers were stopped. In south-east Australia there were no miracles, no crusades, only hard-nosed colonists. Almost all the eucalyptus over 300 feet high were felled to make planks and rafters for Melbourne and Sydney. It was the same story in the region around Perth. Only a handful of giant eucalyptus remain. In northern New Zealand the giant kauris, worshipped by the Maoris as fathers of the forest, were slaughtered in their thousands, leaving barely a dozen for posterity. Further south, as I found when hunting for New Zealand's biggest podocarps a decade ago, the loggers took the lot.

So I was saddened but not surprised to hear that in Patagonia there were only a handful of ancient Alerce, at least on the Argentine side of the Andes. We were told that one of the most accessible giants grew at the western end of the vast (and unpronounceable) Lago Nahuel Huapi. Two hours in a large white catamaran brought us - and a hundred cheerful Argentinan tourists - close to our quarry. Then a second smaller boat brought us to a small, green, reedy lake, Lago Prias, which stretches out an arm to within a few miles of the frontier with Chile, under the shadow of the Thunderer. It is in this narrow belt of primeval forest, its head and shoulders dowsed with 3,000 millimetres (120 inches) of rain a year - four times the rainfall of most of Patagonia - that the Alerce is happiest. But can a giant be happy when confined to a zoo?

With the hundred cheerful tourists we clambered up and down the slippery steps of the boardwalk leading to the giant. Two guides, eloquent, I'm sure (but they only spoke Spanish) marshalled us into files like schoolchildren. The giant alone was silent. He was also largely invisible. He had been confined to a wooden cage inside the wooden boardwalk. We could see his feet and the lower part of his legs. They were certainly impressive: an Ozymandias of a trunk, with strips of red, moss-covered bark like an American redwood, though on a much smaller scale. I would guess he was 25 feet round the waist, a fraction of the girth of an ancient giant sequoia.

Most of his body was invisible behind a screen of coihues and half-dead *Chusquea* (the local bamboo which periodically flowers and dies). His height was anyone's guess. But I would be surprised if he was much taller than the coihues. Our guide, eloquent on the subject of the dying *Chusquea* (when it flowered and died it was a case of 'death after sex'), knew less about the history of the tree. But she told us to look at the large axe-wound on one side. What did this signify? Why was the tree spared?

I gathered that the loggers came here in the 1880s, as soon as the country was cleared of the local Indians by General Roca, the Argentine dictator of that period. (Roca was a man of iron, famous for not taking prisoners. You could say the loggers behaved better to the Alerce. At least they found their victims a home, as rafters and floorboards, in the new towns of Patagonia.) Anyway our guide explained that here on Lake Prias the loggers took every large tree. The stumps were their gravestones. Why was one giant spared? Had the loggers had a fit of conscience? No, she said, somewhat earnestly, loggers were not like that. The trunk must have been cracked. I'm sure she was right.

Three days later we took a boat to a see a second giant Alerce that had survived the loggers. He was hidden away at the western end of Lake Menendez beyond an immense wall of ice and snow, melting, like the Thunderer, into a skein of waterfalls. This new Ozymandias turned out to be even larger than the one with the axe-wound. His height, we were told, was 70 metres (230 feet) tall with a girth to match. But once again the giant was largely invisible. Most of him – head, shoulders, and most of his body – was hidden among the dying *Chusquea* and the surrounding screen of coihues.

I can understand why the authorities lean over backwards to protect the handful of venerable Alerce that survive in the Argentine. But I think they are too protective of these shy giants. If I were a giant Alerce that had survived two thousand years of rain and snow, and the storms that brought down my neighbours, I wouldn't be afraid of a few chattering tourists.

1 February 2013

Back home in Ireland, I am digesting the lessons of the fortnight. What have I learnt that will help me plant, or replant, my arboretum and the woodland gardens around it?

There are lessons from all three of the great southern genera.

In the past I have planted various species of *Nothofagus*, the southern beech, but often in the wrong place. My mistake with *N. alpina* and *N. obliqua* was that I mixed them with our own European beech, *Fagus sylvatica*. In due course our beech outgrows and upstages these intruders from the south. The answer is simple: keep the two genera apart by planting them in separate groups. My mistake with *N. antarctica* was that I had tried to make it a specimen tree, and given it special protection. I hadn't quite grasped that it was the scrubbiest but hardiest of the species. Now I have seen it scrabbling in the rocks under the glaciers high on the flanks of the Tronador. So the lesson is this. plant it as a thicket and let it face the icy blasts on the outside of the plantations. My mistake with *N. dombeyi* was that I had seriously underrated it. Although I had once seen a fine example at Mount Usher in County Wicklow, I had no idea before I saw it in Patagonia that this was the most majestic of the genus. Now it will be given pride of place in my arboretum.

The *Araucaria* or monkey puzzle is quite a different kettle of fish. Our family pet, the great monkey puzzle on the lawn of my parents' house in Sussex - the tree insulted by Vita Sackville-West - had been chosen as a single icon to impress the guests. (It was probably planted by my father's great-uncle, Sir Francis Pakenham, British ambassador to Chile in the late nineteenth century.) After it died in 2009, I planned to plant a successor on the lawn at Tullynally. But now I have seen its cousins growing among the rocks in Patagonia, gnarled and twisted survivals from the Jurassic era, I realise that a mountain is the place to put the tree. I know just the spot at Tullynally - well, a stylised sort of mountain, among some boulders below the grotto. All I need is a packet of wild monkey puzzle seeds from Patagonia. Like Menzies I can rear them in pots. Nature and a warm greenhouse will do the rest.

When I am old I shall look up from my wheelchair, lost in a forest of monkey puzzles.

What of the third species from the Andes, the gigantic Fitzroya or Alerce? For this I don't have long to wait. Today there's a new jewel in the crown of the arboretum: a twelve-inch-high cutting of Alerce, given me by a generous friend who works at Edinburgh's Royal Botanic Garden. It has a noble pedigree. The cutting was taken from a plant collected as seed in the wildest part of the Chilean Andes. Its mother may have been more than two thousand years old.

Yesterday, we had a ceremony to celebrate the planting of the young Alerce. I had chosen a site in the clearing on the west side of the arboretum. It's not an ideal spot because the soil is stony, and bricks are often turned up by the spade - relics, I suppose, of earlier buildings. But it's well protected from winter storms by the wall of the drying yard. I decided to plant it in honour of our seventh grandchild, Julia, now two years old. I hope Julia and the Alerce both live to be more than a hundred. Of course by then Julia will be an old lady, but the Alerce may be only just beginning its life.

My first white goddess, Kanchenjunga (28,000 feet), seen from St Paul's Anglican School, Darjeeling. We were given tea in the bungalow where Joseph Hooker stayed before his daredevil expedition to explore Sikkim.

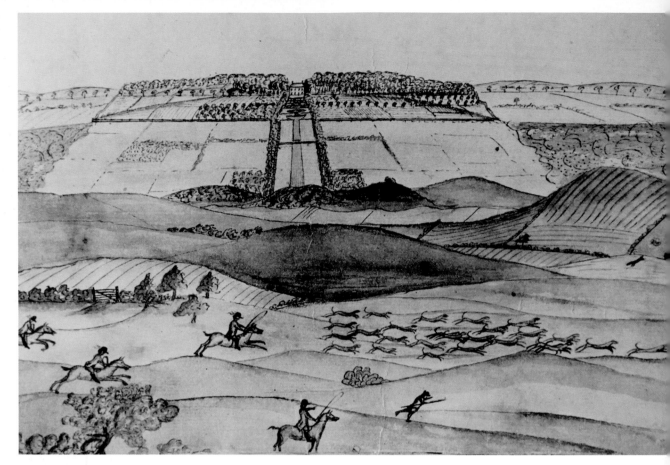

ABOVE: View halloo at Pakenham Hall, now Tullynally, in 1738 (with the fox escaping to the right). From a sketch in the diary of 28-year-old George Edward Pakenham. The demesne then followed the European fashion for axial avenues, basins, cascades and a tree-lined canal.

LEFT: Portrait of George Edward Pakenham attributed to James Latham and probably painted about 1740. His elder brother, Thomas, married a Longford heiress that year and was later created Baron Longford.

OPPOSITE: Tullynally today, photographed from one of the hills shown in George Edward's sketch. The original two-storey house, as plain as a barracks, was given Gothic fancy dress in 1806–42.

LEFT: One of the largest and oldest beech trees in the demesne during the icy December of 2010. Earlier I had counted 220 rings on the stump of one of its brother trees, blown down in a gale.

ABOVE: The upper pond (River Cham) in the pleasure ground during that winter. The mercury fell to -17°C but the water, fed from a deep spring, steamed like a hot bath.

RIGHT: From the balustrade, built by a gardener on wet days, looking towards the Horsepark.

ABOVE: Some of the heifers from our dairy herd grazing on what had been a lawn in my grandfather's day.

LEFT: The Pumpkin House (alias Womb with a View) in the new arboretum. When I commissioned it, I asked Antoine Pierson, a brilliant local French cabinet-maker, what style he would choose and he replied: 'I will only say this. It will be a masterpiece.'

OPPOSITE: Breakfast with Buddha in the Pumpkin House. The conical hill at the end of the vista is Knockeyon, six miles away to the south-east, on the shore of Lough Derravaragh.

Monkey puzzles growing on the cliffs in Patagonia, in western Argentina. In these barren lands they have little competition. On richer soils they are under threat, despite efforts to protect them.

5

Plagues from the East

6 February 2013

I've just been down the Forest Walk and had a long, hard look at the ash tree that
lords it over the first clearing. It's one of my favourites. It's not a champion ash. The
old fellows down in the cows' field at Cruckawn are two feet more round the belly.
But it's remarkably tall and elegant. The trunk rises like a grey column for more than
40 feet before the first branch.

And this week the newspapers are full of the new plague that threatens all our
European ash trees: a fungal disease with the pretty name of *Chalara fraxinea*. In fact
this Chalara is anything but pretty. She has been munching her way through the ash
trees of Europe, starting with Lithuania and the East back in the 1990s and moving
inexorably westwards. Five years ago she reached France and Holland, and now
she's been discovered - to the surprise of the governments' experts - in Britain
and Ireland.

How did this plague cross the seas? Most of the young trees already affected in
our countries were recent imports from the Continent. That's what the experts admit,
somewhat lamely. In other words a timely ban on these imports would have stopped
the plague reaching our shores. Or would it? For we face a double threat. Scientists
believe that, as well as travelling by lorry and ferry, the lethal spores of Chalara have

used the wind to cross the seas – and are spreading invisibly across both countries by the same method.

I'm sorry for the experts who failed to warn us of the impending disaster. They must feel very foolish. But their failure doesn't surprise me. I remember their reaction in the 1960s to the threat from Dutch elm disease, brought here on logs imported from Canada and transmitted by bark beetles. The question was put to them: Would it be prudent to ban imports of Canadian elm logs, unless the logs had first been stripped of their bark – and their fungus-carrying beetles? No fear, said the experts. A ban would be quite unnecessary. Dutch elm disease had visited Britain before and then spontaneously vanished. The same would happen once again. So for a decade people watched aghast as elms died in their millions, and the landscape of many parts of England was changed for ever.

Down in the Forest Walk I looked again at the tall, elegant ash tree. Could I bear to lose it? Fortunately there are other trees hungry for the space: two young lime trees, a battered old beech tree, a pushy young sycamore and a Lawson cypress so tall and handsome that it passes for a redwood. Still, this tall, elegant ash would be a serious loss. We have so few ancient ash trees. I can't think why. This species, the European ash (*Fraxinus excelsior*) is one of the handful of forest trees actually native to Ireland. (In fact we're reduced to only *three* kinds of native trees suitable for timber – two species of oak and this ash – ever since we lost the wych elm to Dutch elm disease.) And the ash grows like a weed in most parts of Ireland. Here in the Midlands the rich alkaline soil suits it to perfection.

Gardeners of course are no friends to the ash. Its winged 'keys' plaster the soil early in spring. But farmers have always encouraged its spread, at least in the hedgerows. The trees grew fast and straight and had a hundred uses: for plough handles, spade handles, shafts for carts, spokes for wheels, hockey sticks, hurley sticks. Perhaps that's the point. Ash provided the small wood that was so valuable on the farm. So here at Tullynally old ash trees were always rarities. Oak and beech, ornamenting the clumps and shelter belts, were allowed the privilege of a long life. Most of the ash were destined to be felled when young.

In my Forest Walk, at any rate, the ash are safe from the sawmill – if not from the dreaded Chalara. Further down the path I encountered another of my favourites: a prodigiously healthy-looking horse chestnut. From its low, twisted branches and slightly dishevelled appearance I would guess it was self-sown, and about eighty years old. Forty-five years ago, when I reopened the Forest Walk, I rescued this tree from a jungle-growth of elder and bramble. It was quite a small tree in those days, and being bullied by a sycamore, which I had to remove.

I have a soft spot for this chestnut and its welcoming, mossy arms. It reminds me of the chestnut in the garden in North Oxford in the first year of the war when I was a child of seven. This was my conker tree - my arsenal in conker duels at prep school - and also my lookout. I remember climbing it, at least the first 6 feet of it, when I heard that German parachutists, disguised as nuns, were expected at any moment. I was determined to die bravely, but glad to find the parachutists (or nuns) were missing. Years later I went back to that garden, now owned by an Oxford college. I wish I had stayed away. The chestnut had been crudely lopped, its head ripped off and all its limbs amputated. It would have been kinder to kill it outright.

The common horse chestnut, as botanists call it, is too common at present for its own good. If it had recently been introduced into Europe we should all be stunned by its appearance: by the many-fingered, paddle-shaped leaves, the fountains of pink and white flowers, the impossibly shiny brown conkers. In fact the species has been naturalised in Britain and Ireland for about four hundred years. (For most of that time its origins were unknown to science, but eventually botanists found it was native to the wilder parts of southern Albania and northern Greece.) Now we all take it for granted - but not for long, I fear. Like the ash, the horse chestnut is also under threat from a plague that is devastating Europe.

There is no treatment. The disease, a form of bleeding canker, can kill large, old trees stone-dead in a year. Two of my favourite horse chestnuts dominated the view of the upper pond in the garden. Three summers ago I was shocked to see these chestnuts turn pale and drop their leaves prematurely. Last year they were standing corpses, and today they are merely stumps. Another huge horse chestnut on the front drive, 16 feet round the belly and perhaps our biggest, seems to have caught the same infection. It must have been planted in the 1840s, when 'Fluffy', the 3rd Earl, commissioned Sir Richard Morrison to extend our towers and turrets another 250 feet to the east. Fluffy had just come of age and was determined to move his mother out of the main house into a new 'dowager's wing'. (In fact the new wing proved so cold and damp that she moved back to England. Perhaps this was Fluffy's plan all along.) At any rate the horse chestnut helped to conceal the junction between the old Gothic and the new. If the bleeding canker kills it now, the house will look as bald as it must have looked in Fluffy's time. And I'm afraid most of this huge tree's buds are rotten. So the tree must be doomed.

This is why I took a hard look at the prodigiously healthy-looking chestnut in the Forest Walk. Will this beautiful creature, too, be a mere stump within a few years?

I'm glad to say there are at least some species of trees not under any threat. Take the common lime, *Tilia x europaea*. It's actually a hybrid (as shown by the 'x' before the specific name) created naturally, it appears, from two European limes: the small-leaved and the large-leaved. Like many hybrids it's somewhat infertile, but good gardeners grow it easily from cuttings. And the tree is long-lived and unusually resilient - irrepressible, you could say.

In the Forest Walk I have a fine young example. It was the first tree I planted - if you could call it planting - in the Forest Walk. The year was 1968 and I had just decided to reopen the Forest Walk. Halfway along, we found a large lime tree lying across the path, blown down, I would guess, by Hurricane Debbie seven years earlier. Some of the roots were still hinged to the ground and there was a flicker of life in its branches. But we cut it up for firewood and removed the logs; the stump fell back into the hole under its own weight. Then I remembered reading that many deciduous trees can be given new life on their old roots. All you need do is cover the stump with soil, and reduce to one stem the thicket of young shoots that follow. The lime tree duly rose from the dead. It's now a fluted column 30 feet high with a perfectly symmetrical crown.

The Forest Walk ends with a romantic flourish: the Swan River or Lower Lake. Three hundred years ago, a generation or two after the first of our family arrived in Westmeath, this had been the climax of a formal landscape. Below the plain classical house a series of small cascades led to a half-mile-long canal, ending in a rectangular basin. A generation later formality had gone out of fashion. The canal and cascades vanished under the plough and the basin was reborn as a romantic river, flowing (or appearing to flow) through the woods of beech and oak. Gliding across the river, I'm sure, was a pair of milk-white swans.

That was the theory. In 1968 the river, rechristened the Swan River in my grandfather's time, had vanished under a thick pelt of reeds and rushes. The resident swans had fled in disgust, back to Lough Derravaragh, a couple of miles to the south. (As I said earlier, this is the lake of the children of King Lir, whom their jealous stepmother turned into swans.) How to persuade them to return? We dug out the Swan River with a drag-line digger and back came the resident swans.

15 February 2013

East of the Swan River are the remains of the woods planted in the mid-eighteenth century at the time the formal basin was being reborn as a romantic river. They must be some of the oldest trees on the estate: two crumbling beech pollards and three antediluvian oaks.

I went down last night to feed some grain to the swans and had a look at these ancient beech and oak. We have had very little frost so far this winter and it looks as if it will be an early spring. Patches of grass are bright green, and you can see the stubby green leaves of the bluebells, although the flowers themselves won't come till May. Sheltered by the stump of a birch, the first primroses are showing their faces.

By contrast the beeches and oaks looked impossibly old and battered. The bigger of the two pollard beech is covered with battle scars; other wounds are fresh and suppurating. The tree was half wrenched from the ground by some gale in the past. But it must have learnt how to ride these westerly gales by leaning away from them. Anyway it was squat by design, for it was a pollard, which meant its head, 10 feet from the ground, was regularly cropped for fuel, while the trunk was free to grow fat. This kept the young shoots safe from the teeth of grazing cows and horses. I expect my ancestors gave up pollarding the tree about two hundred years ago. It was then allowed to grow a new head and keep it. And now the huge, swollen upper trunk and branches are festering with sores, and a trickle of slime runs down its flanks. I'm not sure I envy it for its longevity. But I do admire its stoicism.

The biggest of the three oaks has also suffered a series of shattering wounds. It's not hard to see why. Sixty years ago, this oak was in the lee of a commercial wood of silver firs and Norway spruce planted about 1870 by my great-grandfather. Then the wood was felled, and the shelter vanished - until the next crop of spruce provided it. But oaks are far more long-lived and resilient than beeches. Although crippled by wounds these three ancient oaks may outlive us all by several centuries. Unless, of course, they succumb to one of the two new diseases specifically targeting oak: Sudden Oak Death and Acute Oak Decline.

So far, thank heavens, neither disease has killed any oaks in Ireland. Not as far as we know. But SOD, as the former is called (appropriately enough), has killed hundreds of thousands of red oaks in the United States. AOD, as you might call it, has proved lethal among oaks in Britain. It may be only a matter of a few years before these two newcomers choose to pay us a visit in Ireland.

20 February 2013

Good news, of a kind, about Chalara. We were told earlier this month that Britain's ash trees are under a double threat from the disease: first from affected plants which have been imported from the Continent; second from the lethal spores which the wind carries across the Channel and North Sea to eastern England, and from there to the rest of Britain and Ireland. Well, the second threat doesn't seem to apply to Ireland after all. We curse our cool, wet summers here, but they have given us (and perhaps Wales and Scotland) one precious advantage. It may be too cold here for the killer fungus to breed. So there's a chance this plague won't prove the pandemic here in Ireland that now threatens England – and has already destroyed 90 per cent of the ash trees in parts of the Continent.

25 February 2013

Bad news after all. I have been talking to Gerry Douglas, our friend who sits on one of the official European committees that is trying to keep track of Chalara. He says it's far too soon to be optimistic about this ghastly disease. Even if the spores of the fungus don't blow across the Channel from Wales to Ireland (or haven't already done so), the spores will have already arrived by a different route. They will have been carried on the leaves of the infected young ash trees imported from Europe during the last decade. Hundreds of thousands of young trees were brought over, although the disease was already rampant there. The young ash were planted with the special blessing (meaning the extra subsidy) of the Irish government. You see, these ash trees were 'native', that is, the species was native even if the trees themselves had been reared in Holland or Denmark. And now the government has to spend millions of euros arranging for the infected trees to be destroyed and the owners compensated. But, if Gerry's right, the money will be largely wasted. The infected leaves, spirited away by the wind, will still carry the plague from one end of Ireland to the other.

Die-back for ash, sudden death for oaks, lethal canker for chestnuts: what a cheerful future lies ahead for the trees we admire. Is there no way to escape this scenario, this *Gotterdammerung* of the trees? Recently I attended a lecture by a distinguished American scientist that brought me a glimmer of hope. He pointed to the string of new diseases appearing in Europe and North America – all originating in Asia. Most of them came in container ships, carried in microscopic spores aboard wooden crates. For various reasons it would be impossible to stop every one of these microscopic stowaways from getting ashore. They would certainly wreak havoc in the future. But we should look carefully at the European species under threat. All of the victims – elm, ash, oak, chestnut – are part of a far-flung genus with one or more representatives in the East. And it is with these Asiatic species that we should seek the solution. For millions of years they shared their soil with these same Asiatic diseases and evolved, by natural selection, immunity from them. So these are the trees we should now plant in Europe to replace our dying native species: Japanese and Chinese oaks, Chinese sweet chestnut and Chinese elm, Indian horse chestnut and so on.

I think he may be right, this distinguished American scientist. But there is one drawback. The Asiatic species, proposed as replacements, are certainly attractive. But I can't believe they will grow very large in Europe or live to a great age. The common European species now under threat are some of the most inspiring species on earth.

27 February 2013

Enough of this talk of plagues. Next month will be March, the month when magnolias rule our world – if the weather is kind. These are the giant magnolias from China, Japan and the Himalayas, trees that flower on bare branches before the leaves are awake. And they are safe after millions of years of evolution from all the plagues of the East.

6

Knicker-Pink

18 March 2013

Yesterday, with Charles Horton and Aidan Walsh, my neighbours and fellow magnolia addicts, I left the sombre winter landscape of the Irish Midlands and drove 120 miles southwards down to Waterford where the blackthorn was already in flower. Up here in Westmeath, spring comes like an afterthought. It finally drops in on us nearly a month after it sweeps along the coasts of Waterford. And often a sudden frost in late March descends on my early magnolias, turning the delicate pink or white 'tepals' (as the magnolia's petals are called) to so many brown rags.

Now we were driving to the threshold of spring. Mount Congreve, ten miles west of Waterford city, basks on a sunny bank above the estuary of the River Suir. Here, cradled in an eighteenth-century demesne of ancient oak and beech woods, you will find one of the most sumptuous - and most extraordinary - gardens of the world.

This garden was the only child, so to speak, of Ambrose Congreve, the last and most creative of the six generations of Congreves who owned this estate. As a young man he had married an English heiress - like any sensible Irish squire. Soon he had made a sizeable industrial fortune. His wife's family had made their pile as chemical engineers in the north of England. Ambrose took over the family business and exported engineering plant all over the world. He was young and tough and perhaps even ruthless. But he didn't indulge himself with the usual follies of the rich: with yachts and horses and villas in exotic places. He and his wife Marjorie were childless but shared a passion for gardening. In Ambrose's case it was an obsession - an obsession, above all, with magnolias.

When he was in his sixties he sold up the business and decided to live and spend as if there were no tomorrow. Lesser men (and of course I include myself) buy a dozen magnolias and think they have a collection. Ambrose thought nothing of buying five *hundred* magnolias. Sometimes people asked him why he bought so many large plants from the nursery trade and didn't take the time to breed his own varieties. 'Time?' he would say. 'No, I haven't the time to wait. I want it now.'

He was wrong, as it proved - absurdly and delightfully wrong. He had all the time in the world. He lived to the magnificent age of 104, a flamboyant figure in yellow silk shirt and golden cufflinks, still swapping gardening stories in April 2011, a month before he died. 'Philip bred a *yellow* magnolia,' he told me then, referring to a well-known collector of magnolias. Ambrose made the colour yellow sound risqué and faintly improper. He puffed at a large cigar. 'Philip called the magnolia "Daphne" after his *mistress* . . .' I looked across the room at Ambrose's elegant companion of many years. Was there a yellow magnolia at Mount Congreve and what was its name? I'm sure she guessed what was in my mind. But I didn't dare to ask.

Now that Ambrose has died (he shares a tomb with Marjorie, who died in 1995, inside a Greek temple overlooking the Suir) people ask themselves who owns Mount Congreve. Is it possible that we, the people of Ireland, are the new owners? In fact this was the first question we asked the current curator, Michael White, and it seemed to provoke some embarrassment. It was rumoured many years ago that Ambrose, in return for some tax concession, had agreed to give the estate to the nation. The nation was of course delighted. Who could say no to a bargain like that? This agreement still stands, I believe. But Michael explained that the estate, for the first twenty years after Ambrose's death, will remain in the hands of a trust. (After that it will belong to the nation. I hope this arrangement will work, but it sounds a bit complicated.)

Michael now generously offered to show us the gardens where a mind-blowing forest of early flowering magnolias awaited us. Of course I was anxious to see all the Asiatics, large and small. But it was the giants that made one gasp: the Big Five of the magnolia world.

*   *   *

Why do these plants cast such a spell over us, turning us into helpless addicts? Look at the astounding size of the flowers, which are often as big as soup plates, making them the biggest of any flowers known in the temperate world. And look at their unearthly profusion. A single magnolia tree, as tall as an oak and covering half an acre of hillside, can give birth to three or four thousand flowers. Then consider the astonishing colours and textures of the flowers, which range from a delicate ivory-white to a sumptuous, priestly purple. And compounding it all is the fact that the Asiatic magnolias discard their hairy perules (three layers of miniature fur coats) and come into bloom when winter has hardly left us and the rest of the garden and woodland seems asleep.

The addiction to these seductive creatures from China, Japan and the Himalayas only reached the gardening world in the first half of the twentieth century. In fact magnolia fever spread slowly at the beginning.

The story begins at the end of the eighteenth century. In 1789 Sir Joseph Banks introduced to Europe a small tree with ivory-white flowers, which bloomed on bare branches early in the spring. It was the Yulan magnolia or 'Lily-tree' (in due course christened *M. denudata*, the 'Naked Magnolia'). Joseph Banks was the ebullient young squire and amateur naturalist from Leicestershire who had made his name as the companion of Captain Cook on the voyage of the *Endeavour*. Later he had become the hyperactive President of the Royal Society, and had his finger in a thousand pies. He was the man who had prodded the government to make Botany Bay a station for convicts, and arranged for Captain Bligh of the *Bounty* to hunt for breadfruit in Tahiti. At home he bossed the staff of the royal gardens at Kew and acted as the unpaid botanical adviser to George III.

Apparently Banks imported the Yulan from Japan. But the tree was originally from China, where it was used by Buddhist monks to adorn their temples; I believe they took the white flowers as a symbol of purity. Anyway it was the monks who had brought it to Japan as early as the eighth century. In both countries the startling, goblet-shaped flowers were irresistible to painters, and its naked branches and ivory-white flowers zigzagged across the lacquer screens and porcelain vases exported to Europe. A second species of early-flowering Chinese magnolia, with the confusing name of Mulan (now *M. liliiflora*) was introduced from Japan a year after the Yulan. The Mulan was hardly bigger than a small bush but it had two accomplishments the Yulan lacked. It clothed the outside of its tepals with a lavish purple. And, if it was happy, the generous plant would bloom again and again from spring to autumn.

Neither Asiatic magnolia, it must be said, attracted much notice in Europe from gardeners or the nurserymen who supplied them. Both species were difficult to propagate. So the genus – christened in 1703 in homage to the French botanist, Pierre Magnol – was still dominated by five American magnolias successively introduced to Europe from the seventeenth century onwards. Two of these species were evergreen (*M. grandiflora* and *M. virginiana*) and three deciduous (*M. acuminata*, *M. tripetala* and *M. macrophylla*). But none bloomed in early spring or had the knack of blooming before the leaves emerged.

Thirty years after the Yulan and Mulan had made their debut almost unnoticed, a French landowner and horticultural enthusiast, Chevalier Étienne Soulange-Bodin, had a eureka moment. He was a former cavalry officer who had served under Napoleon and known the sour taste of defeat. It was 'better for both parties to have stayed at home and planted their cabbages', he wrote in 1819 in a letter to the *Gardener's Magazine* published in London. (His bon mot was adapted from Voltaire's *Candide*.) He now looked forward to gardening as a 'guarantee of the repose of the world'. One day, about the year 1820, he took the yellow pollen from the Mulan bush in his garden and smeared it on the green carpels of his Yulan tree.

The result was an artificial hybrid which seemed too good to be true. The colour of its goblet-shaped flowers, different in each clone, ranged from snow-white to dark purple. It was easy to propagate and flowered later than the Yulan, which made it safer from frost. And it proved a triumph of what scientists call heterosis (it sounds like a disease but it means hybrid vigour). The new hybrid, christened *M. x soulangeana* after its creator, was bigger and tougher than either parent. It flourishes where most plants would fail – in the smoke and grime of cities – and seems to revel in neglect. No wonder this hybrid is one of the most popular ever created and now dominates, every March and April, the front gardens of my favourite haunts in Dublin and London.

An equally brilliant stroke in crossing two small, spring-flowering Asiatic magnolias was made exactly a century later. The new species, *M. kobus* and *M. stellata*, had both been introduced to Europe from Japan in the 1870s. But they shared little except their snow-white colour. Kobus was a tough little tree, if rather dull. Its eight tepals were small and spoon-shaped and remarkably resistant to frost. Stellata was delicate and almost always a bush, but exceedingly pretty. Its eighteen long, strap-shaped tepals had provided it with a romantic name, the Star Magnolia. Could the best qualities of each be combined? That was the challenge and in 1919 it was answered by a German horticulturalist in Dresden called Max Loebner. He used the pollen of the tough tree to fertilise the seeds of the delicate bush. It sounds simple, but I'm sure it wasn't. At any rate the result is a small, upright, hardy tree with a snowfall of blossom – perfect for gardens of any size, including of course Mount Congreve.

It remained for the plant explorers to discover the giants of the genus, the Big Five which are the crowning glory of Ambrose's estate.

As I described in Chapter 1, the first giant (the tree that I came to know as Hooker's White Goddess) was discovered in 1849–52 when Joseph Hooker was exploring Sikkim. In due course he named the tree after his companion, Archibald Campbell. But the first seeds of *Magnolia campbellii* were not introduced until 1865, and the first flowering of the tree, twenty years later, attracted little attention. (It's thought to have first seen the light on the balmy shores of Cork harbour at Lakelands, the home of an eccentric bachelor, William Crawford, who specialised in oddities like the Brazilian monkey puzzle and the Tiger-tailed spruce.) Meanwhile daredevil French missionaries exploring central and south-west China, Père David and Père Delavay, made many astonishing botanical discoveries. So did the young Irish doctor, Augustine Henry, who collected thousands of new specimens for the Royal Botanic Gardens at Kew. But none of this botanical loot included any early-flowering giant magnolias. For that the gardening world had to wait till the years just before the First World War. This was when the wilder parts of south-west China and the Himalayas were finally opened up to plant explorers.

The fame of the new discoveries was to be shared between two unassuming young gardeners from Britain, George Forrest and Ernest Wilson. Both were paid a pittance – hardly more than £100 a year when they started – by British nursery firms hungry for new plants from Yunnan and Sichuan. And strong nerves were essential for the job. In 1905 gangs of xenophobic and bloodthirsty lamas swept down the Mekong valley leading from Tibet into north-west Yunnan. George Forrest spent twenty-one days being hunted by these lamas 'like a mad dog', as he put it. Starving and delirious, he was befriended by local Lissu tribesmen. They spirited him out of the valley and across an icy 17,000-foot pass, disguised as a Tibetan. But his feet 'were in shreds' and he only escaped by the skin of his teeth. All but one of his Chinese companions were killed or carried off as slaves, and two elderly French missionaries were tortured before being put to death.

Ernest Wilson was more fortunate. His only narrow escape was in 1910 when his caravan was hit by a landslide in a remote part of Sichuan. No one was killed but Wilson's right leg was mangled by a boulder. It took his bearers three days of forced marches to carry him back to civilisation, with his camera tripod acting as a splint for his leg, but nothing to dull the excruciating pain.

There was no love lost between Forrest and Wilson, and it was perhaps lucky that their hunting grounds didn't overlap. Part of the trouble was that they worked for rival nursery firms: Forrest exploring Yunnan for Arthur Bulley of Ness Gardens, Wilson exploring Sichuan for the celebrated Chelsea firm of James Veitch and Sons. In a few years, as the news of their discoveries spread, they both found more generous employers. Indignant at what he called his callous treatment by Bulley, Forrest realized he could earn a much better salary - ten times what Bulley had paid him at the start - by collecting seeds for syndicates of wealthy plant enthusiasts. These syndicates were organised by J. C. Williams, the millionaire owner of Caerhays Castle in Cornwall (and the man who gave his name to a famous hybrid camellia). For his part Wilson caught the eye of the flamboyant Professor Charles Sargent, the Director of the Arnold Arboretum of Harvard University, who hired him as his official plant explorer in China. Soon both Wilson and Forrest were sending back a treasure trove of unknown plants to their new employers. But the search for a giant magnolia to compete with Hooker's discovery eluded them both.

Then, quite suddenly, Wilson struck gold on his third Chinese expedition, in 1908 - and struck it again a few months later.

In fact Wilson had first glimpsed what was to be the second of the Big Five in the mountains of western Sichuan, when working for the firm of Veitch five years before. He described it in a letter: 'This Magnolia grows to a greater size than any other Chinese Magnolia . . . (I saw) a tree of this species which was more than 80ft tall, with a trunk 10 foot in girth.' When he returned in 1908 to collect seeds and herbarium material, so that he could register his discovery, he found the tree had vanished - cut down for the timber. But he found many 60-foot-high trees had survived in the same area, and the new species was duly named *M. sargentiana* after Charles Sargent, his flamboyant employer in America. Later in 1908 Wilson found another new giant which he called *M. dawsoniana* after Jackson T. Dawson, his employer's chief assistant. This was to be the third of the Big Five.

Strange to say, Wilson had also collected the fourth of the Big Five although he didn't realise this at the time. He mistook it for a pink variety of the famous Yulan. So the honour for discovering this fourth giant, now called *M. sprengeri* and *M. sprengeri*

'Diva' (a violet 'goddess'), passed to an obscure Italian missionary called Father Silvestri. He spotted it in Hupeh, in western China, twelve years later, and gave it the name of an unfortunate German botanist, Carl Sprenger (who lived near Naples, and lost most of his plant collection when Vesuvius erupted in 1906).

For his part, Wilson's rival Forrest had not been idle. After his horrific ordeal in the Mekong valley, a lesser man would have found a different continent to search for plants. But Forrest was made of stern Scottish stock. His work for British plant enthusiasts, like John Williams of Caerhays, brought him a good living and professional acclaim. He introduced a vast number of new species of plants, many of which bear his name. Tree rhododendrons, silver firs, maples, pieris, berberis, buddleias, deutzias, hypericums, more than fifty kinds of primula – the list of his discoveries is probably even longer than Wilson's. His plant-hunting took him on seven expeditions to China – nearly twice as many as Wilson made, for Wilson emigrated to America and eventually succeeded Sargent as Director of the Arnold Arboretum.

And strange to say, Forrest, too, had discovered one of the Big Five without realising it.

Back in 1904, when still new to China, and little dreaming of the ordeal to come, Forrest discovered a new pink-coloured giant a thousand miles to the east of Hooker's. It was 10,000 feet up in a snow-covered grove of silver firs in western Yunnan. At first Forrest's specimens went unrecognised, confused with an entirely different species, but in 1924 Forrest finally managed to send back a new batch of seeds, which were christened *M. mollicomata*. For technical reasons modern botanists don't accept the tree as a new species, but merely as a new variety of Hooker's famous *M. campbellii*, adding the name *mollicomata*. Many gardeners remain unconvinced. To them Forrest's giant seems very different, and many would regard it as the finest of the Big Five.

When this new Chinese magnolia first flowered in Britain in about 1936 it took the gardening world by storm. It had two contrasting advantages compared with Hooker's original version from Sikkim. It flowered earlier, taking only 10 or 12 years to reach that stage in its life cycle, half as long as its predecessor. It also flowered later, meaning a fortnight or so later in the year, when the worst of the spring frosts might be over. And it had a new poise that many found refreshing. The central four tepals clung together to form a cup. The outer seven or eight opened out to form a saucer.

So this was a happy ending to the story of the Big Five. Or was it? Ironically, neither Wilson nor Forrest ever saw their introductions in flower. Both men died suddenly a few years before the first of the Big Five (apart from Hooker's, of course) produced its flowers as big as soup plates. Wilson was driving home from the Arnold Arboretum one afternoon in 1930 when his car skidded and plunged down a ravine. Both he and his wife Muriel died in the crash. Two years later Forrest, aged fifty-nine, took out his gun to shoot some wildfowl at Tengchong in south-west Yunnan, close to the border with Burma. Then he called for help - and died almost instantly from a heart attack. (I have seen the monument at Dali recently erected in his memory by Chinese admirers. The original was destroyed by thugs during the Cultural Revolution.)

*   *   *

We must return to the Big Five, the crowning glory of Mount Congreve. As you would expect, the garden is designed on a princely scale, covering at least 100 acres, or so I would imagine. At first the layout seems conventional. There's an elegant formal garden, with lilies and peonies and other herbaceous plants arranged axially within the original walled garden. But when you leave the formal garden and the lawn beyond, you are in for a shock. The woodland garden straddles the terrace north of the house and the rocky hillside leading steeply down to the estuary of the River Suir. Both areas are crowded - crammed to bursting in fact - with Himalayan magnolias of a gigantic size.

Of course there are lavish helpings of other species which add spice and authenticity to the Himalayan atmosphere: goblets of scarlet rhododendrons, canapés of red and white camellias (some striped like carnations) and dishes loaded with sweet-scented daphnes. But it's the tree magnolias that appear like the creatures of a dream. Where in the world - except in Sikkim or Bhutan or Tibet - would you see a magnolia the size of an oak tree? And not just one. When Ambrose clapped his hands and told his army of gardeners he wanted two hundred magnolias *now*, those men didn't dawdle. Yesterday I tried to count the numbers in the double avenue of magnolias leading down to the Suir. I lost count at two hundred and fifty.

Up on the terrace facing the house are several stunning individual trees. I saw three outsize specimens of the Big Five. There's a twisted old specimen of Wilson's *M. sargentiana var. robusta*. It seems prematurely old and Michael says its huge, drooping mauve flowers are rather 'melancholy'. (I'm not sure that I agree. At any rate I'd give my eye teeth to have it on my lawn.) There's also a sumptuous example of the famous cultivar *M. sprengeri* 'Diva', the goddess that grows 60 feet high, her body adorned with deep-pink flowers. She originated from a single seedling reared at Caerhays Castle in Cornwall. Most striking of all is the cross, called 'Charles Raffill', between two varieties of *M. campbellii* that seems to have the best of every world. It has the double advantages of Forrest's *mollicomata* - flowering both later in the year and earlier in its own life - combined with the deep rose-pink of Hooker's original discovery. But it needs the elbow room that only the most sumptuous gardens can provide.

*   *   *

If any garden in Europe bears comparison with Mount Congreve's it must be the one made by three generations of the Williams family at Caerhays. By chance I happened to be nearby on the morning of 1 March, just over a fortnight before the trip to Mount Congreve. The south coast of Cornwall is kind to tender plants, and spring comes there as early as it comes to County Waterford. So that morning I grabbed the chance and drove down the narrow Cornish lanes to Caerhays. I hoped to be shown at least one famous example of the Big Five. After all, it was John Williams of Caerhays who had sponsored five of Forrest's seven expeditions to China. If I was lucky the tree would be in full bloom.

I also had a personal interest in one of Caerhays' most admired young trees. In 1979 I had the good fortune to be given a two-year-old seedling by Julian Williams, the second owner of the estate. It came from a famous mother tree: a white-flowering form of Campbell's magnolia (in other words Hooker's White Goddess) that been sent as a seed from the Indian Himalaya in the 1920s. The mother tree had already died but had left two very different offspring. The older brother, planted at Caerhays close to the entrance, blooms with flowers as white as its mother's and has proved one of the star performers. I splashed its photograph across the pages of my first tree book, *Meetings with Remarkable Trees*. The younger brother, given me by Julian Williams and planted at Tullynally, is now a prodigy 50 feet high. It's my pride and joy - although I have to admit it's not quite the colour I expected. (This is a sore point to which I shall come back in a moment.) It's the tree, at any rate, that dominates the pleasure ground at Tullynally at the end of this month or the beginning of April. Its flowers are astoundingly large up there in the naked branches - provided the frost doesn't turn them into bundles of brown rags.

At Caerhays that morning I paid my respects to the brother of my prodigy. Unfortunately it was still too early in the season for many magnolias to give us a performance, and the brother was not one of them. But the sun sparkled on the scarlet flowers of the reigning champion of the magnolias: the oldest, largest and most magnificent Campbell's magnolia growing in Britain or Ireland. Its trunk is about 9 feet in circumference, and you could mistake it for an oak or a beech if you didn't see the scarlet flowers. Perhaps there were three thousand individual flowers, and they were not rattling like cups and saucers. They were more like a covey of tropical birds roosting in the upper branches.

31 March 2013

I have just returned from a trip to the south of England where spring is already halfway to summer. Many trees in the London parks - horse chestnuts and sycamores especially - are exhibiting their new leaves. And the magnolias in the front gardens of inner London look magnificent. But this early spring has not been a boon for all magnolias as you might expect. In fact the magnolia zones of both Kew and Wisley are looking very sorry for themselves. Everywhere I see the signs of a searing frost which must have followed an unusually balmy spell in both these great collections. At Kew the delicate pink flowers of the ancient Campbell's magnolia - the twisted old creature facing the giant tulip tree - have been reduced to the colour of dirty cardboard. Even the leathery white tepals of Japanese hybrids like *M. x loebneri* and its cultivars have succumbed. At Wisley there's hardly a white flower left on the famous *M. denudata* by the stream without a brown stain to disfigure it. It's the same with the cultivar of *M. salicifolia*, 'Wada's Memory' (named after a popular Japanese nurseryman believed killed in the Second World War; in fact he was alive after all). Last year I remember the tree shone like a pillar of alabaster. This year it looks as if it has been sprayed with weed-killer.

Back at Tullynally I can only praise heaven that we had no balmy fortnight here. So our magnolias have all stayed safely wrapped in their perules, that is, in their fur coats - except for the first to flower. This is my only giant, and my pride and joy, the great *M. campbellii alba* given me in 1979 by Julian Williams. Unprotected since dropping their fur coats, the huge buds - and I would guess that there are at least three hundred of them - are now intensely vulnerable to the cold. Luckily the weather forecast is for buckets of rain, which means we shan't have frost. But I must keep my fingers crossed.

11 April 2013

This is proving the *annus mirabilis* (you could almost say *annus magnoliensis*) for my garden and woodland. I take back my harsh comments about the Westmeath spring. We've had ten wet days in a row, without an hour of hoar frost. I see the magnolias are deeply grateful. One after another the grown-up ones have thrown off their coats and exploded into flower.

My collection of magnolias, if you could call it that, started almost by chance. I began to plant them nearly forty years ago, after a delightful visit from the late Michael Rosse of Birr Castle, the famous horticulturalist then in his late sixties. Perhaps I had had too much to drink, but I had the cheek to ask him whether he had missed any great opportunities in his life. 'I wish I had planted more magnolias when I was *young*,' he said ruefully. I followed his advice - up to a point. I bought six small magnolias in Winchester. (But why only six? Why not sixty - or six hundred, for that matter? Oh, the reckless parsimony of youth.) Anyway it was a beginning. Four years later I was given my seedling giant by Julian Williams. Another decade and I bought a larger batch. Since I reached my seventies I have been buying magnolias in what the Germans call *Torschlusspanik* ('door-closing-panic'). So now I have about sixty in my collection, representing the Big Five and most of the other twenty-odd species hardy in our climate, as well as a rag-bag of hybrids and cultivars. I think I have done my best for them. I gave them the choicest parts of the garden and woodland: the most prominent corners of arboretum, the pleasure ground and Forest Walk. And, most important, I created a new garden for magnolias only, the Magnolia Walk.

The first six of my collection, now nearly forty years old, are violet and white Japanese hybrids, cultivars of *M. x loebneri*, squeezed into the western corner of the pleasure ground. I bought them at Hillier's, then smuggled them into Ireland. Stupidly, I had lost their health certificates, so I had to take them via Belfast at the height of the Troubles, carrying them strapped to the roof of the car. Now they're 30 feet high and their flowers, brimming with icing-sugar-white tepals, look as edible as meringues. (People say they're considered a delicacy at Japanese tea-parties.) But I now realise I made the typical beginner's mistake. I should have given them room to grow into trees, and I squashed them together as if they were shrubs.

Below them are three other small white magnolias of a little-known species. When I bought them ten years ago from a nurseryman he assured me they represented the *true* species of *M. cylindrica*, introduced from Anwhei in north-east China in the 1960s. He warned me to beware of other trees masquerading under that name. Now I have no idea if my cylindricas are fakes. If they are, they're certainly delightful fakes. Most white magnolias spread their blossoms carelessly across their branches. My cylindricas hold their tubular white flowers as upright as candles on a Christmas tree. Fake or not, this is my favourite small magnolia. It flowers absurdly young: only three or four years from planting. And it looked wonderful this week in the moonlight, when the candles seemed to light up the whole tree.

My favourite medium-sized magnolia graces the Forest Walk and bears the dashing name of 'Star Wars'. It was bred in New Zealand by an enterprising sheep farmer called Blumhardt. It's one of a large group of hardy hybrid magnolias created since the Second World War, mainly the work of American academics and New Zealand farmers. Many are richly coloured, with violet and purple predominant. No one yet knows their ultimate size. It may be enormous – we shall know in the next hundred years. On their mother's side, these new hybrids have the same purple-tepalled Mulan (*M. liliiflora*) as the famous hybrids grown by Chevalier Soulange-Bodin 150 year earlier. But instead of the Yulan (*M. denudata*), which is after all quite a modest tree, these new hardy hybrids have a giant on their father's side, a white-tepalled hybrid form (*M. x veitchii*) of Hooker's discovery, *M. campbellii*.

My own 'Star Wars' is magnificent, if I say it myself. It's only twenty years old and already as tall as a double-decker bus. I have planted it in a sunny, peaty clearing beside the Gingerbread House. This week its prodigious flowers have slowly started to unfold. They are rose-pink and are held up to the heavens like chalices.

Most promising of all my young magnolias are four of the Big Five, all growing like beanstalks. When I planted them four years ago I decided to take back from the farm a sheltered grove in the Lower Horsepark at the end of the Forest Walk. For more than a hundred years it had been grazed by cattle, and (apart from some whitethorns) parkland trees of an earlier generation were the only trees that had survived the chomping jaws of the bullocks. Now it's the Magnolia Walk and a neatly mown path, cut through the long grass, leads you from one magnolia to the next, against the background of ancient oaks and Scots pines and larch and tall, twisted whitethorns.

Only one of these four potential giants is yet conspicuous. This is Fr. Silvestri's goddess, *M. sprengeri* 'Diva'. It's only 8 feet high, but in a week or two it should be carrying a bouquet of fifty deep-pink blooms. Not very large blooms, it must be said, but a good beginning. Its companions, the other three future giants, have decided that, for the time being, they are not going to waste energy by flowering. I see their point. (But I hope they realise that I'm not as young as I was. In fact by mid-August I shall be eighty.)

But what of the first of the Big Five, the Tullynally giant in the pleasure ground, my pride and joy, my towering *M. campbellii alba*? The good news is that the huge buds, shivering in the icy rain, were spared any frost. They opened early last week and now they would bring a cry of admiration from the stoniest heart. Some are fully 12 inches across, and the 10 tepals assume an amazing variety of shapes as they slowly unfold. Up there, high on the branches, you can spot a tea-party of cups and saucers. There are also pheasants roosting, squirrels nesting, cats waiting to spring. And of course there's a barrow-load of cabbages and bananas - especially half-eaten bananas. That's the good news.

The bad news is that, as I confessed in *Meetings with Remarkable Trees*, the flowers of this clone are not white after all, unlike its brother tree at Caerhays. And the insipid, washed-out pink of the flowers seems to offend me more and more every year. Of course I'm being silly. What's wrong with knicker-pink? Well, I must remind myself once again. These flowers are the colour of flamingos.

15 April 2013

'Bad news', I wrote four days ago, and I was moaning about the colour of my magnolias. But bad news is relative. I've just heard that about eighty of our bullocks, penned in the Lower Horsepark, broke down the fence yesterday and stormed into the Magnolia Walk. I suppose they remembered the grass there was particularly tasty. Kevin says that two of the young magnolias were trodden into the ground and six crippled. I don't know yet the identities of the magnolias I have lost. And I haven't the courage to go down beyond the Forest Walk and look. The thought makes me sick.

I shall stay in the Forest Walk. This is where I am planning a new garden in the wild - a Sharawadgi garden - which should provide balm to my soul.

7

Sharawadgi

30 April 2013

May is creeping up on us. But I mustn't grumble. This is perfect weather for planting – or, at any rate, planning – a new garden in the wild.

I'm not sure of the style, but the idea will be to make the new garden follow the principles of 'Sharawadgi'.

It's a strange, paradoxical story. In 1685, Sir William Temple wrote a ten-page essay which he called 'The Gardens of Epicurus'. Temple was an international statesman (he negotiated the peace which ended two disastrous wars with Holland), patron of the wayward young Jonathan Swift (he introduced him to his 'Stella'), and above all a passionate gardener. His essay was a good-humoured, if somewhat rambling piece, part philosophical, part practical, and it included a paragraph that, for various reasons, became famous after the essay was published in 1692. The paragraph described how what he called the 'Chineses' followed diametrically opposite principles of garden design to the rest of the world. They pursued 'Beauty . . . without Order'.

But their greatest Reach of imagination is employed in contriving Figures [i.e. plans], where the Beauty shall be great, and strike the Eye, but without any Order or Disposition of Parts . . . And though we have hardly any Notion of this Sort of Beauty, yet they have a particular Word to express it; and, where they find it hit their Eye at first sight, they say the *Sharawadgi* is fine or admirable . . . And whoever observes the Work on the best *Indian* gowns, or the Painting upon their best Skreens or Purcellans [Porcelains], will find their Beauty is all of this Kind.

So 'Sharawadgi' meant something like 'artful irregularity'. But here's the point. Temple was not saying for a moment that English gardens should be designed in a Chinese style. On the contrary, he was devoted to the formal, geometric style developed in Italy, France and Holland, and universally followed in Europe. He described in the essay his ideal garden: rooted in symmetry and proportion, with trees and walks set out at regular distances, each part answering the other. Above all he loved a house called Moor Park in Hertfordshire with its 300-yard-long gravel walk, descending by regular flights of steps to a parterre of the same length. The parterre in turn was subdivided by gravel walks adorned with two fountains and eight statues, and led to two parallel summer houses and two parallel cloisters, and a grotto embellished with symmetrical rockwork and waterworks.

So Temple had no more idea of designing a Sharawadgi garden than he had of eating with chopsticks or wearing a pigtail. In fact his essay was a warning to gardeners not to try this dangerous and subversive new style. It was twenty to one that the attempt would fail – unless the designer was a genius. But 'in regular figures 'tis hard to make any great and remarkable Faults'. In other words, any fool with a ruler could design a formal garden.

I'm convinced that Temple's rambling essay (though some scholars will dispute this) was the pebble that starts the avalanche. The essay was reprinted several times after his death, and in 1720 was relaunched by his literary editor, Jonathan Swift, now the world-famous author of *Gulliver's Travels*. By 1740, every gentleman's library had a copy of Temple's provocative works. Part of the essay's appeal was that outlandish but unforgettable word 'Sharawadgi'. Was it really a Chinese word? Little enough was known about China in late-seventeenth-century Europe. True, imported Chinese porcelain and lacquer work were already fashionable, and Dutch copies of Chinaware, made at Delft, were already commonplace. But some people thought that Temple had invented the word and was pulling everyone's leg. In fact most modern scholars believe that Sharawadgi is not a Chinese word at all, but a corruption of the Japanese word *Shorowaji*, meaning 'not being regular'. They claim that Temple muddled up the two countries after hearing reports of Japanese gardens from Dutch merchants based at the Dutch trading post at Deshima outside Nagasaki. In other words when Temple wrote 'Chineses' he meant 'Japaneses'.

Temple, at any rate, had inadvertently launched the movement to reject symmetry and go for a more relaxed, informal style. Ten years after Temple's death, Addison denounced formal topiary in the *Spectator* in a famous essay: 'I would rather look upon a tree in all its luxuriance and diffusion of boughs and branches, than when it is cut and trimmed in mathematical figures'. At first his friend Alexander Pope, poet and gardener, was ambivalent about the need for the new style: 'For as to the Hanging Gardens of Babylon, the Paradise of Cyrus, and the Sharawaggis [*sic*] of China, I have little or no Ideas of 'em.' But by the 1730s the architect William Kent, who would have known Temple's essay well, had begun to popularise the naturalistic, anti-symmetrical style in landscape design. Kent 'leaped over the wall', in Horace Walpole's famous phrase, 'and found all Nature a garden'. By the 1750s, Sharawadgi gardens, or their descendants, were springing up all over England. It was Walpole who noisily promoted the new fashion. 'I am almost as fond of the Sharawaggi [*sic*],' Walpole wrote, 'or Chinese want of symmetry, in buildings, as in grounds or gardens.'

Soon Capability Brown took up the lead, and his smooth, bland formula of beech clumps and mixed shelter belts and sinuous lakes was repeated in gentlemen's parks all over Britain and Ireland. Gradually the term Sharawadgi slipped from the imagination – although Chinoiserie itself began to fascinate architects and decorators in most parts of Europe. Nothing was now more fashionable for the garden than a 100-foot-high folly of a pagoda, as you can still see if you visit Sir William Chambers' ten-storey pagoda at Kew Gardens. But no one was trying to *recreate* an authentic Chinese garden.

For one thing, European garden designers had only the haziest idea of what Chinese gardens were like. Even Chambers, who had visited the international trading post at Canton as a young 'supercargo' (agent) and later published an essay on oriental gardening – even Chambers had never seen any of the great gardens of China, which lay many weeks' journey further north. It was not until the mid-eighteenth century that the first dazzling descriptions of Chinese gardens arrived in Europe, in letters written by Jean-Denis Attiret, one of the French Jesuits based in the imperial city at what was then Peking.

And there was an even greater obstacle to recreating an authentic Chinese garden, if anyone had wanted to try. Not a single Chinese tree had yet been exported to Europe which was believed to be capable of surviving the icy winters of northern Europe. (The astonishing Chinese ginkgo arrived in England about 1750, probably via Japan, but it was at first thought to be too tender to survive out of doors.) No wonder, then, that Chinoiserie provided merely *one* of the many exotic features in the new style of European gardens. Often the combination of features bordered on the ridiculous. Incongruously near Chambers' pagoda at Kew was the dome of the Turkish mosque, complete with minarets, and beyond that the elegant Greek temple and the crumbling Roman ruin. A Chinese tourist would have rubbed his eyes in disbelief.

Back in my new garden in the wild, I plan to call it my Sharawadgi garden. It will be a new and improved version of my first Chinese garden, what I call 'Yunnan'. This original garden is in one respect authentically Chinese. Without exception, all the trees and shrubs in this small clearing are natives of Yunnan and Sichuan, in the wilds of south-west China. I collected the majority of them as seeds twenty years ago. It was my first amateurish attempt at plant-hunting in those remote green valleys, botanical treasure houses spread out across the mountains that merge into the eastern flanks of the Himalayas.

Late in September 1993 I took a plane to Kunming, capital of Yunnan, along with a party of fifteen friends who were fortunately a great deal more knowledgeable than I. Our leader, Keith Rushforth, was an expert field botanist, indefatigable in sorting out and naming the seeds we collected in our brown envelopes. (At the risk of seeming ungrateful, I must say I'm glad I didn't share a tent with Keith. He was equally indefatigable, we soon found, in sorting out his own seeds by torchlight far into the small hours.) We had set off in a small green bus for the 1,000-mile, three-week trip to Dali, Tengchong and the borderland east of Burma and Tibet. It was slow going but exciting enough.

Our long-suffering bus plunged in and out of three of the deepest river valleys of Asia – those of the Yangtse, the Mekong and the Salween. As you would expect, there were constant breakdowns and hold-ups. (This was before they built the dazzling new road linking Kunming and Dali.) In every town it seemed to be market day, and every bend seemed to conceal another enormous logging truck taking teak down to the sawmills. But the hold-ups gave us plenty of opportunities for walking – and collecting. When the road to our hunting ground was too rough we hitched a lift in a lorry. And sometimes the bus would leave us at the top of a pass, 10,000 feet high, so that we could continue the hunt, climbing on foot through the thin air and the swirling mists for a couple more thousand feet. This was the way to hunt down the hardiest trees, like the local spruce and silver firs, and the giant-leaved rhododendrons. By the time we were back in Kunming my total 'bag' came to about half a pound of seed, deposited in 150 crumpled brown envelopes. These, I was pleased to hear from Keith, represented over thirty genera and 100 species of trees and shrubs.

In January 1994 I sowed the first batch of Yunnan seed inside our battered greenhouse at Tullynally. To my surprise and delight at least half of the seeds germinated. Two years later the first of the seedlings had become sturdy young trees and shrubs bursting out of their pots. They were ready to transplant. But how would they take to their new home? Our two hard-working gardeners, Jimmy Dalton and Brendan Burke, both born and bred in Westmeath, looked doubtfully at these exotic newcomers. And their doubts were sensible enough, as I soon discovered.

My plan was to create a Yunnan garden with this very amateurish collection. They would be planted in a small clearing in the Forest Walk and kept intact without any changes. No other plants would be added, even if they came from the same wild valleys of Yunnan. For this was to be an expedition garden - the garden of *my* expedition in 1993 - not a more conventional geographical garden, with additions from other collections made at various times. To use a fancy metaphor, I would freeze this Yunnan garden in time and space. That was the idea, and of course it was full of flaws, as gradually became clear.

The first flaw in the plan, as Jimmy and Brendan must have recognised, was the result of our wayward Irish climate. The metaphor of a garden frozen in space and time was all very well. In a harsh Irish winter my Yunnan garden was frozen only too literally. The lowlands of central Ireland, at 53N, are nearer the North Pole than the Equator. In Yunnan, at 25N, the situation is reversed. Of course most of western Yunnan is mountainous - these mountains merge with the eastern flanks of the Himalayas - and altitude can neatly offset latitude. In other words a plant that can survive the winters at 10,000 feet (3,000 metres) in Yunnan may be perfectly adapted to winters a few hundred feet above sea level in central Ireland. I say 'may be'. In fact from the first harsh winter, 1998, I began to realise that Westmeath winters were not so like their Chinese equivalents after all. If I stuck to my guns and refused to add any new plants to my Yunnan garden it would gradually lose plants - and might ultimately wither away, with only half the variety of plants with which I had begun.

The second flaw was the unpromising site of the new garden. I had chosen a clearing on the edge of a plantation of thirty-year-old Norway spruce, whose eastern boundary was formed by the Forest Walk, leading down to the Swan River or lower pond. It had its attractions. It was near enough the main garden; although you often needed boots to cross the farm road, muddied by 500 cows' feet, intervening between the two. It was also well sheltered by a large horse chestnut and several sycamores and a grove of ash – all of which lay to the east of the plantation. Its best feature was that the old millstream from the farm ran through the plantation away to the west. Divert the stream a hundred yards to the east, and I would have ponds and waterfalls for my new garden. But the most important element in any garden is the soil. I had chosen, I soon discovered, an acre of the worst soil in the whole 1,500-acre estate: a thin, mean, black soil, much limier than neutral, with a chalky subsoil ('white marl' they call it in this part of Ireland) waiting just below the surface to ensnare my plants and turn them a jaundiced yellow.

The third flaw was inevitable once I had chosen to make it an expedition garden. All the shrubs, whose seeds had been collected in the same part of Yunnan, would tend to flower in the same months – that is, in May and June. So the garden might be dull enough by August when most of our visitors would come.

The fourth flaw was serious but at least I could deal with it one day – if I had the time and energy. I decided to plant the Yunnan garden without any real plan. There would be no particular style. I would shove in the trees and shrubs and dig out some ponds without a second thought. The plants were Chinese natives. At least that was authentic. But the style of the garden was most certainly not Chinese.

Unaware of these flaws, in the following two years I boldly went ahead and planted my Yunnan garden. The dominant trees were oaks, birch, silver firs, pines, maples; the dominant shrubs philadelphus, deutzia and hypericum. None of the species were exactly commonplace. My oaks included two shy, elegant creatures that looked more like sweet chestnuts than oaks: *Quercus aliena* and *Quercus variabilis*. The latter is the Chinese equivalent of our European cork oak, and develops a rich, fawn-coloured, criss-crossed bark from an early age. The birch were the most pushy. A single powerful species, *Betula utilis* or Himalayan birch, spans the entire range of the Himalayas and beyond, stretching 2,500 miles from China to Pakistan. The leaves, more richly veined than our European birch leaves, look much the same throughout the whole range. And the bark texture is equally sensuous. You could compose a love letter on the flaking sheets that uncoil from the trunks. By contrast the bark colour changes dramatically from east to west, reflecting the steady decline in rainfall. The south-eastern monsoon of China has painted my birch, born in the extreme east of the range, a rich, dark chocolate. The fitful rains of north-east Pakistan paint the birch there an eerie white.

Most of these novel trees and shrubs were only discovered at the end of the nineteenth century by French plant explorers in south-west China. These were the heroic band of French missionaries who hunted plants when taking time off from hunting souls. Three of my best plants were discovered by Père Jean-Marie Delavay who gave his name to them: *Abies delavayi*, a silver fir with the most intense silver markings under the leaves; *Philadelphus delavayi*, the largest and most fragrant, I think, of all this vast, white-flowered genus; *Magnolia delavayi*, an evergreen giant, and one of the few summer-flowering Chinese magnolias.

The most famous of the French missionary-explorers was Père Armand David (1826-1900). He's supposed to have packed up 200,000 plant specimens and sent them back to the herbarium in the Musée d'Histoire Naturelle at Paris. (If the figures are correct, you would have thought he had little time for anything else. Yet he had his souls to hunt. He was also hunting down countless new animals, including the Père David deer and the giant panda.) At any rate, I am deeply grateful to Père Armand David for discovering two of my most captivating trees.

The first is the snake-bark maple called after him: *Acer davidii*. Somehow I managed to grow sixteen of these exotic creatures, and because they were seed-grown (as opposed to being raised as clones from cuttings and grafts) each one is obviously different. The majority are big, colourful bushes, shaped something like a lollipop, with a single mottled green stem rising from the ground. In the autumn they light up the garden like yellow lanterns. The best are tall trees sparkling with bunches of yellow-green seeds; the tallest of mine is already 40 feet high with a striped bark that would make a cobra feel proud.

The second is the blue pine tree, *Pinus armandii*, which now waggles her hips like a dancing girl in my Chinese garden. I don't think I exaggerate. She has sinuous brown hips and a shimmering skirt of blue-green needles. And on a windy day she certainly hums.

To well-deserved acclaim, Père David was safely back in Paris by the 1890s. Other French missionaries were less fortunate. As I mentioned earlier, in 1905 there was a rising in Tibet provoked by the British invasion a year before. Led by a pack of half-crazed lamas, the rebels poured across the mountains into western Yunnan and began to torture and murder any Westerners they found. The Chinese garrison was helpless to save them, although later they put down the rebellion with characteristic brutality. Four of the elderly French missionaries were murdered in horrible circumstances – including Père Soulie (whose wonderful blue-leaved rose I shall come to very shortly). Their heads were stuck on the ruined gates of the French mission. Only one of the European plant explorers in the region managed to escape with his life. This was twenty-four-year-old George Forrest, whose terrifying experience I have already described.

In the years ahead George Forrest was to rival the discoveries of Père David and the French in his own dazzling career as a plant hunter. Magnolias were only one of his specialities. In fact hundreds of Chinese species now common in Western gardens were first introduced by Forrest. And I am proud to say that my Yunnan garden includes a stunning young snake-bark maple, *Acer forrestii*. It's much more delicate than Père David's maple, with long pink lobes as fine as laquerwork, and pale blue lines on the green trunk, like the insignia of an adder. But my Forrest's maple has laughed off the harshest winters Westmeath can throw at it. I admire its courage – and only wish I had grown a hundred of them.

By 2005 the flaws in my Yunnan garden were becoming only too obvious. And I had discovered a new one. My fellow plant hunters in Yunnan – Keith Rushforth and the others – had concentrated the hunt on trees and shrubs, and turned up their noses at herbaceous plants. (You could call them 'woody plant snobs'.) But in spring Yunnan bubbles over with delightful flowers like primulas and irises and astilbes and lilies, all of which are herbaceous. By the autumn these flowers have set seed and are ripe for the plant hunter. Was it now too late to go back to Yunnan to collect some of the treasures I had missed the first time?

In September 2005, I set off on a plant-hunting trip organised by Martyn Rix and including a dozen of his close friends. The plan was to hire a bus and head north-west from Kunming into the wilder parts of Yunnan which I had missed. We would cross the Yangtse close to the famous Tiger-Leaping Gorge, and then cut through into the mountains of Sichuan closest to Tibet. This second trip proved even more eventful than the first.

Much of the country was geographically and culturally part of Tibet. Yaks shared the farmhouses with the farmers. These stone farmhouses looked like small fortresses, flat-roofed, half-timbered, twin-towered. There were no elegant Chinese pagodas, only crude Tibetan shrines decorated with tattered flags. And it was late autumn, so the snow lay deep on the forests of silver fir in the high valleys. We spent one night in a mud-built Tibetan house, huddled against the cold and deafened by the noise of the rats on the floor above. (In fact I fled up a ladder onto the flat roof where I barricaded myself into an attic room.) Despite the cold, I managed to fill about a hundred seed packets on the trip.

One of the most elegant plants I collected was a blue-leaved rose. This was christened *Rosa soulieana* after the unfortunate Père Soulié, the French missionary murdered by the Tibetan lamas. Of course I collected seeds of many plants unknown to me: a violet-leaved ash called *Fraxinus paxiana*, a *Malus* with leaves like a hawthorn, and four or five rare kinds of sorbus yet to be identified. If I struck gold it was with the herbaceous plants. These included two more of Père Delavay's discoveries: a dazzling scarlet peony, *Paeonia delavayi*, and a delicate violet-flowered thalictrum with malachite-green leaves, *Thalictrum delavayi*. My favourites were two species of purple primulas which are rarely seen in Europe: a candelabra species called *Primula poissonii* and a cowslip species called *Primula secundiflora*. Both flower and flower again continuously from June to September – weeks longer than is normal for primulas. And both have proved as hardy as rocks, which is not surprising, as the seed of some of them was actually lying scattered on the surface of the snow.

I must return to Sir William Temple and his Sharawadgi. My first Yunnan garden has no particular style – apart from a steel-and-plywood pagoda created by our enterprising local builder, Michael Fagan. (His design was partly based on a garden pagoda which a friend of mine bought in the Paris flea market. Michael also borrowed ideas from the Chinese cabinet in our drawing room.) It's now too late, I'm afraid, to change the first Yunnan garden.

My new Yunnan garden will be immediately below it in a second clearing. This will be my Sharawadgi garden. How will I design it? I shall follow Sir William's instructions to the letter. As he said in his rambling essay: you have only to look at Chinese 'Skreens' or 'Purcellans' to see what the Chinese mean by Sharawadgi. So I have decided to model my new garden on the famous willow pattern plate first produced in the 1790s by the English firm of Spode. I shall build a new pagoda and a new pond with a three-arched bridge leading to some miniature Chinese mountains. There will be plenty of exotic rockwork and a zigzag fence to keep out evil spirits. (Evil spirits move in straight lines, so a zigzag fence defeats them.) To the right of the pagoda will be the three trees on the famous plate: a tall pine tree, a magnolia and a cherry. In pride of place at the centre of the clearing will be the weeping willow itself, suitably rotten and gnarled. Of course some of the excitement will be missing. Portrayed on the plate in the form of a strip cartoon is the story of the doomed lovers. They escape with the loot from their house. The vengeful father gives chase. They flee to an island. They are saved by the gods who turn them into love-birds. I shall have to do my best with the shy pair of kingfishers who haunt the Forest Walk.

This is my idea for the layout. As for the plants, those frail, pepper-like seeds brought from Yunnan and Sichuan in 2005 are now big-rooted trees and shrubs begging to be moved. These include the pine, the cherry and the magnolia of the famous plate. And I have many descendants from the first Yunnan garden that can be used to people the second. I have made cuttings from the deutzias and philadelphuses, and grown many birch and sorbus from seed. Many of the new herbaceous plants, like the thalictrum and the primulas, are spreading along the stream. In fact they're delightfully invasive. (Of course these plants will be not be true natives of China, but immigrants of the first generation.) But the famous weeping willow will present a problem. In 1993 Keith gave me a cutting of the authentic Chinese species, *Salix babylonica*. It languished and died many years ago. So I shall have to use the European equivalent, *Salix* 'Chrysocoma', which is believed to have at least some Chinese blood in its veins.

Oh lord, perhaps this second Yunnan garden is only a dream. (Valerie's stern comment: 'I hope so.') By Christmas I should know.

* * *

But May is now upon us. I shall take my two-year-old grandchild, Julia, to the upper pond to feed crushed barley to the happy family of ducklings. They'll give her a noisy welcome and she'll enjoy the job. And I shall enjoy feeding black, well-rotted compost to a happy, new-fledged pair of ginkgos beside the pond.

PREVIOUS PAGE, OVERLEAF: One of the ice-blue rivers flowing from the eastern side of the Andes in Patagonia. Despite a century of logging, the mountains here are still covered in dense forests right up to the edge of the glaciers. Southern beech predominate (*Nothofagus dombeyi* and *Nothofagus antarctica*).

LEFT: One of few giant Alerce (*Fitzroya cupressoides*) in Patagonia that somehow eluded the loggers.

ABOVE: In Sichuan, in south-west China, very few old-growth forests have survived. Here's the next generation: smashed silver firs left behind by the loggers and now colonized by rhododendrons.

Some of my favourite magnolias at Tullynally: (top left) the white Campbell's magnolia from Caerhays (white in theory, actually knicker-pink); (top) the rose-pink Campbell's magnolia that I bought from a local nursery; (right) the exuberant young *Magnolia cylindrica*.

A ride with Grandma in the buggy. My wife Valerie with two of our grandchildren – Anselm and Matilda – photographed in 2005.

LEFT: The pagoda in Yunnan in my Chinese garden at the beginning of the Forest Walk. All the trees and other plants here were grown in our greenhouse from seed that I collected in Yunnan in 1993.

ABOVE: The Gingerbread House in the centre of the Forest Walk, based on a design by Samuel Hayes for his garden at Avondale (1794).

RIGHT: A colony of snakeshead fritillaries in the Forest Walk, flowering in early April, if the weather's kind.

OVERLEAF: Gabriel, aged 4, and a friend celebrate the flowering of the giant Himalayan lily in the Forest Walk. You can smell its wax-like flowers long before you see it.

8

To the Rescue

1 May 2013

The leaves of my favourite tree, the ginkgo, are beginning to emerge at last from their squat green buds. To say that I am infatuated with the ginkgo is to put it too strongly. But I am certainly fascinated. Everything about it is strange.

Look at the shape of the leaf. It's usually cleft in the middle, with the line of the veins fanning out from the stalk. You could compare it with a butterfly's wing. (The Chinese, rather prosaically, call the tree a 'Duck's foot', or more romantically 'Grandfather-grandchild tree'.) Or feel the spikiness of its branches. The long brown shoots alternate with short grey shoots criss-crossing like barbed wire. Then there are those weird growths from the trunk, hanging down like woody stalactites. (The Japanese call them *chi-chi*, meaning breasts.) As for the nuts from female ginkgos, I know the smell of the fleshy casing is somewhat pungent. In fact many people find it repulsive. But the kernels inside are delicious. And the age of the tree would boggle your mind. The ginkgo was old, at least fifty *million* years old, before the Alps or the Atlantic were born.

The list of its wonders would fill a book. Indeed Peter Crane, the distinguished palaeobotanist and former Director of the Royal Botanic Gardens at Kew, has written a biography of the ginkgo so compelling that you would think every gardener in the world would become a ginkgophile.

But there was one obvious reason why I had to restrain my own passion for the tree. In Ireland, I was told, our summers are too chilly for the tree to be really happy. It comes from what geographers call the 'warm-temperate' zone, and we are definitely cool-temperate - if we are temperate at all. In summer and autumn it needs a Continental sun to beat down on its green leaves and bake its spiky branches. Did I know any happy ginkgos in any of the great gardens of Ireland? Of course not. So why waste time planting a ginkgo that would only feel resentment to be shivering in Ireland instead of basking in the pavements of London, Paris or New York?

Now this was all thirty years ago before anyone started to talk about climate change and global warming. We had had a long run of cold, wet summers in the 1960s; the 1970s had shown little improvement. In 1984 a miracle occurred. In Ireland the sun shone almost the whole summer long. Over in Hampshire I remember seeing the toxic results of this heat: fields of spring barley not a foot high, stunted by the drought. In Herefordshire I was shown a line of ancient beech that had given up the struggle and died. But in Ireland there were spells of thundery rain to share the summer with the Saharan sun. For us it was the harvest of the century: a thousand tons of barley spouting into the scarlet trailers, spewed out by our green dragon, the John Deere combine. And I celebrated the miracle by the reckless decision to plant three ginkgos.

Of course it was madness - as was clear the very next year. The summer of 1985 was a brute. By July our wheat fields were squashed so flat by the rain that the roots tried to throw up a new crop, which was good for nothing. By October the sugar beet was afloat, and impossible to harvest. The unfortunate ginkgos didn't actually die - not at first. I had planted them on what I thought was a sunny bank on the Grotto Hill. It's a fine, theatrical site, and important too. It commands the roses and maples and dogwoods of the Flower Garden below - part of the garden exclusively under the control of Valerie. She herself watched me planting the three ginkgos with a certain cynicism. 'Why on earth didn't you listen to the experts?' she asked me. 'Listen to the croakers, you mean.' But by 1985 I was beginning to think the croakers (and Valerie) might be right.

At first the ginkgos merely moped. Then one died, and a second became a moribund bush, which Valerie insisted must be removed. The third, mysteriously, began to show promise. Perhaps it was the first hint of global warming. Or perhaps I had struck lucky with the placing of this third tree. It was under the protection of an ancient beech. Fifteen years passed. The third tree began to grow astonishingly well. It grew slowly, of course, by Continental standards. But it was tall and upright with regular whorls of spiky branches, and a slim, handsome finial to cap them, rising a foot a year. Then the sky fell on it - that is, the sky in the form of the 20-ton beech tree, chosen as its protector, skittled over one night by a storm.

I hurried down to the Grotto Hill as two men were cutting up the beech tree for firewood. Its monstrous, lichen-encrusted arms, contorted in death, covered most of the hill. There was no trace of my ginkgo. All that day the men continued to cut up the monster and load the chunks of orange wood onto a trailer. I stood anxiously beside them, brushing the sawdust off my face. 'Watch out for the ginkgo, watch out for the ginkgo,' I shouted from time to time. When the last trailer load was complete we saw a tragic sight. The ginkgo had been decapitated 12 feet up, its arms mangled, its trunk gashed in numerous places. It lay on its back among the sawdust. Then something extraordinary happened. The tree - what remained of it - slowly rose to its feet. And today, fifteen years on, the tree has regrown its head and arms, and now stands proud, 25 feet tall, on the flanks of Grotto Hill. I'm sure it's good for another two centuries. No one would guess that the protecting beech had ever touched a hair of its head.

Resilience is a quality you would expect to find in a tree that has survived at least 200 million years of our planet's history. Reading the fossil record, illustrated by leaves elegantly imprinted on stone, palaeobotanists like Peter Crane can plot the rise and fall of ginkgodom. Its golden age was about forty to 100 million years ago. It was then one of the most successful colonists, whose empire straddled both hemispheres. There was a chain of ginkgo settlements from Siberia to Washington State with outposts as far south as Tasmania. Europe had little attraction for it. Perhaps the climate there was generally too warm, although there was a ginkgo outpost on the Island of Mull, off the west coast of Scotland. Greenland then provided the perfect temperature for the tree and the country must have lived up to its name. But the next forty million years saw a slow decline in the ginkgo empire - a fighting retreat, if you like - as fewer and fewer areas of the world could provide it with the climate it needed.

Of course the ginkgo was only one of hundreds of genera of trees that needed the warm temperate zones of the world if they were to breed and survive. Many of these trees, it seems, are now extinct - unable to adapt to the double trauma of shifting climates and shifting continents. But evolution had taught the ginkgo the trick of survival. It knew how to move with the climate. When the northern provinces of its empire - Greenland and Iceland and Arctic Canada - became too cool, it headed south to make new conquests in Europe, including mainland Britain. But *how* does a tree move? Obviously progress is slow, perhaps only a few yards every year. It all depends on how efficiently the seeds can be moved. This in turn will depend on what particular agent the tree can exploit (or persuade) to disperse its seeds: wind, water, or some bird or animal.

Pioneer trees like the birch produce up to a million fluffy seeds in a season, exposed in thousands of delicate catkins. So the birch can rely on wind alone to push forward the frontier of the birch forest. Trees that live on riverbanks - willows, alders, aspens - can expect the current to carry their seeds (or bits of branch capable of rooting) to colonise a new territory. But ginkgos have a heavy seed, enclosed in a hard shell, and covered in an edible casing - like other nut-bearing trees. Only a hungry bird or animal can move it. And this brings us to the first of many evolutionary puzzles facing the palaeobotanist dealing with the ginkgo. When the ginkgo needed to move, as the climate became hotter or cooler or drier, what bird or animal did it recruit to carry this heavy seed?

I like the idea that it was the dinosaur that was recruited by the ginkgo for this important task. The idea comes from an American academic, Bruce Tiffney, who believed he could explain, in evolutionary terms, the appalling smell produced by the rotting, rancid flesh of ripe ginkgo nuts. The dinosaur needed that special smell, says Tiffney, to sniff out its next meal of ginkgo nuts. The seeds pass through its gut and are deposited in the dinosaur's lair, transformed in due course into a grove of ginkgos. There's only one weakness in this theory, as Peter Crane was quick to point out. The dinosaur died out during the ginkgo's golden age, the ginkgo lived on to be prized and cherished by Man. So even if Tiffney's right, the ginkgo must have found another recruit (or other recruits) to be hooked by that smell and swallow its seeds in the next seventy million years. Could monkeys have done the job? Or elephants? Or badgers? (They eat ginkgo nuts in modern Japan.) Sad to say, the fossil record is silent. We can only assume, from the ginkgo's gradual decline, that whoever was doing the job was not doing it very well.

All we know is that the gradual decline of the ginkgo ended in almost total extinction. In the last million years there were four separate ice ages which only the most nimble and athletic genus of tree could survive. Each time the world cooled the tree had to take refuge further south - and then return to the north each time the world warmed again. Clearly this ice-dance was too much for the poor ginkgo. When the historic record begins - on the cusp of the second millennium AD - the only ginkgos in the world were confined to a few parts of China. And some botanists believe it was already extinct in the wild. Let me explain.

The first undisputed reference to the ginkgo in Chinese literature is in an exchange of poems, during the eleventh century, between a poet, Mei-Yao-Chen and a historian, Ouyang Hsiu. Known then as *ya chio* ('Duck's foot'), the tree is already prized by the two scholars, who know about its delicious nuts. But when some trees are planted in the emperor's capital the nuts create a sensation. 'They were presented to the throne in a golden bowl,' the historian tells the poet. 'The nobility and high ministry did not recognise them and the emperor bestowed a hundred ounces of gold. Now, after a few years, the trees bear more fruits.'

Mei-Yao-Chen, the poet in this literary encounter, tells us he collected nuts in the wild, and we know he lived in Anhui province in east-central China. But botanists doubt if there were still wild ginkgos as far north as this. The two areas now regarded as the likeliest refuges for wild ginkgos then - and indeed now - are Tianmu Mountain near the coast in Zhejiang province and Jinfo Mountain in Chongqing, close to the border with Sichuan. But it's possible that, by the eleventh century, the ginkgo had already lost its place in the Darwinian struggle and was no longer a true native of these mountains. What is certain is that, at some earlier period, the last wild survivors were saved and admired and multiplied by man. For once our own species behaved like gentlemen!

By the later Middle Ages the ginkgo was being cultivated for its nuts in many parts of China - and not only for its nuts. It became the tree of choice for Buddhist temples and shrines of other religions. Perhaps it was the mysterious fecundity - those strange *chi-chi* hanging from the trunks of the older trees - that attracted Buddhist monks and worshippers. And there was the belief that those odd-looking leaves of the tree, the shape of a duck's foot, had miraculous properties. It was claimed that extracts could cure ailments of many kinds, an optimistic belief that has spread, with the tree itself, to many parts of the world today.

Inevitably, as cultivation of the tree spread northwards in China, it came to be exported with other exotic goods to Korea and Japan. We can only make a wild guess at when it arrived there. There are huge, ancient ginkgos in the temple precincts of both countries. But their planting dates are no better than old wives' tales, and no one can date them within a hundred years or more. Probably the tree arrived there about the end of the fourteenth century. The first literary reference to ginkgos in Japan comes from a dictionary of the mid-fifteenth century. A century later a Japanese poet,

Socho, describes his gift of a ginkgo's beautiful yellow leaves.

It was from Japan, four centuries later, that other temperate regions of the world finally received the gift of the ginkgo. The story is operatic. In fact there is more than a whiff of *Madam Butterfly*. By the end of the seventeenth century Japan's first brief flirtation with Europe had ended in disaster. In 1543 the first Portuguese traders, sailing from their Chinese foothold at Macao, had landed their trade goods. Their ships' holds were stuffed with guns, bread, tobacco and other intoxicating novelties. Jesuit missionaries followed on their heels with no less intoxicating promises of eternal life. But Christianity proved as potent - and divisive - as the guns. After a mere forty years the missionaries were expelled by the Shogun, Toyotomi Hideyoshi, the real ruler of Japan behind the shadow-emperor. He then ordered twenty-six of their Japanese converts at the southern port of Nagasaki to be crucified; it was claimed they had been plotting a European invasion. Early in the seventeenth century Christianity was totally banned and its converts hunted down and killed without mercy. Portuguese traders were still tolerated - up to a point. To keep them out of mischief they were now confined to a kind of prison island, Deshima, artificially constructed in the harbour at Nagasaki. In due course, Dutch traders, who had broken the monopoly of the Portuguese, replaced them at Deshima. And it was from this far-flung outpost of the Dutch, hardly wider than two streets, that all trade between Europe and Japan was conducted for the next two centuries.

We owe our knowledge of Deshima - and the ginkgo, and other plants in Japan - at this period almost entirely to the writings of three remarkable botanist-physicians who lived, and suffered, on that wretched island.

The first of these, Engelbert Kaempfer, landed at Deshima in 1689. The son of a Protestant pastor from Lemgo, just inside the borders of Germany, he was already much travelled. He had studied medicine and natural sciences in Prussia, Sweden and Russia, and roamed the world, serving on a Swedish mission to Isfahan and the court of the Sultan of Persia. How claustrophobic he must have found life as the doctor at Deshima. For a scholar and botanist, however, there were compensations. Once a year the head of the Dutch mission was allowed out of his prison to pay his respects to the Shogun at Edo (the modern Tokyo). Kaempfer joined the retinue, snapping up anything that caught his fancy: books, paintings, porcelain, plant specimens, including of course specimens of the ginkgo. When he returned to Europe two years later he brought the first drawing of the tree known to the West, now treasured in the British Museum. It shows the spherical fruit, the sharply pointed nuts, and eight of the elegant leaves with a cleft at the centre, the cleft leaves (*biloba* in Latin) that were to fascinate the great Carl Linnaeus. In due course these leaves provided Linnaeus with a specific (that is, second) name to give the tree.

But what was the origin of the generic name *Ginkgo*? Kaempfer had called it that. But where on earth had he got that strange name with two 'g's? The word makes no sense either in modern Chinese or Japanese. (The Chinese, as I said, call it various names, including 'Duck's foot' and 'Grandfather-grandchild tree'.) Peter Crane has now sorted out the puzzle. Kaempfer had transcribed the seventeenth-century Japanese name 'ginkyo', using his own North German dialect in which 'g' is pronounced as 'y'. (So, I suppose, we should all be talking of 'ginkyos'. Fortunately this discovery has been made too late.)

In the two centuries after Kaempfer's return to Europe, Carl Thunberg and Philipp von Siebold were the two other botanist-physicians who embraced life on the prison-island of Deshima. And each man put to good use the tantalising glimpses of Japan when they were allowed to join the mission to the court of the Shogun at Edo. Thunberg was an inquisitive young pupil of Linnaeus. Back in Europe in 1775, he published *Flora Japonica*, the first comprehensive account of Japanese plants, including a full description of the ginkgo. He was followed by Siebold, who published his own *Flora Japonica*, and numerous other works on the people and plants he had met and the little-known culture of Japan. And it's here that we encounter more than a glimpse of Madam Butterfly.

For seven years he endured the life on the prison-island. As a doctor, however, he was allowed more freedom than the rest of the Dutch inmates. He was allowed to treat Japanese patients – he was both ophthalmologist and obstetrician – on the mainland at Nagasaki. After all it was only a few hundred yards away, across the bridge from the island. And in Nagasaki, on a house visit, he fell in love with a Japanese girl called Sonogi. She was sixteen and he was twenty-seven. The authorities allowed her to visit him on Deshima and she gave birth to a daughter, Oine.

When Siebold's contract was up he set sail from Nagasaki intending, it seems, to return later to visit (and perhaps collect) Sonogi and their child. By bad luck the ship was forced back into port by a storm. His luggage was then minutely inspected to see what he was taking out of Japan. There was no problem with the specimens of the ginkgo and other plants, the drawings, the porcelain, the netsuke, and the rest. But he was found to have two highly sensitive items: maps of Japan and Korea, given him by the court astronomer and librarian at Edo, and a gown with the crest of the Shogun.

The authorities at Edo were obsessed, paranoid you could say, about the risks of invasion. So it was treason to give a map of Japan to a foreigner. All hell now broke over poor Siebold's head. His friend, the court astronomer, was thrown into prison, where he died soon after. Siebold and many officials were arrested, and interrogated for weeks. His sentence, in 1829, a year later: to be expelled from Japan, leaving Sonogi and their child – expelled never to return.

But strange to say, the story ended not unhappily. By 1855 Japan was a different country. Commodore Perry of the US Navy had tied up his black ships in the harbour and put his boot in the Shogunate. After two hundred years, foreigners were once more in fashion. Back came Siebold, now married with five children, to enjoy a belated reunion with Sonogi and their daughter Oine. He must have been proud to be told that Oine was training to become Japan's first woman doctor.

But I am getting ahead of my story. A century earlier, long before Thunberg and Siebold had written their scientific studies of the ginkgo, the tree itself was flourishing in Europe. No one knows who first brought the seed, where it was first planted or whether it came from Japan or China. But scholars are prepared to guess. There's good reason to think that the first seeds were imported by the Dutch East India Company from Japan, by way of Deshima Island, and were planted in Holland and in England. There's a celebrated ginkgo in the Old Botanic Garden in Utrecht which fits the bill nicely. It was probably planted in the 1750s or 1760s. However it has a rival in the so-called 'Old Lion' of a ginkgo at Kew Gardens.

According to folklore (which fooled me, too, until I read Peter Crane's book) the ginkgo, with a handful of other Old Lions, came down the Thames, travelling by barge, dispatched from the 3rd Duke of Argyll's estate near Richmond. The truth would appear to be less exciting. The tree was probably sold to Kew in 1760 by a London nurseryman, James Gordon, who specialised in importing exotic seeds from China and Japan. Whatever the origins of the seeds, and of the cuttings struck from the first plants, the fashion for ginkgos spread slowly across Europe – and beyond. As you would expect, the botanic gardens were first in the field: after Utrecht and Kew, it was Leiden in 1785, Pisa in 1787; Rouen, Paris and Montpellier soon gave chase. In due course European botanists discovered the ginkgo was dioecious, meaning that, to produce seeds, two separate trees were needed, one male and the other female. However it was possible to graft a female branch onto a male ginkgo, and many seeds were produced eventually in the warmer parts of Europe.

In France the tree was known as *l'arbre aux quarante écus* ('the tree of forty crowns'). The explanation for this strange nickname is given by John Loudon. In 1780 a Parisian gardening enthusiast called Pétigny went over to London and visited a nurseryman known for dealing in rare plants. The man showed him five ginkgos in a single pot, and claimed these were the only ginkgos in England; he had grown them from nuts imported from Japan. After a bibulous lunch, Pétigny bought all five for 25 guineas and took them away with him. When the effects of the wine had worn off next day, the nurseryman realised what a fool he had been. He was desperate to buy back the ginkgos, and offered M. Pétigny the extraordinary sum of 25 guineas (40 crowns) for a single plant. But Pétigny proudly refused the offer. He took the ginkgos home with him to Paris, and in due course it was from these five ginkgos that all the first ginkgos in Paris were propagated.

The first ginkgo to sniff the air of the new United States was planted in 1784 by William Hamilton at his country estate, Woodlands, south of Philadelphia. Hamilton was a keen plantsman, landscape architect and political insider who had just come home, dazzled by a tour of English gardens and estates. He was determined, he said, to make Woodlands 'smile in the same useful and beautiful manner'. Woodlands itself has now vanished under bricks and concrete, but one of Hamilton's ginkgos is still alive today. It was presented by him to a neighbour, the American naturalist John Bartram, and is now the jewel in the crown of Bartram's Garden; it must be the oldest ginkgo in North America. Soon the fashion for ginkgos spread across the country, beginning with the political elite. I expect Jefferson, Franklin and Washington admired them and planted them. When Hamilton's ginkgo was still only a baby, his estate at Woodlands was the scene of a huge patriotic demonstration attended by everybody who was anybody in the new republic. On 4 July 1788 no less than seventeen thousand young Americans saluted the new-born United States Constitution in the grounds of Woodlands. I should like to think they also saluted Hamilton's new-born ginkgo.

In the last twenty years I have been fortunate enough to see many of America's noblest ginkgos, including female ones that produce those seeds with the controversial smell. And I owe to one tree in particular a special debt. It's the ancient female ginkgo planted in Mount Auburn Cemetery, on a wooded hill within sight of Boston. This delightful place, founded in 1831, is one of the earliest fruits of the 'garden cemetery' movement in Europe and America. The idea was to replace the cramped burial grounds of the city with healthy landscaped cemeteries out in the country. A friend took me to Mount Auburn in 2002 and I was fascinated by the Gothic tombs (where many eminent Bostonians were given their last farewells) and dazzled by the exotic trees, especially by this female ginkgo. 'Would you care for some of her seeds?' I was asked by the director, and he handed me a dozen, already clean and mercifully odour-free.

Back at Tullynally, I decided it was time to have another go with ginkgos. Last time two had died, and one had survived a near-death experience. Well, everything would be different now. Global warming had reached even the misty shores of Ireland. Our springs often came earlier, and our summers were warmer. I would grow my own ginkgos from seed – those seeds from Mount Auburn, fertilised by the bones of the great and the good, the Brahmins of nineteenth-century Boston.

To my surprise and delight, my new ginkgos grew up uniformly tall and strong. Perhaps it was the effect of our new climate. Perhaps two of the original plants, which I had bought from a nursery, had simply been duds. Or should I attribute my success to the richness of American bones? Six of my ginkgos, at any rate, have grown better than I could have dared hope. I gave two away as presents. The remaining four have all been given places of honour.

The first pair were planted with due ceremony in the sunniest part of the pleasure ground close to the upper pond. This is the happy pair to whom I fed black compost when I took my grandchild Julia to feed the ducklings.

The second pair were given a bay of the arboretum, in the ante-room so to speak. This is where I plant the trees to honour my human saplings – eight grandchildren at present (with, who knows, perhaps more to come). As I said earlier, Maria's twins – Anselm and Matilda – have been given twin ginkgos as companions of their own age. Perhaps I, too, will be remembered when people admire these trees. After all, the Chinese call it the 'Grandfather-grandchild tree'.

*   *   *

A few hundred yards from my two pairs of ginkgos, I have planted other genera of trees whose last survivors were rescued, in the nick of time, by man.

The ginkgo, as I have said, was saved from extinction a thousand years ago by Buddhist monks and other discerning Chinese. Now the trees are safely back in their old haunts, after millions of years in exile, back in the temperate regions of Europe and North America. We can call them 'Living Fossils' and the 'Trees Time Forgot'. Equally appropriate would be 'The Trees That Came Back'. But the story of the ginkgo's rescue has an echo in our own era, two echoes in fact.

In 1941, during the war with the Japanese, a group of Chinese partisans found themselves in a remote valley in Hubei province close to the River Yangtse. One of them, called T. Kan, was a forester by training. He was intrigued by a tall, gaunt tree next to a shrine in the village of Mo-tao-chi, a deciduous conifer which the villagers called a 'water fir'. But it belonged to a species he could not identify. It was not until 1944 that the first specimens of the tree's feathery leaves and cones were sent to Peking for identification and not until 1946 that it was realised that the tree was not only from an unknown species, it was a survivor from a completely unknown genus. Meanwhile, in 1941, in wartime Japan, a Japanese palaeobotanist called Shigeru Miki had peered into his microscope and discovered a new genus of fossils. This was based on the fossilised leaves of a deciduous conifer once widespread in North America and beyond, a conifer that had died in the Piocene era millions of years earlier. He called the fossil tree *Metasequoia*, meaning 'like the sequoia', the giant redwood of California. When the Chinese botanists in Peking read Miki's article they reached an astonishing conclusion: Miki's metasequoia was alive and well in Mo-tao-chi five million years after it had died out in the rest of the world.

By 1948 the Arnold Arboretum at Harvard had sponsored - for a mere $250 - an official Chinese expedition to collect seeds in Mo-tao-chi. These were at once dispatched to the Arnold Arboretum, and then forwarded to botanists and tree enthusiasts all over the temperate world. The new tree, *Metasequoia glyptostroboides* (alias the Dawn Redwood), was welcomed everywhere. And its appetite for life was unmistakable. From that one gaunt old tree at Mo-tao-chi hundreds of thousands of youngsters were reared in Europe and North America, many from seeds and many more from cuttings. Like the ginkgo, it seemed delighted to return to its old haunts. And like the ginkgo it seemed surprisingly well adapted to modern urban life. Within thirty years of its discovery, tall conical specimens - pale green in spring and foxy pink in autumn - crowded many of London's pavements.

My own experience of the metasequoia astonished me. For once a newcomer seemed perfectly at home in my garden. Forty years ago I planted three young saplings beside the upper pond in the pleasure ground and a fourth in the Forest Walk. Today they are my pride and joy. The soil is poor enough: a limy clay. But the trees have grown 45 feet tall, and are sturdy enough. What I admire especially is the fluting in their lower trunks, which gives them a wizened Chinese air. But it's hard to choose between the tree's host of admirable qualities.

It's one of the first deciduous trees to burst into leaf. The pale green, feathery leaves remind one of those of the American swamp cypress, *Taxodium distichum.* But the metasequoia decides it's ready for spring a month before its American cousin, and grows at double the speed – at least in our cool climate. And it makes me feel good, I must admit, to be giving life to a tree that found itself, so recently, on the edge of the grave. I think I know what those Chinese monks felt like, back in the eighth century, as they snatched the ginkgo from the brink of extinction and gave it pride of place beside their temples.

My other attempt to honour a newly rescued genus of tree has proved a lot less fortunate. In 1995 a forest ranger and bushwhacker called David Noble abseiled down a rope into a canyon in the Wollemi National Park in the Blue Mountains near Sydney, Australia. 'Wollemi' means 'look at me' in the Aboriginal language. No doubt David Noble looked – and gasped. There in the canyon was a group of less than a hundred trees of a completely unknown genus. In due course they were found to be a member of the *Araucariaceae*, the monkey puzzle family, and the genus was christened, somewhat controversially, *Wollemia nobilis.* (Its specific name would have been *nobilii,* I have been told, if David Noble had been a botanist, but he was only a park ranger, poor man, so they settled for the pun on his name instead.)

Anyway the tree caused a sensation. It was another one of the 'living dead' – a tree known only from fossils, and presumed to have died millions of years earlier. Unlike the Chinese, who did little to safeguard the metasequoia after its discovery, the Australian authorities bent over backwards to protect the newcomer. The whereabouts of the canyon was kept a close secret for fear visitors would damage the trees – or, worse, infect them with a fatal disease carried on their boots. Meanwhile commercial cuttings were taken and multiplied on an enormous scale, so that young Wollemis could be planted throughout the temperate world. Even if the original trees were killed by disease, the genus would be safe.

Of course there was one huge question mark. The tree had a home in a frost-free canyon somewhere north-west of Sydney. It would probably be happy in California. How would it cope with the icy winters of north-west Europe?

Sad to say, I can answer that question only too easily. In 2008 I bought a Wollemi for the exorbitant sum of £150 (some people paid thousands of pounds for the privilege) and planted it in a place of honour in the arboretum. Next winter was mild enough, but the tree looked distinctly pale and homesick by the following spring. In 2010 we were assaulted by two brutal winters within twelve months: in January and November–December. What were the feelings of the Wollemi when the thermometer sank to minus 17 °C on Christmas Day? None, I'm sure. The poor creature was already a blackened corpse.

9

Pity the Poor Sycamore

10 May 2013

Today the thermometer reached 20 °C and spring is advancing with delightful speed. Of course every young leaf is not equally welcome.

Pity the poor sycamore, I thought this morning, as I surveyed the army of twin-leaved, 3-inch-high seedlings that are marching across the arboretum. Pity the poor sycamore. It has no friends in the gardening world.

When did you last plant a sycamore, I asked one of my sisters recently. She looked at me with amazement. Even a devoted fan of the species, as I regard myself, must confess that they spend a great deal more time pulling up sycamores than planting them. Of course they plant themselves without being invited. I reckon there must be half a million seedlings from this year's crop spreading out across the 5 acres of the arboretum. (The figure might seem exaggerated. But when we have a bumper crop, as we did this year, just try counting the number of seedlings in *one* square yard.) Most of these uninvited guests will die of their own accord, suppressed by the grass which will grow faster than they can. But enough would survive, I think, to turn the arboretum into a thicket of sycamores if I did nothing to stop them.

In fact I shall be generous to a selected few. They can find a billet under the shade of the grove of twenty mature sycamores on the north side of the arboretum. These hundred-year-old sycamores are less showy than the towering beech on the south side of the arboretum. But the grey-brown bark of their trunks, flaking and cracked with age, provides a home for lichens and many kinds of insect. These in turn provide a winter meal for blue tits and bullfinches. The finest sycamore, pink-trunked and plated like an armadillo, looms over the Pumpkin House at the centre of the arboretum. Unlike many sycamores, its leaves turn a rich lemon-yellow in autumn – rather than a muddy brown. It's from the progeny of this tree that I shall select my replacements. Some at least of its seedlings should inherit the rich colouring of their parent. The rest of the vast army of seedlings will be hunted down and dispatched without mercy.

Perhaps I am a brute. Now from the arboretum the road leads to the rising ground of the demesne and the plush fields of ryegrass grazed by our inter-racial dairy herd. (We have crossed Friesians with Jerseys. But not out of goodwill. The aim is hybrid vigour: to boost our income from milk.) Anyway it's here, among the graceful clumps and shelter belts of beech and oak and larch, that our sycamores come into their own. The finest clump of sycamores was planted, about two hundred years ago, in the ancient rath (or ringfort) overlooking the rectangular fields laid out a century earlier. To balance the design, a second rath was planted with oaks at about the same date. Overpopulation out here poses no problem. On the contrary, the sharp teeth of the dairy herd make sure no seedlings survive, which means these sycamores will need replacements one day. (I feel sure one of my successors will devote himself to the task.)

Out in the demesne the sycamores have certainly found an honourable place. And so they should. They come from an ancient line of European maples which was introduced into Britain and Ireland hundreds of years ago. They are what botanists label as 'archaeophytes', meaning they were apparently introduced by man at some time date before 1500. In other words they were naturalised here – got their passports, if you like – long before the Tudors ruled Britain. They are one of the huge and glamorous maple family, the Aceraceae, spread across Europe, America and much of the northern hemisphere. Botanists reckon there are about 150 different species worldwide, with at least double that number of sub-species and varieties, most of which are happy to be allowed to grow in Europe. And the sycamore is king. It's the maple that grows biggest in our world, lives longest and supplies the best timber. The list of its accomplishments – of all the uses supplied by its alluring white wood – would fill volumes.

When I first came to live in Ireland, in the 1960s, there was a craze for 'wavy-grain' sycamore cut up as a veneer for panelling. A single tree could fetch over £1,000, the equivalent of £10,000 in modern money. But there was no sure way of telling which tree had the magic figure in its wood until it was sliced up in the timber yard. (I learnt this to my cost. Rogue timber dealers would descend on our woods and chop pieces out of the bark of the sycamores, in the vain hope of finding the precious stuff.) The smooth white wood was also once fashionable for all kinds of joinery and cabinet-making, as well as, incongruously, for gunstocks and violins.

No parkland tree, at any rate, can boast a more colourful bark than the sycamore, nor a bark endowed with such mysterious patterns. (I know one tree whose bark flakes off like pieces of a jigsaw puzzle.) And look at its young leaves in spring. Can the leaves of beech and oak offer any comparison? True, the leaves of *every* species of tree are glowing with colour in early May. But the design of the sycamore's leaves is more subtle. In fact like almost all maples, its leaves unfold in spring etched into a series of lobes or fingers. The sycamore has five lobes, giving it an elegant, five-fingered look. Now look at its flowers, which appear at the same time as the leaves, and compare them with those of the beech or oak. The flowers of the beech and oak are unexciting. Maples by contrast have clusters of miniature flowers which protrude between two of the leaves. And the sycamore's flowers are among the most elegant in the whole far-flung maple family. They hang in yellow-green tassels (or racemes) with up to fifty minute flowers in each tassel. Each flower can produce a winged samara or 'key': a fat little pair of seeds, joined at the centre, with curved wings at each side. Of course it's with this army of winged seeds that the sycamore launches its airborne invasion of our gardens.

The sycamore, as I have said, is king of our European maples. In parkland it had originally only one competitor: its cousin, the Norway maple, introduced from northern Europe in the late seventeenth century. This never becomes a giant like the sycamore. But it has some delightful features. The flowers come *before* the leaves and open a brilliant yellow. The leaves themselves are even more elegant than those of the sycamore. They are shinier and have sharp points to the five lobes and the extra teeth. I have planted one in the arboretum, a tree now 25 feet high, which I'm proud to say I grew from seed. Part of the tree is edible. I mean, you can tap the trunk of a Norway maple to make maple syrup – just as you can tap the trees from the east coast of America, the red maple, the silver maple and the sugar maple. (But I shan't dare tap my own Norway maple for many years. If I am spared, it would be a nice way to celebrate my hundredth birthday.)

It's these three pushy East Coasters, introduced in the seventeenth and eighteenth centuries, that brought the wild colours of the American 'fall' to British and Irish gardens. The finest, I think, is the red maple, *Acer rubrum.* And it was one of these, planted about a hundred years ago in our pleasure ground, that gave me the dangerous addiction to maples from which I have never fully recovered.

The tree rises out of the rhododendron jungle below our pink Campbell's magnolia, facing an elderly horse chestnut. In winter it would not catch your eye. It's a stubby creature, about 40 feet tall, and the bark is a dull grey. But in late March or early April it celebrates spring by covering its entire canopy in small scarlet flowers. These are followed by small five-fingered leaves and bright red, winged fruits. By September the leaves begin to turn, each leaf a miniature rainbow of scarlet and yellow and green. By October the whole tree is on fire. Who could resist such a prodigy?

For thirty years I have indulged myself by accumulating maples from the far corners of the world. I have planted about forty different kinds of maples, that is, different varieties as well as different species: in the pleasure ground, the flower garden, the arboretum, in Yunnan and Tibet. In fact I have gorged myself on maples. And somehow I still have an appetite for more.

In the pleasure ground the star performers, I think, are a contrasting pair discovered in California in the 1820s by the celebrated David Douglas. His tragic death is well known. In Hawaii he fell into a concealed pit used for trapping wild bulls, and a wild bull gored him to death. (The Australian convict with whom Douglas was staying later insisted it was a complete accident, and vigorously denied that Douglas was having an affair with his wife.) But in his short life as a plant explorer Douglas introduced dozens of American giants to Europe and other parts of the world. These included the Sitka spruce, the grand fir and the fir that bears his name. He also found time to collect two of the maples that grew under the shadow of these giants. The first was the big-leaf maple, *Acer macrophyllum*, a bully-boy of a tree with leaves cut into deeper lobes and even bigger than the sycamore's. There's a famous pair of them, planted in the inner quad of Trinity College, Dublin, sometime in the mid-nineteenth century. I grew half a dozen from the seed of these trees and planted them as a grove. They are growing like beanstalks. The second is calmer and more graceful: a seven-lobed vine maple, *Acer circinatum,* which turns reddish-yellow in autumn. You could easily mistake it for one of the more delicate maples from Japan.

In the arboretum the largest and beefiest are a pair of twenty-year-old oriental thugs: a spiky maple from Japan, *Acer pictum*, and a muscular Chinese maple, *Acer cappadocicum sinicum*. I grew both these myself from seed. (If you look closely at the labels, you'll see they're stamped with a mysterious duck symbol. In fact this means that I picked up the seed in Kew Gardens without permission, while I was pretending to feed the ducks.) But the prize maples in the collection are the more delicate ones from China and Japan. The snake-barks, *Acer forestii* and *Acer davidii*, carry a white stripe down their green or red stems. We owe these two, as you would guess from their names, to the plant explorers Père David and George Forrest. Best of all, for form and colour, is the downy Japanese maple, *Acer palmatum* and its countless varieties.

This miraculous tree was first described by Engelbert Kaempfer in the seventeenth century, but not introduced to Britain until 1820. At first it was believed to be unable to cope with frost. In Loudon's day people were advised to plant their specimens with their backs to a wall. But it turned out that the enemy of the tree was the wind not the frost. Soon it came into fashion. And why would this graceful creature ever go out of fashion? In spring the colours of the varieties range from jade-green to lobster-pink. In autumn they turn to mixtures of purple, crimson and gold. Indeed an avenue of Japanese maples, like the one at Westonbirt in Gloucestershire, can boast as many colours as Jacob's famous coat. And maple-lovers flock to Westonbirt to pay homage to them in October, just as Japanese tourists flock to Kyoto to pay homage to the originals.

To return to the sycamore, the king of our maple kingdom, often mocked and humiliated in the garden, but usually welcomed as an honoured guest in the park. Technically it's not a native. To a botanist, a native is a species that found its own way from the Continent after the last ice age. Probably the sycamore was introduced by a man (or even a bird) about one thousand years ago. But it has been naturalised for so long in Britain and Ireland, and is so ideally suited to our soils and climate, that most people would agree it had earned its passport by now. I say, most people. Unfortunately there is a small group of environmentalists, influential in official circles, who would like to cancel its passport and drive it from these shores.

In Northern Ireland, I heard recently, the authorities are trying to cleanse the shores of Lough Neagh of every sycamore, although this would mean removing most of the natural tree cover. Fortunately, many landowners love these trees and will fight the planners tooth and nail. In the Irish Republic, where I live, millions of pounds of government money have been spent trying to eradicate sycamores – and indeed beech trees, too – from the last surviving demesnes. The government, under pressure from the lobby of environmentalists, have introduced a so-called 'native tree scheme'. Landowners are paid large grants, spread over twenty years, if they agree to cut down ancient sycamore and beech and replace them with young oak and ash, both of which are native, at least in theory. In fact, as I said in Chapter 5, this scheme has proved to have fatal flaws. The nursery trade in Ireland could not provide from local sources the millions of saplings needed for the scheme. So trees were imported from nurseries in all parts of the Continent – including nurseries invaded by *Chalara fraxinea*, the lethal ash disease. It was too late by the time the enormity of this error was discovered. By then the infected ash saplings had had ten years to spread the spores of Chalara far and wide. So much for the good sense of these environmentalists.

When I feel angry, I call these people 'the Talibans'. With puritan zeal they are trying to root out the trees in Britain and Ireland that 'don't belong'. There are only thirty-two true-blue natives (only twenty-six in Ireland), we are told – the ones that arrived on their own feet after the ice ages and before the Stone Age. The rest are aliens.

There are two ways to answer this fundamentalist argument. The first is that the Talibans have chosen to set the clock at the end of the last ice age. You belong if your ancestors arrived between 10,000 and 6,000 BC. You are an alien if you arrived about the time of Christ. But evolution didn't begin with the Stone Age. In earlier periods – before and between the four ice ages – Britain and Ireland had a much more exciting stock of native trees. From the point of view of the ginkgo, native to Britain in about four million BC, the oak and the ash are interlopers. In fact, viewed in geological time, Britain's tree population was once incredibly rich. It included the spruce and sycamores now found in Europe, as well as many of the exotics like giant sequoias and Douglas firs and magnolias that have only been reintroduced from America or the East within the last two centuries. Who are we to say that the earlier natives have lost their passports and only the (geologically) recent arrivals are given the rights of citizenship?

The second point is a more obvious one. Botanists tell us that only thirty-two British trees are what they call native. But most of the large trees that we cherish in Britain and Ireland are long-naturalised. Think of the walnut, probably introduced by the Romans from south-east Europe. Think of the sweet chestnut brought over from Italy and the Alps. Think of the horse chestnut that came from Constantinople - or so it was believed. (Later it turned out it came from a corner of Greece and Albania.) Think of the 'London plane' - probably an immigrant from Spain. Our landscape is dominated by long-naturalised immigrants: larch, spruce, silver fir - the list is endless. Even the Scots pine is an immigrant to England, Wales and Ireland, brought down from Scotland or brought over from the Continent. And the beech, the queen of our forest trees, is thought to be an immigrant, too, north and west of an unknown line somewhere in southern England and south Wales.

Yes, say the Talibans. We can tolerate some of these aliens. What we can't stand is *invasive* aliens. Of course there is a mafia of plants that threaten the environment. Everyone has their personal blacklist. Up on the rain-soaked moors of western Scotland, *Rhododendron ponticum* from the Caucasus has alienated most of its friends. Japanese knotweed and giant hogweed have equally few admirers. But these are not trees. In my experience trees soon strike a balance with their neighbours. The three dominant and longest-lived communities inside my arboretum - oak, beech and sycamore - don't encroach unduly in each other's territory, despite the apparent threat from that army of sycamore seedlings.

One invasive alien, it's true, was the terror of our trees. But it was an animal not a plant: the North American grey squirrel. For years I watched helplessly as the delicate trunks of young beech and oak and sycamore were mutilated by these gangsters. Oddly enough, they never touched the ash trees. Then the gangsters suddenly left us and have never returned. The experts say that the native pine marten has polished off the grey squirrel. I have my doubts. One year we were infested with squirrels, the next year no squirrel was to be seen. (How many pine martens would you need to polish off thirty thousand squirrels, I asked. 'Ah,' came the experts' reply, 'the pine martens don't need to *eat* all the squirrels. They just frighten them so much they can't have sex.') Anyway, free from these gangsters the arboretum and our deciduous woodlands in general are now able to muddle along as they like. I think they find a kind of equilibrium, although each year the balance between oak and beech and sycamore must shift as their seed harvest fluctuates.

Unfortunately the battle with these green Talibans continues worldwide. When I was last in Brussels there was a move to cut down the famous forest of beech, the Forêt de Soignes, which encircles the city to the east. It was originally planted in the late eighteenth century by the Austrians who occupied that part of the Low

Countries, and many of the beech are prodigies of height and elegance. The Talibans were not interested in that. They said the natural vegetation was a mixed oak forest, and this should be restored as soon as possible. At present, there is a stand-off, I understand, between preservationists and Talibans. But the authorities have agreed not to let the beech reproduce themselves. So, unless the preservationists find new allies, the Talibans will gradually win the battle by default.

I witnessed a similar struggle a few years ago when I was last in South Africa. Cape Town is rightly celebrated for its heart-stopping site on the lower slopes of Table Mountain. At the end of the nineteenth century much of this land was owned by Cecil Rhodes, the attention-seeking Prime Minister and gold magnate. Rhodes built and rebuilt his palatial barn, Groote Schuur, on these magical slopes, and ornamented them with thousands of European pines. The pines - cluster pines from south-west France and umbrella pines from Italy - grew to a magnificent size, taller even than they would have grown at home. Today Groote Schuur is the official residence of the President and the slopes are the jewel in the crown of Cape Town University. But the planners designated the slopes as part of the Table Mountain National Park. As a result the vociferous local Talibans insisted the alien pines should all be removed and the slopes allowed to revert to natural *finbosch* - mainly thorn bushes of one sort or another. (Ironically, these local Talibans are usually white South Africans whose families must have left Europe about the same time as the pine trees. Black South Africans have no time for these distractions.)

Fortunately there was a roar of protest from the people of Cape Town. I happened to be giving a lecture there at the time and asked for hands to be raised if people supported the attempt to save the pine trees. Up went a thousand hands, while two wretched Talibans slunk from the hall amid howls of derision. The pine trees were saved - but for how long? Like the beech forest at Brussels, the pines at Cape Town have been treated like dangerous immigrants. They have been sterilised, that is, they are not allowed to replace themselves with seedlings. Once again the Talibans will win by default.

Sometimes I tremble at the thought of what the Irish Talibans would do to me if they had the power. I'm sure they would have me prosecuted for giving comfort to sycamores - as well as for introducing scores of dangerous aliens from Yunnan and Tibet.

I will explain.

10

Lost Horizon

Tullynally, 20 June 2013

Some morning this week (I tell my friends who are staying) you should go down to the upper pond, alias the River Sham - the serpentine-shaped pond in the pleasure ground. If the sun's shining and there's a gentle wind from the south, you'll be aware of a strange but delightful scent. It's coming from the cowslips in a new garden below the pond, a garden I created about fifteen years ago. These are no ordinary cowslips. This is the great Tibetan cowslip, *Primula florindae*, the giant of the primula genus, a sulphur-yellow thug that grows five feet high with leaves like cabbage leaves and a scent that's nothing short of ambrosial.

Tibet, as I call this new garden below the River Sham, is the counterpart to Yunnan. Twenty years ago I flew with some friends to Yunnan in the Himalayan corner of south-west China, and returned with a treasure trove of seeds collected in the wild. This was the origin of my own Yunnan, the pagoda garden at the head of the Forest Walk. Two years later I went on a similar quest to Tibet hoping to collect enough seeds to make my own Tibet a few hundred yards upstream from Yunnan.

Today you can't miss the Tibetan cowslips beside the boggy stream. The species is a voracious coloniser of bogs and marshes. Yet it's only found as a native plant in one small corner of Tibet. We encountered a little colony on the banks of the mighty River Tsangpo, under the shadow of two grim snow-mountains, Gyala Peri and Namche Barwa. In due course I managed to grow a handful of the plants in my greenhouse. And today there are several hundred giant cowslips upstaging even the most exotic of my trees. I shan't complain.

But I am getting ahead of my story. I must explain this quest for trees and other plants in Tibet.

Keith Rushforth is one of the leading field botanists in Britain. He's tall and bald, with the build of a footballer. In his manner he is quiet, self-assured, optimistic. Trees and other plants are his obsession. In fact he's an expert on Himalayan flora and has led half a dozen expeditions to China, Bhutan and Tibet. It was Keith who led our expedition to Yunnan in 1993. Two years later he asked me if I would like to join the small group of British and Irish and Australian enthusiasts collecting seeds in Tibet. I jumped at the idea. Keith had somehow wangled permission from the Tibetan authorities (really the Chinese, I suppose, as they control the country) to cross the pass over the main chain of the Himalayas, a pass called the Doshong La. This would mean we could at least get a glimpse of parts of southern Tibet that few explorers have ever been allowed to see: the lost valleys of Pemako only a few miles from the border with India.

Ever since the border war between China and India in 1962, this has been a military zone jealously guarded by the Chinese. But Frank Kingdon-Ward described it in the 1920s as a 'plantsman's paradise'.

It was Kingdon-Ward who made his name as a plant hunter and explorer by leading expeditions to this remote corner of Tibet. Like Joseph Hooker, eighty years before him, Kingdon-Ward was the son of a well-known academic botanist – in his own case, the Professor of Botany at Owens College, Manchester. And like Hooker he wanted to make his father proud of him for his success in exploring remote corners of the world. But there the parallel ends. After his return from Sikkim, Hooker became an academic and an administrator – and eventually, like his father, the celebrated Director of the Royal Botanic Garden at Kew. Kingdon-Ward had no such desk-bound ambitions. For over forty-five years, from 1909 to the mid-1950s, he ranged the Himalayas, exploring the remotest regions, discovering new trees and other plants, often at great risk to himself. On one occasion his tent was squashed flat by fallen trees. At another he found himself at the centre of an earthquake rated more than 9 on the Richter scale. But somehow he survived, wrote twenty-five books about his discoveries, and died peacefully in his bed aged seventy-two.

Today no one can deny the importance of these discoveries. He was the first to travel all the way down the great canyon of the River Tsangpo - 19,000 feet deep at one point, which makes it the deepest in the world - in his search for a gigantic waterfall rumoured to rival Niagara. The Tibetan Niagara proved a gigantic disappointment for poor Kingdon-Ward. It was barely 50 feet high. But down in Pemako he discovered a botanical Shangri-La with vast numbers of plants of all kinds, many unique to Tibet.

Who knows, I thought, after reading his book, *Riddle of the Tsangpo Gorges*, we, too, might dazzle the world with our discoveries. You can see why I found Keith's invitation irresistible.

We met in London: Keith and five others, including my close friend Patrick Forde (who had created a professional plant nursery on his family estate in County Down), a lady orthodontist called Peta, and her adopted son, a young Vietnamese boy called Vinh. We were a cosmopolitan band. Bob Cherry, a cheerful plant expert from Australia, asked if we knew what we had let ourselves in for. I asked what he meant and he said he meant Keith.

'What's wrong with Keith?'

'He's only interested in plants. He's not a *leader*. He'll leave everything to the Tibetans.'

'What's wrong with that?'

'You'll soon see.'

But I had no qualms about Keith, after our successful trip to Yunnan.

That evening we set off via the steamy plains of Bangladesh to fly to Lhasa airport - a featureless little airfield in Tibet's vast, icy plateau 10,000 feet above sea level. Then leaving Lhasa itself to the north (we hoped to enjoy its fleshpots on our return) we started on the 250-mile drive towards Kingdon-Ward's Shangri-La. The River Tsangpo was our companion for most of the drive. It rises far to the south-west and runs eastwards, parallel to the main range of the Himalayas, for hundreds of miles - a docile giant, blue-grey from the glaciers, brown after recent rain, gliding between sandy, yellow banks. Below the pass of the Doshong La, the giant turns crazy. It hacks its way *between* two enormous snow mountains, Gyala Peri and Namche Barwa. Then it makes a dash for the plains of India, where it re-emerges as the Brahmaputra, the second largest river in the world.

For the first part of the trip Keith had arranged for us to travel in style. We coasted along in three white Toyota Land Cruisers, while our Tibetan companions followed in a pale-blue and green lorry, loaded with our food and tents. In three days we reached Pe, a huddle of small tin-roofed huts, among meadows grazed by yaks, at the foot of the Doshong La.

It would be most unfair to blame Keith for what followed. He was in the hands of the Tibetan authorities – I mean the Chinese. We had Sherpas to carry our food and tents and two Nepalese to cook the food. But, astonishingly, we had no local guides. Our Tibetan companions came from a different region; two of our three guides were townees from Lhasa itself. Worse, we had started perilously late in the season. The pass of the Doshong La is relatively low: a mere 14,000 feet, which is nothing much in the Himalayas. But the pass is notorious for its bad weather. A deluge of rain surges up the canyon from the plains of Assam. In autumn, as soon as it reaches the pass, the rain turns to snow. By late October it snows every day. By early November blizzards have blocked the pass, and Pemako is cut off from the world for the winter. All this was clear to me from reading Kingdon-Ward's chilling account of his adventures, *The Riddle of the Tsangpo Gorges*. I discussed it with Keith. The dates we had chosen were designed to give us a narrow window. We should arrive *after* the seeds were ripe and *before* winter set in. Keith admitted it would be a near-run thing. Couldn't we leave a fortnight earlier? No, we had been given our dates by the Tibetan authorities, and we must trust to luck. Keith was always an optimist.

Two days after reaching Pe we started to make the ascent of the pass. A dense cloud hid from us the gigantic snow mountains, Gyala and Namche Barwa, and the mighty Tsangpo itself, only a few miles north of the pass. One by one we ourselves vanished into the rain and the mist: six Europeans, two Nepalese and fifteen Tibetans (including the Sherpas carrying the boxes of food and the tents). We thought we were well prepared for the weather. I was wearing two sweaters, a black balaclava hat (too much like a terrorist's, I fear) and an anorak. But the mist was so dense that I soon lost touch with my companions. The track was barely visible. It was a steep, slippery path flattened by boots and the hooves of yaks, winding up through the rough grass and dwarf rhododendrons. We had passed the last belt of trees, lichen-covered silver firs cringing in the wind, an hour or so earlier. Soon the rain turned to sleet, and then to snow. I continued to climb, as the track became steeper and rockier, stopping often to catch my breath.

Where were my companions? I presumed I was somewhere in the middle of the caravan. As the snow became deeper I was at first reassured to find footprints to follow. But who was I following? One of our party? Or could I have strayed from the track and be following the footprints of some villager? (Or, for that matter, the footprints of the yeti, the Abominable Snowman? Nothing was impossible.) By this time the mist was even thicker, and it was blowing a blizzard. The snow was now so deep that it concealed clefts in the rocky track. I fell repeatedly and had to crawl out of these clefts on my hands and knees. Soon the snow covered the footprints, too. It was obviously time to halt and look for my companions. I sat down in the lee of a boulder the size of a house. I had to admit I was lost – lost in the Himalayas in a blizzard through nobody's fault but my own.

I sat there in the lee of the boulder for perhaps twenty minutes. It seemed like a lifetime. Then I saw two snow-encrusted figures emerge from the mist. It was the two young men from Lhasa, the guides who knew as little about these mountains as we did. Apparently I had been leading the caravan without realising it. The guides were followed by the rest of our party, the Europeans, the Nepalese and the Sherpas – all except our leader, Keith. He was last seen collecting seed from the silver firs in the valley below. By this time the Sherpas had put down their loads with a certain finality. It was too dangerous, our young guides said, to continue. The Sherpas' loads weighed about eighty pounds, and the snow was forming crevasses in the track.

Just then a trio of local hunters appeared, one of whom carried a gun. They told us they had taken three hours to climb down from the top of the pass. It would take us five. And at least three more to a campsite. The snow was much deeper on the Pemako side. Their own companions who were carrying loads had been forced to turn back. We, too, must turn back.

At this difficult moment, Keith finally emerged from the mist. He was striding along with his collecting bag as if he were picking blackberries up a country lane in England. I told him the bad news. The Sherpas refused to go on. If we crossed the pass ourselves, which the hunters said might take a further eight hours, we should have no food and no tents. How could we go on? Keith faced our dilemma with the sang-froid expected of British explorers. 'No comment,' he said. I put to him the grim facts once again. No Sherpas, no food, no tents. In fact, no choice. Reluctantly Keith nodded. Two hours later we were back on the road to Pe, a defeated column marching through the sombre forests of spruce and silver fir in the gentle rain.

It was a rebuff, certainly. And we learnt a somewhat obvious lesson. Shangri-La does not give away its secrets too lightly. If we had wanted to gain admission to that paradise of plants we should have started a fortnight earlier. But was it a defeat? To explore the grassy banks of the Tsangpo among the yaks was a privilege for which I must be grateful to Keith. It was more – it was one of the great experiences of my life. Nowhere else have

I seen two immense snow mountains rise, like genies, out of the mist at dawn. And in the next few days we made a number of exciting discoveries. We found the gigantic Tibetan cowslips close to the village of Pe, as I said earlier. These had been first spotted by Kingdon-Ward in the 1920s – he christened this primula species *florindae* after his first wife – and they are now common enough in the gardens of temperate Europe and North America. However, many of them today have been muddied by crossing with other species of primula, losing both the brilliance of their sulphur-yellow flowers and their ambrosial fragrance. Our seeds would be the real McCoy.

Within a few miles of Pe we also found a mass of stunning Tibetan trees: white pines called *armandii* after the famous French missionary, Père Armand David, who discovered the giant panda; blue-stemmed maples called *giraldii* after an Italian missionary; and half a dozen rare species of rowans with shiny pink or white berries. All these trees, I knew from Yunnan, would be well suited to our wet and sunless Irish summers. Their seeds littered the grass in the small valley, grazed by yaks, beside the Doshong River. It was the work of a moment to collect the sticky green pine cones, the double-winged maple seeds and the rowans' shiny berries.

Keith now told us his new plan. All was not lost, not by any means. There was another valley which Kingdon-Ward had explored – not so secret but almost as full of treasures as Pemako. It was called the Rongchu valley and was only two days' march to the west beyond the Tsangpo. He was assured by our guides that we had full permission to go there. Of course there might be difficulties. At 15,000 feet, the Nyima La – the pass that led to the Rongchu – was 1,000 feet higher than the ill-omened Doshong La. But our guides had told him there would be less snow so far west of the main chain of the mountains – perhaps none at all. The Land Cruisers and the lorry would have to take a 150-mile detour by road. They would cross the Tsangpo by the main bridge. Meanwhile we could march straight there, crossing the Tsangpo by the ferry at Pe, and taking ponies to carry our tents and baggage. We would meet again in two days.

I liked Keith's plan, although I was becoming a little wary of his optimism, and the fecklessness or inexperience of our guides. I had already heard something of the Rongchu. It was lyrically described in Kingdon-Ward's book, *Land of the Blue Poppy*. That astonishing poppy had originally been discovered by Colonel Bailey, the British adventurer who led an expedition to Tibet in 1912. But it was Kingdon-Ward who made the blue poppy famous. (The same could be said in reverse.) The poppy's blue was purer and more intense than any other. So the gardening world took the poppy to its heart when Ward introduced it on his return from Tibet in the late 1920s. But the species, like the Tibetan cowslip, tends to deteriorate when cultivated in Europe and North America. At least the purity of its blue petals tends to be muddied as the result of interbreeding. So Keith told us. And of course this suited me fine. The poppies grown from my seeds, if I found any seeds, would be as blue as a blue diamond.

The mud huts of Pe straddle the east bank of the Tsangpo, now barely 10,000 feet above sea level. On the opposite bank the ground rises steeply and the rocky slopes are dotted with larch, yellow in autumn. You can also see thousands of stunted evergreen oak, *Quercus semecarpifolia*. (The species is little known in Europe although hardy and elegant enough. It's sometimes called, because of its gilded underleaf, the golden oak of the Himalayas.) The Tsangpo itself takes a breather here. Soon it will turn east and go crazy, leaping into the canyon and heading for India. But here it's several hundred yards wide and looks more like a lake than a river. In fact Pe is one of the few places where the river is placid enough to be crossed by a ferry. Late next morning, with half a dozen ponies and ponymen, we clattered down to the riverbank and embarked, somewhat gingerly, in a pair of dugouts lashed together. The ferryman looked as old as Charon and so did his oars. But a long steel cable, attached to the other bank, helped offset the force of the current. We landed safely and, after a delicious lunch of beer and chicken chapattis, belatedly began the 5,000-foot climb towards the pass of the Nyima La.

Five hours later darkness found us still struggling through the heart of a forest. Of course the plan was that we should pitch camp somewhere in open country. The ponies could graze, and there would be room enough for tents. But the climb was stiffer than any of us had anticipated. When climbing hills in Cumbria or Kerry I had always found the secret was not to hurry. Put the machine in low gear, I would say to myself, and up she would go. But here the thin Tibetan air had begun to defeat me. I suppose we were already more than 12,000 feet up. I found myself needing to stop, every few minutes, to catch my breath. Would I make the top of the pass?

I was also alarmed by the series of makeshift bridges over the river which criss-crossed our track. My companions seemed to find no difficulty in negotiating them. I proved less agile. The river was in spate - hacking a zigzag path through the forest, plunging over rocks and boulders and fallen trees. The bridges were simply trees that had collapsed across the river and been left there to help people to cross. No one had removed the bark and sawed flat the slippery trunks. Luckily the two Nepalese cooks saw my predicament. Without their help - and they each took one of my arms - I would have certainly slipped and fallen on the jagged rocks below.

At least darkness put an end to my troubles for that day. And as the light faded I was, for the first time, able to take in my astonishing surroundings. I thought I had seen a wild forest before. I had been to Rothiemurchas in the Scottish Highlands and seen something of the original Caledonian forest, marvelling at the ancient Scots pines on the hillside. I had tramped through the great beech forest outside Brussels, the Forêt de Soignes, astounded by the tall, straight trunks and the cathedral-like calm. But those forests were managed and tamed. Most dead trees had been disposed of - cut up for firewood, removed for safety or simply to tidy up the place. Standing trees stood upright. The few recumbent corpses lay flat on the ground. Here in Tibet was a forest in the raw. The spruce and fir lay at all angles, stitched together like giant brambles. Half them seemed to be dead or dying - having collapsed from old age or been smashed down by storms. And no one had touched the wreckage. (I suppose the nearest village was too far below us for the villagers to come up here for firewood.) The forest was a Gothic jungle, as it might have been imagined by Edgar Allan Poe. I began to recover my appetite for Tibet.

After supper I lay in my tent listening to the music of the small bells attached to the ponies' harness. Bob and the ponymen had lit a fire with the spruce branches in our clearing and the sparks rose in a resinous fountain. Perhaps we shared the forest with bears or snow leopards. I felt secure enough in my sleeping bag. One of the ponies was munching grass a few feet away. I could hear the insistent jangle of its bell close to my ear. But, after that climb for five hours through the Gothic jungle, nothing could keep me awake very long.

Next morning we crossed the pass of the Nyima La without too much trouble. I was alarmed by the thought of the height - over 15,000 feet. But the stony track soon emerged from the forest, which was a blessing. Now I could see the rocks on the summit of the ridge. Perhaps I was only a couple of hours from the pass. There was no sign of snow, thank heavens. The guides were right: away from the Doshong La the weather was clear as a bell. I followed the column of ponies and ponymen, and pressed ahead up the track, stopping often to catch my breath. I could soon see Keith and the rest of the party in the valley far behind me. (I think they were collecting seeds of giant rhubarb and dwarf rhododendrons.) By midday I had panted up to the summit. What a relief! And what a reward!

Over to the east, beyond the great blue abyss cut by the Tsangpo, were those two amazing snow mountains once more: Gyala Peri and Namche Barwa. They must be now about thirty miles away from us, and already they seemed almost benign in the midday sunshine. At least they had lost that air of menace they had maintained when we tried to push open the door they guarded, the door to Shangri-La. But what awaited us now in the Rongchu valley to the west? Our first sight of this new paradise was not particularly encouraging. A straggling line of huts followed the line of the river and the metalled road beside it. The good news was that the lorry and Land Cruisers, carrying our main supplies, had made the long detour to the west and were ready to greet us. Already the ponymen had set up the tents. A spiral of woodsmoke from the campfires rose in the thin, frosty air. By morning, I thought, those tents would be blue with hoar frost. But not perhaps quite as blue as *Meconopsis baileyi*, the poppy we had come so far to find.

The next few days were spent in exploring the valley and it proved full of treasures after all. There were many trees and other plants with seeds ripe for the collecting bags of Keith, Patrick Forde and myself. I had already snapped up half a dozen cones of the white pine, *Pinus armandii*. Now we got the cones of the equally beautiful silver fir, the local form of abies. Keith scrutinised these abies carefully and told us that some of them differed in an exciting way from the normal form of the species. He *might* have stumbled on an entirely new species. He couldn't promise anything yet. (More than ten years later Keith announced that this was indeed a new species of abies and he christened it *Abies fordei* in memory of our friend and companion, Patrick Forde, who had died, sad to say, in the meantime.)

We also collected seeds from several species of trees that, earlier in the trip, had tantalised us from the far side of the Tsangpo. These included the miniature cones of a weeping form of the local larch, *Larix potaninii*, some tiny acorns, already germinating, of the golden oak, and the delicate catkins of seeds from the local Himalayan birch; some of these birch trees have mottled green bark, others have bark the colour of chocolate cake. Best of all, Patrick found the seeds of an elegant little tree called *Lindera obtusiloba*. The Latin epithet, meaning 'blunt-leaved', hardly does justice to the extraordinary leaves. They end in three chubby fingers, growing from a scarlet stalk, and they glow like yellow lanterns in autumn.

To make a Tibetan garden, when I returned home to Ireland, I would need more than Tibetan trees. I would need the Tibetan shrubs and other plants that would be their companions in the wild. Soon I had bagged over a hundred species. The shrubs included two kinds of rose, *Rosa macrophylla* with outsize orange hips, and *Rosa sericea pterocantha* with huge, blood-red thorns; also three rare kinds of berberis including the glaucous-leaved *Berberis temolaica*. The two most outstanding of the herbaceous plants, apart from the giant Tibetan cowslip we had found at Pe, were an aggressive redhead called *Rodgersia aesculifolia* and an elegant *Iris chrysographes*. (Of course this iris didn't look particularly striking that autumn. But its flower, I was soon to discover, is a delight: a rich, imperial purple inscribed in gold with what look like Chinese characters.)

But where, oh where were the blue poppies which Kingdon-Ward had found in this actual spot seventy years earlier?

On the second afternoon after our descent from the Nyima La, I felt I had earned a respite. Keith and my other energetic companions had decided to pursue the search for the blue poppies five miles upstream. I told them I would stay in the camp to write up my diary. I wandered down to the stream, shaded by a grove of willows. The sun was hot and the water delightfully cool. I decided to wash my feet. But before I had removed my shoes and socks I sprang up in amazement. I had sat down on a clump of something familiar, yet different - something with the unmistakable coronet of the poppyhead, yet larger and more exotic than any I knew. Could it be . . . no, I could hardly hope . . . yes, by God it was! I had sat on the famous *Meconopsis baileyi*, the blue poppy itself. The poppyheads were overflowing with black seeds and it was the work of a moment to fill my envelope from the hoard.

An hour later Keith, Patrick and my other companions returned, and they were not in the best of tempers. They had tramped ten miles up and down the Rongchu valley - and they had found nothing. I held out the plant I had sat on. 'You weren't looking for this by any chance?'

'Where on earth did you find it?'

'Oh, by the stream. I suppose I have a nose for that sort of thing.' (I wasn't foolish enough to admit I had sat on it.)

Keith and Patrick were incredulous. Of course I didn't deserve these seeds. I was the duffer of the team. But there were enough blue poppy seeds for everyone, and enough Chinese beer that evening to celebrate in style my moment of glory.

*   *   *

When I flew home to Ireland in late October 1995, I brought back with me over a hundred small brown envelopes. Each brown envelope was marked with a time and date, an altitude (supplied by Keith) and a tentative botanical name (supplied by one or other of my companions). And each contained the seeds of one species of Tibetan tree or other plant that I had collected in the wild. Some of them - the envelopes with birch and rhododendron in particular – contained more than a thousand individual seeds. For two months I left my precious Tibetans to cool their heels in the refrigerator. This was to give them a winter, needed by many seeds if they are to break dormancy. Then I sowed them in green plastic seed-trays, carefully labelled them (two identical white labels for each tray in case one label disappeared) and told them to wake up: winter was over and now it was spring. In fact they had just exchanged the rigours of the refrigerator for the joys of the heated greenhouse. By the April of that year, 1996, the Tibetans in nearly half the trays had sprung to life. (The other half had, for various reasons, including my own inexperience, failed to germinate.) By the second autumn, 1997, I had hundreds of boisterous Tibetans raring to be planted out. But how should I choose the site of their new Tibet?

I thought two principles were important. The site of the new garden must be big enough, and secluded enough, for it to have a life and character of its own. And it needed plenty of water. South-east Tibet has a monsoon climate (as we had found to our cost when trying to cross the Doshong La), and many of my new plants had been born within sight of the Tsangpo and its tributaries.

There was a corner of the pleasure ground below the River Sham which had previously been stocked with peat-loving plants like azaleas and rhododendrons. It had once been called the 'American Garden', meaning a garden for peat-loving American plants. Maria Edgeworth, a distant cousin but close neighbour, gave a lyrical account of the place in the 1830s (though she was less lyrical about its owner, Lady Longford). But by 1996 it was a marsh and a wilderness. Sallies dominated the wetter bits, brambles the drier ones. This, I thought, would be perfect for Tibet – I mean, once I had disposed of the sallies and brambles. Yes, this would be just the place to make a new stream garden. It would need a few dozen tractor-loads of black peat from the bog. Water I could provide by diverting the stream from the pond above it. Then I could grow acid-loving plants from Tibet as well as those which could cope with lime. I could even create a bit of gorge scenery by digging out the banks of the new stream. It may sound a bit whimsical. But I wanted the Tsangpo to be reborn in Westmeath beside its two grim companions, those snow mountains, Gyala and Namche Barwa, which still troubled my dreams.

To dig out the Tsangpo was the work of only a few hours for a large yellow JCB. Then we built a concrete dam to divert the outflow from the River Sham back into the new channel. Making the snow mountains, Gyala and Namche Barwa, was more of a problem. It's surprising how many tractor-loads of soil are needed to make the smallest hillock. I settled for two black mounds of peat, fully 9 feet high, with red and blue and green prayer flags to decorate their flanks. (The effect was, I thought, a little too cheerful. I should have liked the mountains to look more menacing.) More successful was a miniature Tibetan temple whose six-sided pillars were made from the limbs of an old sweet chestnut that blew down that Christmas. The design I took from the porch of a Tibetan shrine, torn down by Red Guards during the Cultural Revolution and then reconstructed by benefactors from Thailand. We painted the temple scarlet and commissioned a Romanian painter, who was living in one of our flats, to add some Tibetan dragons in lieu of several months' rent. They looked most authentic, these fiery dragons. (I asked Mikael, the painter, how on earth he knew what a Tibetan dragon looked like. He turned to me, astonished by my ignorance. 'I got it from the Internet, of course.')

It only remained to arrange my forty species of Tibetans - trees, shrubs and herbaceous plants - in what I hoped would appear a natural manner. The site was an oblong. I planted three small groves, combining the new trees with the old beech and yews and horse chestnuts along the fenceline. In the first grove, to greet you at the gate, I put the two rarest trees: the golden oak (*Quercus semecarpifolia*), and the Tsangpo cypress (*Cupressus gigantea*). The golden larches and the white pines and the blue-stemmed maples brought up the rear. Between them were the white-berried rowans and the scarlet crab apples and most of the more exotic shrubs including the pudgy-fingered *Lindera obtusifolia*, the pink-flowered *Rosa macrophylla* and the glaucous-leaved *Berberis temolaica*.

Had I introduced scores of alien invaders, as the Talibans might claim? In fact none of my exotic new introductions proved invasive - meaning that they posed no threat to the environment. None of them grew where they were not wanted. It was as simple as that.

Yet almost everything I planted survived and many grew astonishingly well. On Christmas Day 2010 the thermometer at Tullynally fell to -17 °C. My Tibetans shrugged off the frost and the blizzards. And in the last fifteen years it's been the primulas and the poppies that have stolen the show. The Tibetan cowslip, *Primula florindae*, the sulphur-yellow flower with the ambrosial scent - this is the giant that spreads itself majestically along the banks of the Westmeath Tsangpo. And Kingdon-Ward's poppy, *Meconopsis baileyi*, glitters on the summit of Namche Barwa, its petals as blue as the ice from a glacier.

ABOVE: From Yunnan, in south-west China, we headed north to Sichuan, close to the borders of Tibet. Young larch trees have occupied the mountains cropped by the loggers.

RIGHT: *Sorbus hupehensis* seizes its chance in a newly created clearing in Sichuan.

ABOVE: Old larch trees (*Larix potaninii*), battered by storms, at the summit of a pass we crossed, 12,000 feet up in southern Sichuan.

OPPOSITE: A large sycamore that has planted itself next to the Pumpkin House in my arboretum. If only it wasn't so generous with its seedlings. But its flaking bark is pink and its leaves are banana-yellow in autumn and I forgive it everything.

OPPOSITE: An eighteenth-century beech in the parkland. I confess to killing its brothers in order to see the view of Knockeyon.

ABOVE, RIGHT: The hut in my Tibet modelled on the porch of a Buddhist temple I photographed in 1995. The dragons came from the Internet.

RIGHT: Blue poppies (*Meconopsis baileyi*) grown from seed that I collected from Colonel Bailey's old campsite in the Rongchu Valley, Tibet.

OPPOSITE: Ancient yew trees in Kingley Vale, Sussex. Edward Lear made a drawing of them for his friend, Alfred Tennyson. But their age is a mystery.

ABOVE: A one-woman balloon launched, with some difficulty, from the lawn at Tullynally. I got a ride in one of the safer, man-carrying balloons.

OVERLEAF: Balloon view of Lough Derravaragh with Knockeyon six miles away at the end of the lake. You can see the large ring-fort and the Millennium Wood at the foot of the picture. Above them, 100 yards into the lake, is the small, round *crannog* (man-made island) where the Viking ingots were discovered by illegal treasure-hunters.

11

How Old Is an Old Yew?

1 July 2013

Yesterday they cut down one of the yew trees that used to stare at our windows from across the fence beside a large beech tree. I had known it for years. It was not one of my favourite trees: long ago someone had lit a bonfire too close to its feet and it still bore the scars. But I don't think I would have agreed to its summary execution if I had been at home.

I was away in London and our farm manager, Kevin, asked my wife if he could cut it down. It was just across the fence in the demesne. And it had poisoned two of our calves, according to Kevin. Regular menace, he said. Then move the fence, I would have replied. But I wasn't there, and down it came: 115 years of staring at our windows reduced to a couple of tons of cherry-coloured wood blocks in ten minutes. (I had often wondered when it was planted. Now I know. You can see the creature's exact age from counting the annual rings shamelessly exposed on the stump.)

Probably Kevin was right and it had poisoned the calves. Sometimes a dose of yew leaves can be fatal to cattle and horses. And sometimes a yew has to take the blame for an animal's death that the vet can't explain. Guilty or not, the tree has always had a sinister reputation among farmers. No other tree has so many ways of killing you or your animals. Lethal alkaloids lurk in the soft green leaves, the withered brown leaves, the flaking brown bark and the bitter black seed hidden in a scarlet coating. Only this scarlet coating of the seed, the aril, is safe to eat – a concession offered by the tree for one very good reason. Birds find the aril delicious, and the poisonous seed passes safely through their gut before finding a well-fertilised home in a new territory.

In the Middle Ages the longbow made of yew was Britain's national weapon. In fact it dominated medieval warfare. But English yews were never sufficient, nor did they meet the high standard needed for the English arms industry. Strips of Spanish yew (taken as a payment in kind for the tax on wine and spirits) were brought in attached to barrels of wine. These longbows carved from Spanish yew were astonishingly powerful machines. In the hands of an experienced Welsh archer a steel-tipped arrow, fired from a longbow at the rate of eight arrows a minute, could puncture a knight's visor or breastplate as efficiently as a bullet. No wonder the French knights bit the dust at Agincourt.

Of course it was not long before the discovery of gunpowder made the longbow an anachronism. Yew trees, no longer a strategic resource, took refuge in the churchyard. Here they were safe from farmers and were welcomed for their pious associations. The grove of yews had been revered from the time of the Celts, consecrated as a place for their temples and for exposing the heads of their enemies. In Christian times, the yew served as one of the few evergreens available for religious rites. It was the palm for Palm Sunday and the wreath for the Mass of the dead. As a Christian symbol, it could play a double role. It was the tree of death, like the cypress in the Mediterranean. It was also the tree of redemption, of life after death and of immortality itself.

To return to my own humble yew, summarily executed, I could see Kevin's point. Farmers have enough troubles without having to worry about yew trees. That tree had the misfortune to be in the wrong place. But I must now plant a sapling yew on the right side of the fence. After all, the common yew, *Taxus baccata*, is the *only* evergreen tree, apart from holly and juniper, indigenous to England, Wales and Ireland. (Scotland has the Scots pine, *Pinus sylvestris*, as well as yew, holly and juniper. Nobody knows why the pine survived in the icy Caledonian forest when it died out in all the other parts of these islands.) And there's another reason why I should plant more yews. Ireland was once famous throughout Europe for the abundance of yew trees. Let me explain.

In 1183, only a decade after the Normans had invaded and conquered Ireland, an enterprising Welsh monk, Giraldus Cambrensis (alias Gerald de Barry) set off to tour the new colony. In due course he wrote a best-selling account of his travels, *Topographica hibernica*: a racy mixture of facts and the fabulous. There are marvels of many kinds:

from bearded ladies to men who turn into wolves, and from islands of fire to corpses that defy decomposition. The less sensational part concerns trees and other plants.

'In all the lands I came to [in Ireland],' he writes, 'the yew with its bitter fruit grows far and wide – and you may see masses of this tree most of all in old graveyards, and the sacred places of holy men by whose hands they were once planted for the beauty and ornament they could add.'

It sounds authentic all right, his description of medieval Irish churchyards teeming with yew trees. But today, sadly enough, ancient yew trees are rare enough in Irish churchyards. England and Wales, by contrast, have ancient yews in plenty. Ireland, tormented by civil wars, must have lost its heritage of yews during the last few centuries. A few exceptional yews have survived in churchyards dating from before the Reformation, although most of the biggest (and perhaps oldest) have depended on the protection of private gardens and demesnes.

At Tullynally, I must confess, our common yews are ordinary enough. No, that would be unfair to the species. Yews are never ordinary, even when they are young and take a conventional shape. What I mean is that we don't have any champion yews. But we have a decent number of oddball yews scattered about the place. My favourite is (or rather was) an old yew tree, near the Forest Walk, that found itself alone in a new plantation of Norway spruce. Presumably the workers who planted these youngsters took pity on the old fellow. At any rate they left him to his own devices. For years he must have risen like a handsome green obelisk above the heads of the pushy young spruce. But commercial spruce grow at least twice as fast as yews. Desperate to survive, the old yew concentrated all his energies on trying to keep his share of daylight. The race for the sky made him unusually symmetrical and elegant. But slowly the life was squeezed out of him – until the dark green obelisk became a grey-brown skeleton. Perhaps he was more beautiful in death than he had ever been before. At any rate I hadn't the heart to have him consigned for firewood. The corpse, propped up in a mossy clearing among his enemies, now commands the ride through the forest. And there he will stay, I hope, till the day of doom – which means the day when the ten-wheeled forwarders arrive to harvest the spruce and all hell is let loose in the forest.

Of course that old yew was a creature of the wild. What of the cultivated yews at Tullynally? The other day I did a kind of census and was surprised at the score. We have no less than twenty-five common yews in the garden: modest creatures that give us a backdrop for the lawn and the trees of the pleasure ground. We have also nineteen Irish yews that are far from modest. In fact they are born attention-seekers. Freakishly upright, they punctuate each section of the garden like so many dark green – and glittering gold – exclamation marks.

Let me begin with our common yews. These are all middle-sized examples of the common yew, girthing at least 6 feet and reckoned at least one hundred years old. The largest two take the edge off the east wind when it threatens the pleasure ground. They share that duty. Otherwise they are opposites. The wilder of the two, 14 feet 6 inches in girth and ribbed like a Gothic column at the base, splays out like a fan-vault above. The other tree, 12 feet in girth, looks at first sight conventional: its trunk rises straight as a chimney for 50 feet. But the branches have an odd habit of making right-angle bends whenever they have a chance. I cannot say I admire this quirk, although it must follow Darwin's rule of natural selection. In certain situations, I suppose (though I can't quite envisage one), a yew with a kink would be fitter than a yew with conventional curves. There was also a third large yew tree in this part of the garden until ten years ago. It was decidedly Baroque: its trunk twisted like a column of barley sugar.

How old are old yews of this kind? In 1990 I put the question to Alan Mitchell, the leading dendrologist of his generation and the guru we all depended on. Almost single-handed, he had created the Tree Register of the British Isles – an idiosyncratic charity which kept the score for champion trees and others of unusual size. For thirty years, wearing sandals on the coldest of days, he tramped the length of Britain and Ireland with tape measure and hypsometer. By 1989 he had recorded the measurements of 84,000 separate specimen trees of 1,670 different species. If anyone knew the answer to the riddle of a tree's age, it was Alan Mitchell. So I believed.

Now I had been told that his friends teased Alan with the claim that if you gave him a good lunch he would make your trees taller and fatter and older. It was midday when my hero arrived at Tullynally. I took him to see my three old yews. 'Do you want me to guess their age? It could be seven hundred years.' Of course I was thrilled. Seven hundred years. That was only two centuries after the Norman invasion – and three hundred years before the first Pakenham carpet-bagger had set foot at Tullynally. I took Alan in to lunch. But perhaps the beef and potatoes and boiled cabbage weren't quite up to standard. Alan drew me aside after the coffee and said: 'I've been thinking of your three old yews. I may have exaggerated. Shall we say five hundred years?'

Sad to say, Alan died five years later. His life's work, the Tree Register, continues to expand under the care of enthusiastic trustees, among whom I am proud to have been included. (Its digital archive in 2011 recorded 250,000 measurements for over 190,000 noteworthy trees.) But there was an odd sequel to Alan's visit to Tullynally. The third old yew – the Baroque one that twisted like a barley-sugar column – was infested with ivy. Could you please cut the ivy, I asked one of our men. I should have known better. When I next saw the yew its trunk was scored with two deep cuts made by a chainsaw. Gangrene, or its woody equivalent, followed soon after – and death after two more years. I felt miserable about the whole business. Then I realised there was one compensation at least.

Here was a rare chance of finding out the actual age of an old yew – as opposed to making an inspired guess, like Alan's, based on the size of a living tree, which in this case had been 11 feet in girth at the base. The yew was dead. So we could count the annual rings and discover whether Alan was right. It sounded simple, but I was in for a shock. The yew was not seven hundred – or even five hundred. It was only a hundred and ninety. Alan had been generous to a fault – nearly three times too generous.

Was this an unusual case? Or is it impossible to make meaningful estimates of the age of any living ancient yew? I shall come back to this baffling question in due course. First let me say something about the other kind of yew, the upright Irish yew, of which we have nineteen attention-seeking examples at Tullynally. This is the peculiar mutation (*Taxus baccata* 'Fastigiata') which originated here in Ireland about two hundred and seventy years ago and has now spread from Britain to the Mediterranean and from the Atlantic to the Antipodes.

Sometimes I wonder if we boast enough about this remarkable tree, which represents Ireland's most striking contribution to the world of horticulture. Perhaps the association with graveyards casts a shadow on its reputation. But let me say a word about its origins. It was about 1740 (*not* 1780, the date often cited) when a tenant farmer called Willis noticed two very rum-looking yews growing on a rock high in the Carricknamaddow ('Rock of the Dog') Mountain above Florence Court, County Fermanagh. Florence Court was the 'very costly and sumptuous' home of his landlord, Lord Enniskillen. In due course Willis dug up the rum-looking yews and gave one to Lord Enniskillen, then planted the other in his own humble garden. I assume his lordship was grateful. In some respects these freaks were distinctly superior to the common yew. The foliage was a richer and darker green. And (somewhat incongruously for an Irish tree) every single twig grew upright. The result was a massive pillar of dark green, crowned with spires and pinnacles. Both trees flourished in their new homes, although Willis's died after about a century.

Meanwhile Lord Enniskillen's tree at Florence Court had become famous. Although the tree didn't come true from seed, it was easy to propagate from cuttings. The great London nursery firm, Lee of Hammersmith, began to mass-produce cuttings at the turn of the eighteenth century. Once the Napoleonic Wars were over, the tree took the Continent by storm. Its uprightness made it perfect for a formal garden. Those dark green pillars and spires were equally adaptable for the palace or the graveyard. It was hardier than the Mediterranean cypress and took the pruning knife just as well as its half-brother, the common yew. By the mid-nineteenth century a golden form had been discovered and mass-produced from cuttings. Soon the craze for Irish yews spread to America and beyond – and the Irish yew continues, I think rightly, to have its admirers. Meanwhile Lord Enniskillen's original tree, the natural mother of every Irish yew in the world, lives on in honourable retirement at Florence Court.

At Tullynally an avenue of eight tattered old Irish yews, 40 feet high and as broad, leads you down the main axis to the greenhouses in the walled garden. I say old, and I mean that they appear on the first detailed estate map, dated 1835. I should expect them to have been planted in the 1820s when my great-great-grandfather, the 2nd Earl of Longford, was keen to cut a dash in the fashionable world. Living mainly in London, he had seemed like a confirmed bachelor. Then at forty-nine he had married at last. His young English bride – the family's first bride for two hundred years not born in Ireland – was Georgiana Lygon, daughter of the Earl of Beauchamp. What would these modish Lygons make of Tullynally? As a house it had been unpretentious enough in the eighteenth century – in fact as plain as a barracks. Now Lord Longford transformed it into a Gothic castle, and redesigned the garden to fit. I hope his new father-in-law, Lord Beauchamp, was suitably impressed by the eight young Irish yews.

Today they are looking their age, with many of the upper branches missing or broken by storms. Valerie says she would like them rejuvenated – meaning decapitated and pruned back to the shape of pillars. I am alarmed by her talk of getting a good tree surgeon to do the job. I think that we should respect the feelings of old trees as we would respect the feelings of other veterans. If this sounds too anthropomorphic, I can put it another way. We should be sensitive to the patina of age, as we would be with the wall of a castle or a piece of old furniture. But I fear this is an argument that will not be settled easily. I may well lose it – after my funeral.

To return to the common yew, and the contentious subject of its longevity. It's over a hundred years since the lines were drawn in a debate between the distinguished Swiss botanist, Professor Augustin de Candolle (the man who anticipated some of

Darwin's work on evolution) and a tree-loving English clergyman called John Lowe. In fact de Candolle had died in 1841, some years before Lowe was born, but the debate rumbled on throughout the century and continues today. In essence the argument is about estimates of a yew tree's age based in turn on estimates of a yew tree's speed of growth. De Candolle claimed that yew trees often grow so slowly in their later years that they are capable of living far more than a thousand years. He estimated that a yew that girthed 10 feet was already 480 years old; with a girth of 20 feet it was 960; and with a girth of 30 feet it was 1,440. Rubbish, declared the Reverend John Lowe. His estimates were not much more than a third of de Candolle's: 190 years, 380 years and 570 years respectively. He cited cases where the exact planting dates in the seventeenth and eighteenth centuries were known. The trees had grown at rates between a foot in girth in seventeen years and a foot in girth in twenty-four years.

Modern research, such as it is, has tended to side with Lowe. But although Lowe's estimates for trees up to 12 feet in girth seem sensible enough, he doesn't appear to have made sufficient allowance for declining growth in very old trees. The eighth and last edition of W. J. Bean's *Trees and Shrubs* - the Bible for tree enthusiasts like myself - cites an estimate that old yews very gradually decline in their growth rate, from 5.5 inches of girth for every ten years when they are young, to 3.5 inches when they are old. This would mean a 30-foot giant was 800 years old, compared with Lowe's 570 and de Candolle's 1,440. And a handful of even bigger yews - like the 34-foot giant in the churchyard at Tandridge in Surrey - might possibly have taken root before the arrival of William the Conqueror.

What makes this debate even more complicated is that both Lowe and de Candolle assumed a clear connection between the age of a tree and its size. But modern research into the age of other long-lived species, like oaks and pines, has shown that the connection is not clear at all, once a tree has passed a certain stage. Dr Schulman, the pioneering dendrochronologist, studied the Bristlecone pine in the White Mountains of California during the 1950s. This project involved drilling the trunks with an auger and then counting the annual rings under a microscope. He found that the oldest tree yet recorded in the world, the 4,700-year marvel dubbed 'Old Methuselah', was of quite modest size. By contrast, the biggest in the groves - 'the Patriarch' 2,000 feet higher up the mountain - was also the youngest.

Other scientists have made similar discoveries more recently. In Scotland a research team studying the Scots pine in its native fastness, the Caledonian forest, were surprised to find that, in one of their plots, the younger trees were actually bigger-girthed than the older ones. In general they reported that 'neither tree height nor tree dbh [diameter at breast height] can be used to calculate the age of pine trees with any accuracy'. One thing that did emerge was that longevity was more closely linked to slow growth than to size. Some of the smallest pine trees, stunted by the icy winds, were proved to be nearly three hundred years old. Scientists have found much the same is true of oaks doomed to scrape a living on icy mountainsides. They linger on to a riper old age than their cousins living off the fat of the land. (I believe the same rule of longevity applies to rats that have been starved. Perhaps it even applies to the human race.)

So where does all this leave us? I mean, is it too much to hope we can *ever* know the age of a huge ancient yew tree? My own feeling is that we need some eager young scientist – a man fired up with the zeal of Dr Schulman – to give us the real facts. Too much time has been wasted on guesswork. I know that ancient yews inside or outside churchyards in Britain or Ireland are usually hollow. It should be no surprise that yew trees in a warm, damp climate decay much more quickly than Bristlecone pines 10,000 feet up in the icy White Mountains of California. Dr Schulman was lucky: to count the tree-rings of a pine he could drive his auger through a trunk that was solid to the core. How then can we count their tree-rings? I believe there are ways around this problem. A tree hollow at the base will often be solid enough 10 feet from the ground. You could drill through the upper part of the trunk and adjust the ring-count accordingly. Or you could drill through the lower branches and adjust the ring-count. It is up to modern dendrochronologists – tree archaeologists in effect – to develop the right techniques. Or must we remain for ever in a scientific limbo, while experts debate longevity like medieval schoolmen debating how many angels could perch on the point of a needle?

To pursue this matter I set off recently for a tour of some of the better-known yews in Ireland and England. I was well aware that almost all the largest known yews are in churchyards: cavernous giants like the great yews at Tandridge in Surrey and at Much Marcle in Herefordshire. (See my wanderings in the 1990s, portrayed in *Meetings with Remarkable Trees*.) But on this new expedition I decided to pay my homage to secular trees in groups rather than to individuals in churchyards. I had two reasons for this. Churchyard yews are sacred yews, at least by long association, and some people would feel squeamish about driving an auger through the stomach of a tree of that sort. I also wanted to test the hypothesis that bigger doesn't necessarily mean older – that, after a certain stage in the life of a tree, there's no clear connection between size and age.

I began my tour at Loughcrew, which is only a step or two north of Tullynally –

well, twelve miles, hardly further than a good Irish giant could throw a decent-sized boulder. This corner of north-west Meath is unusually rich and mysterious. The rolling hills conceal a full-blown megalithic necropolis – one of the biggest in the country – dating from at least 3000 BC. Unfortunately the local landlords, the Naper family, found their way into the passage graves in the early nineteenth century, too soon to know the techniques of modern archaeology. But many elegantly decorated stones survive today, including a form of megalithic sundial which floods one of the tombs with magical sunlight at dawn on the spring and autumn equinoxes – provided, of course, it's not raining. The yew trees, thirty-five of them, are even more magical.

In the early seventeenth century the tower house at Loughcrew was the childhood home of Oliver Plunkett. He became the martyred Archbishop of Armagh recently canonised by the Pope – Ireland's first new saint for seven hundred years. But by 1673 the high-minded Catholic Plunketts had been replaced by the high-living Protestant Napers. Cromwellian carpet-baggers like the Pakenhams, the Napers carved out a huge estate from forfeited Catholic land and built themselves a Carolean longhouse beside the Plunketts' crumbling tower house. Next to it was a still earlier feature, a Norman motte (or mound) shaped like a pudding basin. It was here, between motte and longhouse, that the thirty-five yews were planted in four more or less regular lines. The effect is dramatic, although the longhouse was swept away two hundred years ago. Fortune had smiled on the Napers: I presume they had hunted down an heiress. Anyway they built themselves a Greek Revival palace half a mile to the east, a melodious echo of Athens and the Acropolis in the rolling hills of County Meath.

But when did the Napers plant those yew trees? The present owner, Emily Naper, is an enthusiast who has, despite every obstacle, made Loughcrew a honeypot for tourists. She believes the trees are contemporary with the long-vanished longhouse and are therefore now more than three hundred years old. But were they in fact planted decades later? All we know for certain is that John Lowe singled them out for attention in his meticulous survey of yews in Britain and Ireland. This was published in 1897 and Lowe reported that the biggest yew at Loughcrew was then 11 feet in girth. I uncoiled my yellow tape and measured each of the thirty-five carefully round the base. Which was Lowe's tree? Presumably the biggest, a dramatic column of a tree nearest the tower house, with roots contorted like Medusa's serpents. Its girth was now 15 feet 8 inches. So this yew had apparently grown nearly 5 feet in the last 115 years – at roughly the speed Lowe had predicted. But the variation in the girth of the trees was very striking. The smallest of the thirty-five girthed only 7 feet 8 inches – less than half the size of the biggest. From the symmetry of the planting, I assumed they were all contemporaries. So this seemed a dramatic confirmation of the rule that bigger is not necessarily older.

My second conclusion was that the trees were younger, perhaps much younger, than Emily Naper (and most other people) believed. You see, the *average* girth of all thirty-five yews came to 11 feet. This was the girth of my own yew with barley-sugar columns, the one which defeated Alan Mitchell, the one which proved to be only 190 years old. Could these thirty-five trees really be more than 300 years old? Surely they had not grown so slowly as that, and were late-eighteenth-century not late-seventeenth-century trees. I began to have more confidence in Lowe and less and less in de Candolle. But here was an argument that could be settled so easily by a man with an auger. Or even without one. A few years ago, I was told, several yews in the group were gnawed by sheep and died soon after. The trees were cut down and the stumps removed. But, sadly, no one bothered to count the rings.

Down in the south of England I visited three famous groups of yews growing in the wild: at Newlands Corner and Druids Grove in Surrey, and at Kingsley Vale in West Sussex.

Newlands Corner is a clearing carved out of a romantic ridge a few miles east of Guildford. The site is a magnet for picnickers and is efficiently managed by Surrey Wildlife Trust. There's a car park and an interpretation centre eager to keep you up to date with the latest news about birds, butterflies and slugs. But, strange to say, there's no mention of the famous yews. Fortunately I found someone who knew where they were hidden – in a hollow a few hundred yards behind the car park.

The Newlands yews were a revelation. Here in a tangled acre of suburban Surrey, sheltered from the gales by beech and sycamore and other forest trees, are some of the most important – and wildest-looking – yews in Britain. I counted a dozen which could have served as demonic caricatures of the species. Eyes popping, tongues lolling, mouths spitting – there seemed no limit to the fantastic shapes which the tree could assume. How to explain this devil's carnival, this danse macabre? If only one could discover how these yews were managed in the past. Perhaps the owners sold all the more conventionally shaped yew trees to the timber trade. The wood was always prized by cabinet-makers for its pink colour and its speckled figure, and they paid a high price for it. If the straightest trees were sold, it happened more than a century ago, as there's no sign today of their stumps. Thank heavens the yews are now safe from the chainsaw in their hidden hollow. And perhaps, after all, it's sensible of the authorities not to shout too loud about the whereabouts of these yews. Picnickers' feet can compact the soil and slowly asphyxiate ancient trees.

Druids Grove hides its head in a wooded valley between Leatherhead and Dorking. I found it even more elusive than Newlands. In fact it's part of the same little empire, controlled by Surrey Wildlife Trust, and once again there's a notice telling you of all the delights in store - butterflies, snails, slugs and so on - without a mention of the yews. Fortunately I had brought an Ordnance Survey map and eventually found the narrow track leading to the grove. I can understand why the Trust keeps the public in the dark. The yews here are particularly vulnerable. Feet cruelly exposed, they crouch on both sides of the path. Many were wounded in the famous hurricane of 1987: their crippled limbs still litter the steep, chalky hillside. But the Trust's policy of benign neglect - of keep-out, nature-knows-best - seems to have failed at Druids Grove. The grove itself is disappearing fast under a thicket of newcomers. Ash trees are the main intruders, reinforced by beech and box and elder. Unless these upstarts are removed, the wounded yews will eventually succumb. Young yews are needed, but there's no natural regeneration - except by the upstarts.

And what a legacy will be lost if the upstarts win! I counted a dozen ancient yews in 400 yards. They looked distinctly less demonic than the Newlands tribe, these solemn, whiskered old men - as solemn as a community of monks. I suppose that's why they were thought appropriate for the ceremonies of the Druids. I climbed up the hillside to the biggest, the high priest, relying on the ash saplings to help me keep my footing. (Even an upstart has his uses.) The high priest had splayed feet, crooked shoulders and an abbot's belly, but his back had rotted to dust. On the other side of the path was the tallest yew: perfect for a Druid sacrifice, a naked giant at least 50 feet high. Somehow he had escaped the eyes of the timbermen.

My third visit was to Kingley Vale, a 200-acre wooded chalk escarpment dominating the garish yellow rape fields above the town of Chichester. This, too, is a nature reserve, but managed with more self-confidence (and no doubt more resources) than the other two. Its managers are happy to blow their own trumpets: after all, this is the finest surviving yew forest in the whole of Britain. In fact Kingley Vale is brimming over with yews of every size and age. High up on the skyline, immediately below an Iron Age fort, you can follow a track leading to acres and acres of young yews. It's a place to delight the heart of a poet or painter: there are grassy clearings, yellow with lady's bedstraw and pink with common spotted orchids. (I suppose these are the descendants of the orchids that grew here a hundred years ago, when this was still open downland cropped by sheep.) Further down the track you reach a much earlier generation of yews. Many of them are hollow with age, others bulbous and pneumatic, others again twisted like Laocoön and his sons, writhing in the coils of the sea monster. But most seemed poetic enough to me that afternoon.

I was thinking of how much Kingley Vale meant to Edward Lear, the artist and nonsense poet. He had agreed to illustrate the poems of his friend Alfred Tennyson and decided that these twisted yews at Kingley Vale would be perfect for Tennyson's elegiac poem 'Oriana'. The engraving is not one of Lear's most inspired works – perhaps he came on a dark, cold day – but Tennyson was happy with it. Years later, long after Lear had died, Tennyson and his son, Hallam, came to Kingley Vale and paid homage to those ancient trees that Lear had painted.

Ancient trees! But exactly how ancient? We are back to the unresolved debate between Lowe and de Candolle, and their modern counterparts like Bean. I measured some of the biggest and some of the smallest trees at Kingley Vale. Their girths range from more than 20 feet to less than 10 feet. The biggest, according to Lowe, would now be a mere 360 years; according to de Candolle it would be 960 years, and according to Bean some figure in between. But these wildly conflicting estimates would only be estimates for *average* growth. Even if Bean is correct, he can tell us little about the age of any *individual* tree. This is because, as we now recognise, individuals of the same age vary so much in the speed they grow. So bigger does not necessarily mean older. And the smallest yew on the hillside, like those stunted Scots pines in the Caledonian forest, may well be one of the oldest.

The mind boggles at these difficulties. Oh for a modern Dr Schulman and his auger. Just let him count the rings on the trees and he'll settle the debate about longevity once and for all. But it's just possible that I've missed the point. Tales of 5,000-year-old yews are part of their mystique. How old is an old yew? Perhaps people would rather not know.

16 July 2013

While I was away hunting yews in southern England, the weather in Ireland has been unnaturally warm. I believe we have had no rain for a month. I hear that on Tuesday the thermometer rose to 80 °C, oven-hot by the standards of County Westmeath. Now I am stripped to my shirt. At night we sleep with our windows wide open. And still it feels hot. I wonder how long this strange Saharan wind will persist.

12

Flames at My Heels

21 July 2013

Yesterday was another scorcher, a day - and indeed a night - to remember.

It began gently enough. At a quarter to seven I walked out to the arboretum in my pyjamas and dressing gown. Was this extraordinary month of dry weather beginning to take its toll on my newly planted Japanese maples and other delicate creatures? Of course I had done my best. But it's a laborious job dragging hose-pipes and water-cans through hogweed and scutch grass. And now the yellow clay in the bare ground was beginning to crack. Even the Pumpkin House was complaining about the heat. The thin sheets of local oak, the elegant brown outer skin of its curved walls and domed roof, had started to emit strange creaks and groans.

Still, most of the trees seemed to be enjoying the heatwave. When oaks are happy they thrust out a second tier of green shoots in the middle of summer, called 'Lammas shoots' after the Anglo-Saxon harvest festival of that name. Well, most of my twenty-year-old oaks looked happy - and so did the pushier of the maples, including the painted maple, *Acer pictum*. The Japanese maples, being young and delicate, needed a cold shower-bath. But I saw no casualties.

In the main gardens, on the other side of the house, the heat was more menacing. In Tibet the larger trees and shrubs were holding their own – including the chocolate-barked Himalayan birch (the Eastern form of *Betula utilis*) and the rowan with pearl-white berries in summer (*Sorbus arachnoides*). But normally the giant Tibetan cowslips (*Primula florindae*) light up this glade in summer with their bunches of 4-foot-high stems, their sulphur-yellow flowers and their stunning fragrance. Now their stems were kinked by the heat. All I could do was rig up a barrel and a drip-feed for the worst affected. But fortunately most of them grow very sensibly beside the stream in the lower part of the glade. (It was there that they found their own way. I had foolishly put the first plants on a dry bank after I brought back the original seeds from Tibet.)

In Yunnan, below the farm road, one of the 30-foot-high Himalayan birch was dying with heatstroke. I dowsed it with water from the pond below the pagoda, although I knew it was a gonner. The rare purple primulas, *Primula poissonii*, were also in distress. These are as essential for Yunnan as the giant cowslips are for Tibet. For three months, from June to September, they light up the place with their candelabras of ruby and yellow flowers turning to purple and yellow. More hose-pipes, more water-cans. It's astonishing how quickly a cold bath revives an apparently dying plant. By lunchtime my trees and other plants were in great spirits, although I was wilting myself. I decided to spend the afternoon in the shade of some sixty-year-old Norway spruce in Number 3 plantation at the southern end of the Forest Walk.

Now plantations of conifers are not much admired by the public – unless people want trees to make money for them, which conifers can do very efficiently. And I have to admit that when a plantation of spruce is young it is no beauty. The trees are planted in grim, regimented blocks, an affront to the soft curves of nature. Hills and dales are wiped from memory. All is masked by a curtain of spiky young Norway spruce (or young Sitka spruce which is spikier still). Inside, the young spruce wood is impenetrable to humans – unless someone has left the ghost of a ride through the wood. But the native plants seize their chance while the aliens are young. A native insurgency attempts to smother the young spruce: coarse grasses of every description, ably assisted by cohorts of nettles, thistle, bramble, whitethorn and blackthorn. Chemical warfare is the usual form of reprisal. The native insurgency is put down by a disciplined deployment of herbicide, originally including the infamous 24DT, pioneered as Agent Orange in Vietnam.

But I must pass over this painful beginning. In sixty years the wood is unrecognisable, the chemical warfare and the insurgency long forgotten. The spruce are now fully mature, elegant brown columns supporting a canopy of jade-green branches 100 feet above your head. The floor is carpeted with moss and wood sorrel (a kind of shamrock) and dotted with inverted cones of pale green lady fern. It's a secret place, silent apart from the whispering branches high overhead, a green time-warp. You could imagine that no one had been here for years, apart from the badgers, whose tracks meander across the moss from one badger sett to another, and a grey squirrel who has left a half-eaten fir cone on a tree stump.

Then you recall (that is, if you own the wood) that it was for money, not ornament, that these trees were planted. The trees are now commercially mature, meaning ripe, or over-ripe for harvest – ripe for the chainsaw. And in a year or two this beautiful wood will look as if it were the scene of the Battle of the Somme. Corpses of spruce will be flung everywhere, as huge machines gouge out timber, grinding stumps, sawing, heaving, hacking, amputating. The machines will leave at last, but the wood will not be left in peace for long. Back will come the planters with their two-year-old spruce and the grim cycle of havoc-peace-havoc will continue as before.

Would I really let this be the fate of these beautiful Norway spruce at the southern end of the Forest Walk? Of course we needed the money. Yet I found the dilemma peculiarly painful. Number 3 plantation, as you would guess from its name, is not our only wood. About 30 acres in all, it represents less than a sixth of the commercial woodland at Tullynally. Most of the other spruce plantations are younger and have not been looked after so well. I suppose I can only blame myself for that. I planted these younger trees soon after I inherited the estate in 1961. My priority, beset by those 62 per cent death duties, was to make the farm pay. Commercial spruce came second. (Dairy cows could make money for you the year you bought them. Trees took half a century.) All this explains why the old plantation, Number 3, was so close to my heart. Of all our plantations it's the best and the most mature and the most beautiful. Should I sacrifice these trees to Mammon? And the painful questions only multiplied. Would time provide me with another plantation of equal quality? Would I live to see it flourish?

All the later plantations are poorer in various ways. Only one part of the woodland can be compared in beauty, and that, paradoxically, was never planted. It is 50 acres of wild peat-bog, on the north-east boundary of the estate. Sixty years ago, the experts told my predecessor, Uncle Edward, that it was too wet and too poor to be worth planting. These days it is, I recalled on that sweltering afternoon, a self-sown paradise of pink-flowered heather and white lichen and blue-green Scots pines.

It was now just after 5 p.m. I could find no answer to these dilemmas. Filled with gloomy thoughts I set out to walk back to the house up the Forest Walk. Just then I became aware that something odd was happening on the north-east boundary of the estate. My mobile phone hummed a childish tune. Our farm manager, Kevin, was ringing to say that there was a fire *somewhere* in the wildest part of the woods. People reported seeing puffs of grey smoke blowing from near the eastern boundary. Could I find where the smoke was coming from?

The 80-foot-high Gothic tower crowning our battlements is more practical than it appears. The lower octagon now houses the 2,000-gallon water tank that feeds all the taps and basins and bathrooms in the house. The upper turret makes an excellent, airy lookout. It was years since I had dared to climb the two external steel ladders that lead to the top. But was I a man or a mouse? I climbed slowly up the rusty steelwork until I could command the whole south and eastern part of our estate and the rolling hills that mask Lough Derravaragh. I could now see the mushrooms of grey smoke clearly enough. They sprouted from the north-east boundary. The 50 acres of wild peat-bog were on fire. So it appeared.

The self-sown paradise was *on fire*. And the fire now threatened to spread to the heartland of the estate – to the main commercial spruce woods to the west of the peat-bog, including Number 3 plantation.

The Castlepollard Fire and Rescue service is based less than a mile from the peat-bog. Two scarlet fire engines trundled into the neighbouring field, the Bog Meadow, and the crew waited for orders. I took the fire-chiefs to the north-west corner of the wild bog but they said it would be too dangerous to try to enter that way, as the smoke and flames were blowing straight in our faces. Was there no other way into the bog? But it is surrounded on all four sides by a solid wall of rhododendrons. No machine could enter, so it was impossible to attack the flames. By 8 p.m. the fire-chiefs told Kevin and me that they were leaving us. But all hope was not lost. Either the fire would burn itself out without breaching the green wall of rhododendrons. Or it would spread into the main woodland, and then they would come back in the morning. They could fight the fire there, provided we cut a track for their machines.

Faced with this second, disastrous prospect – of the fire spreading – Kevin and I hired a local contractor with a powerful JCB. He agreed to spend the night, if it was necessary, hacking and smashing through the jungle to make a path for the fire-engines. He would arrive just before dark. Meanwhile Kevin asked me to go down to the fire itself and tell him the situation. Was the fire spreading? Or had the green wall of rhododendrons defeated it and was it slowly burning itself out?

I think it took me half an hour to reach the wild peat-bog. It was still full daylight, and the flames lit the evening sky as I pushed my way down the barely visible passage cut through the wall of rhododendrons. But these flames, thank heavens, marked the end of the fire. This had skinned the entire bog from east to west, burning the heather, the bilberry plants and the lichen and the smaller Scots pines. But the defences (if you could call them that) had held firm. The green wall of rhododendrons, 40 feet high in some places, had acted like a fire-curtain. It was burnt brown at ground level but still very much intact. The surface of the bog itself was black and smoking but cool enough to walk on. In ten minutes I had crossed it. And *there* was indeed the source of all the trouble. Under one of the largest Scots pines, on the extreme east of the bog, were the blackened embers of a small bonfire - and a slightly charred packet of potato crisps and two empty cans of fruit juice. (Teenage picnickers, no doubt, and abstemious ones, I had to admit.)

There are times when one trivial mistake can have serious consequences, especially if one's alone in wild country. Impatient to reach the bog before daylight failed, I had forgotten my mobile phone. And now luck turned against me. The wind had changed while I was out on the bog, and the last of the flames had now backed round to the south. My path through the green wall of rhododendrons - the narrow passage down which I had squeezed half an hour earlier - was now blocked by a new line of flames. I think I remained calm. I knew I wasn't really trapped. I could retrace my steps across the bog in the hope I could find the way the firemen had come. But it would soon be dark. And if I tried to return this way it would mean a long walk and at least an hour's delay. I wanted to get back home quickly to tell Kevin the good news. No need for the contractor with the digger after all. The fire was nearly out. And then I made a second mistake even stupider than the first.

That green wall of rhododendrons looked impenetrable. But it was only about 50 yards wide. Beyond it, my blue Volvo beckoned, barely ten minutes away. Of course I had brought nothing to cut a path with. But couldn't I break through that green wall by brute force? In the event it took a full hour to go 20 yards, mostly on the flat of my stomach. Inside the maze of branches I lost all sense of direction. There was an alarming moment when I found the flames only a few yards ahead. I must have done three-quarters of a circle! On I went, burrowing like a rat, my bare arms (the day had been a scorcher) scratched and bruised.

By 10.30 p.m. the worst was over. So I thought. I was somewhere in an old, half-derelict plantation. The road must be near. Yet it all seemed strangely unfamiliar. I couldn't recognise these trees. Was I really in some part of my own woods? The spruce trees seemed much larger than any I remembered. And they were not the elegant brown columns of Number 3 plantation. They looked twisted, spiky, malevolent. It was now hard to see more than a few feet ahead of me. Of course darkness falls quicker in a spruce wood than in a sunny glade. And I suppose it was now nearly 11 p.m. I had found no trace of a track. I was feeling my way through the wood at the pace of a snail, stumbling over tree stumps and jabbed by the jagged ends of the lower branches. A few minutes later I stopped somewhat ruefully. Benighted, that was the word! I was lost in my own woods, beaten down by darkness. All I could do was bed down somewhere in a soft patch of leaves and wait for daylight. Dawn, I imagined, would break in about six hours. *Only* six hours. But what an ass I had been to let myself become benighted - and without a mobile telephone.

Survival experts (as I discovered too late) say that the first mistake people make when they are lost is to fail to recognise it. They continue walking - usually in the wrong direction. Darkness had in a sense saved me from that fate. However I now did my best to make a bad situation worse. In the last faint glimmer of light I saw what I thought was a low hill on my left. I decided to grope my way towards it. It might be only a hummock 10 feet high or a lofty gravel ridge; it was too dark to tell. But there was a faint chance I might find a landmark I knew. Failing that, it would be a safe place to make my nest and wait for dawn. This was my third - and most painful - mistake. The nest I had chosen for myself had already been chosen by a swarm of well-armed enemies.

Fortunately I am not allergic to bee-stings, or perhaps I am, and my attackers were wasps, not bees. I was soon punctured in a score of places on my left leg and thigh. The pain was at first overwhelming. I lay on a stony terrace just below the nest of my attackers, wondering how I could possibly survive the next six hours. Luckily my invisible enemies didn't renew their attack. And after an hour or so the pain became bearable. I was now anxious about the cold. It had been such a scorcher that day - probably the hottest day for a dozen years - that I had no coat of any kind, only a short-sleeved shirt. This was soaked with sweat after the hour-long struggle with the green wall. Suddenly I began to feel the cold. But there was little I could do except wrap myself in leaves and huddle in a foetal position on my stony bed. Sleep would be impossible, I knew, what with the hard ground, the cold and the pain of the stings. But at least I would be home in little more than six hours. Home and in my own bed and dumbed down with painkillers.

What about Kevin and the news I had failed to give him: that the fire was nearly out? I was alarmed to think of how my disappearance would seem to Kevin, and what he would tell Valerie. In fact this was now the worst part of my predicament. It's one thing to know you have made a fool of yourself and are paying the price. Much worse to imagine that your friends may believe you are dead, or are lying with a broken ankle or scorched by the fire somewhere in the blackened bog. If only I had remembered to bring that wretched telephone.

Of course it was all out of my hands. I felt calmer when the moon rose, shining in flecks of pale light through the thick canopy above my head. I knew the moon rose in the south-east. Well, I would find my way home easily enough in the morning. And just now something rather odd happened to me, something that I still cannot fully explain. I saw three pale figures standing about 20 feet behind me. They were not all threatening. I felt mildly curious to know who they were. My guardian angels coming to the rescue? Surely they were a bit late. No, I decided that it was a trick of the moonlight shining on three dead trees. Soon the apparitions vanished - and so did the moon. I lay on my stony bed, sore and sleepless. If only I could see my watch. Was the night half gone?

And then I saw something that proved a great deal more substantial than any pale figure in the moonlight. Four bright lights appeared in the darkness immediately below my hill, and there were four people waving them. 'Who are you?' I shouted, incredulous. My rescuers stumbled up the hill towards me. It was Kevin, my son Fred and two others. 'Are you OK? Nothing broken?' Then their mobile telephones began to chatter. 'We've found him. Nothing broken. Call off the main search party.' They told me that in a couple of hours, at 4.30 a.m., half the town of Castlepollard was due to come out and search for me. It was the final time I felt a fool that evening.

24 July and after

The rain came three days later, dowsing the last surviving flames in the wild bog. Today, when the rain had stopped, I gingerly drove down to the wood, then retraced my steps on that fatal night.

The flames had indeed cleaned out the bog, but this was not altogether a disaster. The delightful white lichen, it was true, would take years to recover - except for a few patches at the corners that were protected by large pine trees or birch. But the various species of sphagnum moss growing in the bog-holes looked cheerful enough. (Those bog-holes, excavated by turf-cutters a century ago, are deep enough to drown you in a wet winter.) Most of the small green bilberry plants had also survived in the shelter of the bigger Scots pines on the edge of the bog. Called *frochain* in Irish, bilberry flourishes among the heather on Irish bogs. Its blue-black fruit, which could pass for a miniature blueberry, tastes delicious in August.

But the best thing about the fire was not what it left but what it destroyed. Over the years I had watched helpless as a horde of self-sown intruders - natives like the downy birch, aliens like the pines and rhododendron - gradually took over my wild bog, suppressing the bog-plants like heather and bilberry. Why didn't I reach for my chainsaw? Too expensive, I thought. You cut down a birch and it bounces back within months. So I had steeled myself to the thought that, in the long term, I would lose the bog. And now the fire had given it back to me, doing in a few hours what it would have taken me months, and a great deal of money, to do for myself.

I set off to return to the car elated by this discovery. But there were other unanswered questions. How far was I from the road when darkness overwhelmed me? It didn't take long to find the stony hill. It loomed up in a trackless jungle-growth of ash and sycamore - yet it was only a few hundred yards from the path through the spruce plantations I should have followed. I suppose it was a glacial hill, part of an esker ridge, and covered with beech and silver fir that blocked any view into the plantations below. I realised, to my surprise, that I had never been in that part of the wood before, and could have lost my way even in daylight. I clambered up to the top of the hill, perhaps 80 feet from the ground. There was the dent in the leaves where I had made my nest. And there was the rival nest hardly 10 feet away - with my old enemies rising in a spiral ready to defend their home. I retreated hurriedly, and was stung twice to punish my curiosity. So I failed to discover if my enemies were bees or wasps. Another question I failed to answer was the identity of those three ghostly apparitions - guardian angels, I had thought - that I had seen standing in a glimmer of moonlight 20 feet from my bed. I searched in vain for three dead trees that could have acted the part. The stony hill did not reveal its secrets.

14 August 2013

A month has passed. Ireland has enjoyed an uncharacteristically dry and sunny August, but lacking the drama of the heatwave. Today's my birthday, my eightieth, and we have a large party staying in the house: Antonia, Michael, Rachel and Kevin (that is, four of my five brothers and sisters), Maria, Eliza, Ned and Fred (my own four children) and eight grandchildren, all eager to celebrate the occasion.

I wasn't so keen on the idea myself. After all, why *celebrate* it? Better to say nothing in the hope the Reaper doesn't notice. But I cheered up when we had speeches from the grown-ups and songs and poems from the children and the champagne began to flow. And I was persuaded to take three of my grandchildren whose ages range from ten to sixteen - Gabriel, Ciaran and Aidan - to see the scene of the fire and the stony hill where their poor grandfather had laid his head.

We pushed our way through the jungle of ash and sycamore to the stony hill. The grandchildren were not impressed. How *could* I have got lost so close to the road? Anyway, why *had* I failed to bring my mobile telephone?

By contrast, the wild bog looked strangely beautiful. The smaller trees and bushes were charred ghosts. The larger Scots pines had survived, burnt black to about eight or ten feet from the ground. Above that height the trunks were still pink, the foliage still blue-green. It was as if a tsunami of flame had washed over the bog submerging everything up to that height. But the spongy surface of the peat was black no more. In a month it had covered itself in a soft green pelt of bog-cotton. We tramped across to the *frochain*, the green bilberry bushes that had survived the fire. I had never made bilberry jam. This was my chance. We collected almost a pound of these miniature blueberries. On our return to the house, we boiled them up with a pound of sugar and three lemons. The bog-jam tasted wonderful, I thought. Could you call it ambrosial? The grandchildren said it was OK - just like any other jam.

13

Lake of the Oaks

10 September 2013

Today I am setting off, in my battered rowing boat, for the Millennium Wood on the delightful shores of Lough Derravaragh.

I suppose Westmeath is spoilt rotten with lakes. At any rate it's brimming over with lakes carved out by the glaciers in the last million years: Lough Lene, Lough Ennell, Lough Owel, Lough Ree and many more. But Lough Derravaragh ('lake of the oaks') is surely the most beautiful. Strange to say, it's also the least known.

If you want to appreciate Derravaragh, then take a flight across the lake in a balloon. Last June we were fortunate enough to persuade a covey of balloonists to hold a balloon festival in our demesne. In the mist before dawn the pilots unrolled the vast, limp, scarlet and yellow and green envelopes on the lawn and in the Horsepark below. Fed by their gas burners, they began to come to life, swelling like pears and glowing like Chinese lanterns. Then the sun caught them, and they rose, one by one, and vanished over the beech trees in the pleasure ground.

To my delight, a young, bearded pilot gave me a place in the pannier of a green balloon, one of the last to take off. We headed south-west across our plantations, with the gas burner roaring like a blast furnace. Soon we were flying at about 1,000 feet over the northern shore of Derravaragh. It was a view to die for! Six miles away to the south, jade-green in the early morning sunshine, rose the sacred hill of Knockeyon and its ancient oak trees. Below us you could see the rushy fields and blue-slated roofs of Coolure (an old family house bravely restored by Valerie) and the stony inlet, amid the spotted orchids and the curlews, where I keep my rowing boat. Beyond Coolure, the rushy fields resumed, then gave way to a field of young oaks, planted only thirteen years ago, the Millennium Wood.

* * *

Forty years ago I bought the 15-acre field ('Reilly's Field', it was called) for what we would now call a song – as far as I remember, for £5,000. If I had a plan, it was rather negative. I was afraid some local farmer would buy the field and wreck the view with a crop of bungalows. So I bought it and rented it out for bullocks to graze. But in the Millennium year I thought of a bolder and more original plan. What about a modern oak wood as a counterpart to the ancient oak wood on the flanks of Knockeyon? By this time the Irish government, subsidised by the EU, was leaning over backwards to persuade farmers to convert farmland to forestry. The government paid the whole cost of the planting. More astonishingly, if the farmer chose a slower-growing and therefore less profitable species, a hardwood like oak, he was paid a twenty-year premium to compensate. So my Millennium Wood would cost me nothing to create, and would pay me rather better than bullocks – at least for the first twenty years.

Now, by the year 2000, lots of other farmers were taking the bait and planting trees where their bullocks used to graze. What was original about my plan was in the *provenance* of the trees. Many 'Irish' oaks are not Irish at all. The acorns, collected from the same species on the Continent, are French or German or Dutch oaks grown in Irish tree nurseries. By contrast I would insist on choosing a series of real Irish sources for the acorns. In fact I decided to plant an All-Ireland wood, or if you like it, a 'United Irish wood'. Of course my wood was not making a republican statement (although it might have looked racier before the Good Friday Agreement of two years before). If a wood can make a statement mine was merely a cultural one. I wanted to celebrate the diversity of Ireland's culture expressed in her native oaks.

We have only two native species of oaks in our country, both of which are wide-ranging in Europe, and even western Asia: the common oak (*Quercus robur*) and the sessile oak (*Quercus petraea*). And there are numerous forms of hybrid between these two – so much so that the hybrids are probably commoner than the pure species. I would hope to get good examples of oaks from north and south, east and west, from Wicklow to Westport, from Killarney to the glens of Antrim, that is, from all four provinces, including Ulster. Many would probably be hybrids. The richness and diversity would, I hoped, be enlightening - perhaps even stunning.

That was the plan in the Millennium year. And now, in September 2013, I can row across the bay to that stony shore and savour the result. To say the result is mixed rather understates the case. Part of the wood has grown far more vigorously than I would have dared hope. Part of it is, from most points of view, little short of a disaster.

* * *

I will explain. What they called 'Reilly's Field' was actually three small grassy fields, separated by hedges of unkempt whitethorn and ash, and descending gently to the stony shore of the lake. The lowest of these fields included an exceptionally large ringfort (or rath) dating from some time in the Early Christian era. I shall come to this wonderful earthwork in due course. I had no wish to plant it with young oaks - nor would the government's archaeologists have allowed me to do so. It has its own mysterious wood to protect it: half a dozen ancient oaks, beech and horse chestnut, with an understorey of bluebells eager to grab the light before the trees come into leaf. What I needed was shelter for my young trees - shelter from the storm winds that accelerate across Lough Derravaragh and the peat-bogs beyond. And the ringfort did the job perfectly. This is where I had planted the first contingent of the Millennium oaks, all grown from acorns taken from Westmeath oaks in the autumn of 1999. Thirteen years ago they were 1,500 frail little seedlings no bigger than my hand. Today they are broad-chested, muscular creatures 20-30 feet high, broader than Westmeath bullocks and upright as guardsmen - in a word, magnificent.

Why had this first contingent succeeded so well? Of course I had loaded the dice in their favour. Their parentage was far from typical of Westmeath. Our finest oak trees at Tullynally are some of the tallest and most elegant in the county (if not the whole of Ireland). And all the Westmeath acorns which we collected were collected from our finest trees. I filled a sack myself, choosing the largest brown acorns that had fallen from each tree. To my surprise, the finest acorns came from the tallest tree, nicknamed 'The Squire's Walking Stick'. (It's believed to have been planted in 1748, eight years before the family was promoted to the peerage.) I think I could recognise those acorns anywhere. They looked more aristocratic, if that doesn't sound absurd, as they were longer and tapered more elegantly to a point. Today, the oaks from those acorns must be the elite of the Millennium Wood: young giants that will dominate – and eventually suppress – all their rivals.

Of course the life of trees that are planted to be part of a wood will never be like the life of the pampered creatures planted in gardens or parks. In the woodland it's Darwin who rules. The life or death of a tree is decided by natural selection, a euphemism for the brutal struggle for survival. You plant *seven* times as many saplings as you need to fill the forest – 1,500 for every acre, planted roughly six feet apart. Then you let them fight it out. In an astonishingly short time the main battle is over. Today, thirteen years after the wood was created, it is already full of dead and dying losers. The winners are cock-a-hoop. The sight is enough to turn one's stomach – as it would on any other kind of battlefield. And it seems so extraordinarily wasteful. But this is nature's way of moving forward and it works for us in two different ways.

First, it's a struggle for supremacy in *form* as well as size. It's about transforming the shapes of the winners. These oaks will grow far taller and shapelier than if they had been allowed to stand alone. And this means, of course, they will make better planks in the sawmill – and, in due course, better beams and bedsteads and chairs and tables. Second, it's a question of economics. Why would any businessman put money in a new oak wood which will pay no dividends for a century or more? Even with the government subsidies, and a trickle of income from thinning, it sounds a crazy investment. But this is where nature comes to the rescue. The cost of creating a wood would be much higher if the process of selection were done by man. Why pay a man with a chainsaw to thin the lines of young oak? Nature will do the job – or at least most of the job – for you, perfectly free.

Delighted with myself, I usually follow the track that winds up through the Millennium Wood past a gap in the whitethorn hedge and into the next compartment. This is the first of the six small compartments whose acorns were collected in the autumn of 2000 in all parts of Ireland. The list is a roll call of famous woodland names beginning with Killarney. I walk down the lines of this first compartment – and am appalled. These trees are only a year younger than the young giants from Westmeath. But they are stunted dwarfs by comparison. Few of them have what foresters call 'apical dominance', meaning the possession of prominent leading shoots. They lack all the qualities that foresters value: the vigour that makes timber quickly and the uprightness that makes the planks long and straight. Of course the great majority would be eliminated by natural selection. But where are the winners? It's hard to imagine any worthy victors emerging from this Darwinian struggle. There are large gaps between trees, gaps which willows and scrubby ash and whitethorn are beginning to fill. Nature will do a job here, but not the one that is needed to produce an oak wood. I can picture the scene in fifty years. This part of the wood will be impenetrable. Most of those stunted dwarfs from Killarney will have been beaten down by a rabble of scrub. Perhaps I exaggerate. But I feel that the wood will fail on every count, aesthetic as well as commercial. The surviving oaks will be as large and misshapen as trolls.

I am equally appalled by the sight of four of the other five compartments, whose acorns came from Counties Wicklow (Glen of the Downs), Kerry, Laois and Limerick. However, in the fifth compartment, from County Antrim, I find some comfort. The trees are not nearly as uniform as those from Westmeath. But enough of them are straight and vigorous. This contingent from the North will stand proud - I feel reasonably sure of that. But the mystery remains. How to account for the success of these trees, and of my own trees from Westmeath, and the sickening failure of all the rest?

I know several things for certain. The differences cannot be accounted for by the way the young trees were planted. It's true that we used the ploughing method when we planted the Westmeath trees, and the mounding method for all the other compartments. These are two alternative ways of protecting very young trees from encroaching grassland. But they both worked equally well in the rich, brown, boulder clay of Reilly's Field. And it's also true that this soil is not of a uniform depth in all parts of the field. (It would be strange if it was, for the boulder clay was dumped here in a rather slipshod manner by an ice-sheet.) But these variations in soil don't explain the pattern of failure and success any more than the different methods of planting.

I assume the explanation must lie in the genes of the tree, in nature rather than nurture. But let me qualify that. These elite trees from Westmeath are neither 'natural' nor a product of 'natural' selection in the sense that a wild whitethorn or gorse bush would be. They are the result of a process of human selection that goes back hundreds of years. Whoever sowed the acorn that produced the Squire's Walking Stick in 1748 knew what he was about. He chose an acorn from a straight and vigorous mother tree - just as I did 252 years later. He and I rejected the acorns from scrubby bushes and trolls and stunted dwarfs and all the other forms of oak we regarded as aberrations of nature. So did the people who collected the acorns from County Antrim. By contrast the acorns from Killarney and the other southern counties were more typical of the oak woods from which they came. They were, I assume, relatively unselected acorns, collected to fill a sack by men being paid by the hundredweight. No one worried whether the parent was a fine tree or a troll. But were these acorns in every sense 'natural'? I suspect those southern oak woods had been managed and mismanaged over the centuries. Natural selection can make trees taller and straighter. Human selection, if it means systematically removing the best timber trees, has the reverse effect. The trees get smaller and the woods get scrubbier. No doubt I should have known what to expect when I chose acorns from these famous southern woods. I should have set off with my sack and made my own selection. I hope I will have another chance. And perhaps the southern oaks in this sun-smitten year, 2013, will bubble over with acorns.

This afternoon the weather's perfect, with a south wind caressing the lake. I shall retrace my steps to the great ringfort in Reilly's Field below the Westmeath oaks. I have said that Westmeath is spoilt rotten with lakes. Well, it's also spoilt rotten with ringforts. If you look on the Ordnance Survey you'll find mile after mile of them, provided the soil is rich: circular banks-and-ditches stamped on the fields like the footprints of a gigantic animal. We have at least three of them on our farm, beyond the wall of the demesne. As I said earlier, the two best-preserved ones were borrowed to make clumps in the landscape: the first planted c.1800 with a ring of sycamore, now coming to the end of their lives; the second with a ring of oaks now in their prime. Why so many in the richer parts of Ireland? The ringfort was apparently the normal form of agricultural settlement in the Early Christian era - an unpretentious affair of thatched huts and cattle pens protected by a paling planted on a circular bank. (The fields of England, too, must have once sprouted ringforts. But most of them would have been ploughed out long ago.) The normal diameter of an Irish ringfort is about a hundred yards. The great ringfort beside the Millennium Wood is double that size.

I have often wondered why such a gigantic earthwork was scooped out of this remote corner of the Irish Midlands. Of course it's less than a mile from the mouth of the Upper Inny, the river that connects Westmeath to the Shannon and the south. So this was the ringfort that must have commanded the lake - and its forests of oak - from the north. I suppose that in the first millennium Derravaragh was the Great North Road of these parts and boats made of oak supplied the means to use it. In fact in 1965, soon after I had come to live in Westmeath, we made a remarkable discovery connected with these oaks.

It was the year the government wooed the local farmers (and shocked the local fishermen) by robbing the lake of half its water. This was a half-baked scheme for draining farmland and bogland beside the lake. It had been begun as part of the government's River Inny drainage scheme 150 years ago. About 1865 they took 8 feet off the level of the lake, leaving a new shoreline to be slowly colonised by scrubby ash and Scots pine. In 1965 they took a further 12 feet off the lake, leaving a second shoreline of mud and stone. What was half-baked about the scheme was that no one had bothered to strike a balance between the needs of farmers and the interests of the community at large. But some of its results were better than we could have hoped.

As I have said, Derravaragh was permanently lowered by a further 12 feet. This was done by blasting out the rocky mouth of the Lower Inny that drains the lake. And lo and behold, beached on the new shore by the ringfort at Coolure – the stony shore that had been the bed of the lake since the end of the last ice age – we discovered two ancient-looking dugouts. Were these the boats that had once been the pride and joy of a Celtic chief? Both were carved from solid oak. The smaller of them was an elegant canoe, repaired at the stern with an iron nail; the larger a punt, 20 feet long, and fitted with a socket at the centre – apparently to hold a mast and a sail. We showed photographs to an archaeologist in Dublin who seemed surprisingly unimpressed by our discovery. Ancient dugouts, it seems, are nearly as common as ringforts and just as little is known about them. Could they be dated? The archaeologist said our boats probably came from the first millennium. So they could have belonged to a Celtic chief. (I wonder if a modern archaeologist could use dendrochronology to date the boats. I must remember to ask.)

That same year, Derravaragh, robbed of its water, laid at our feet an even more exciting discovery – in fact a treasure. One day a small boy knocked on the front door at Tullynally and held out something wrapped in a muddy cloth. 'Will ye buy it from me?' It was a small bronze sword, more like a dagger, elegantly curved, with fluted edges to both sides of the blade. But part of the hilt was missing, and the sword had snapped in two. 'I dropped it,' said the small boy, then added, 'What will ye pay me?'

'Where did you find it?' I asked, dazzled by the beauty of the sword, despite the damage.

'Under your boat on the shore.'

Of course I would buy if it was authentic. I telephoned the National Museum in Dublin to ask for advice. In due course the Director, Dr Rafferty, came down to have lunch and see the sword. 'Yes,' he said, 'that's a Bronze Age sword all right. Could be

1000 BC. We've plenty in the museum. Thank you. Belongs to us, of course.' And he took the two pieces from me and - to my astonishment - pocketed them.

'But what about the finder?'

'Oh, give him £20.' And he handed me the notes, leaving me distinctly crestfallen.

Next day there was another knock on the front door. It was the small boy again. 'I found another one under your boat.' He handed me a second Bronze Age sword that must have been cast in the same clay mould as the first. But he hadn't dropped this one. It sparkled like Excalibur. The small boy was delighted to get £40 for the two swords - a small fortune for a child in 1965. Did I telephone the Museum again? I really can't remember. All I know is that the second sword has been sitting on the mantelpiece in the library for nearly fifty years, and must belong to me by now.

To return to the Celtic dugouts and the great ringfort at Coolure, nothing more was discovered about either of them till the 1990s when there was a dramatic twist to the story. Out in the bay, a few hundred yards south from the ringfort, lies a small circular island whose stony surface is hidden under a jungle-growth of scrubby oaks, white willows and a large horse chestnut. It is actually a *crannog*, a man-made island from the Dark Ages, and a counterpart to the great ringfort opposite. Derravaragh is rich in crannogs, which were used by local farmers as a safe retreat during troubled times. I have counted the remains of six crannogs along the eastern shore, and no doubt there were more. Some are now high and dry on the shore, a mere heap of stones, others a pile of rocks a few hundred yards out in the lake. This one by the great ringfort is by far the best preserved. And it's no surprise that it was this one which attracted the attention of illegal treasure hunters, soon after the invention of metal detectors.

By the 1990s only professional archaeologists were allowed to use metal detectors in or around an archaeological site. Nonetheless a group of amateur treasure hunters took a boat to the crannog. They were armed with frogmen's equipment, including metal detectors that work under water. A full report of what they found has never, I think, appeared in print. But I gather they found an amazing hoard of Viking silver strewn on the bed of the lake beside the crannog. Of course they could not sell it in Ireland - or even report its existence. They flew to California and tried to sell their hoard to the Getty Museum. The next part of the story is missing, perhaps lost in a legal black hole. All I know for certain is this excellent news: the Derravaragh hoard of Viking silver is now a prize exhibit of the National Museum in Dublin.

What does the discovery of these Viking silver ingots tell us about the crannog and the ringfort and the oak trees that helped to construct them in prehistoric times? I have talked to the archaeologists from Dublin who, legally of course, excavated the crannog a decade after the hoard was found. Dendrochronological analysis of the oak piles showed that the crannog is unusually ancient. It was first used as long ago as the first century AD. It was then built and rebuilt for more than a thousand years, layers of oak alternating with layers of stone and mud. The Celtic chief who owned it during the Viking era must have been rich. No doubt he traded with the Viking colony in Dublin, selling cattle and slaves, and was handsomely paid in silver. But why did he cast these silver ingots into the lake? Was it done for display - an expensive form of conspicuous consumption? Or was he making a ritual offering to his gods? Or was he merely trying to hide them from his enemies before fleeing in his dugout canoe? Perhaps we shall never know.

Later this afternoon I shall row out into the bay and circle the crannog. It's early September - on the cusp between summer and autumn. Normally few trees would have thought of shedding their leaves by this time. But this summer has been delightfully dry and the trees have paid the price. On the stony crannog both the willows and chestnut are looking sick and pale.

Six miles away to the south, the trees on the flanks of Knockeyon look green and fit. Tomorrow I shall borrow an outboard engine. It's time to take a boat and revisit my holy mountain, Knockeyon, and its ancient oaks.

Bacchanalian scenes at Castlepollard, a mile from Tullynally. Satirical drawing by William Lygon Pakenham (later 4th Earl of Longford) in 1858. The caption reads: 'Ye Revd Father O'something by various powerful and highly Apostolic hints prevails upon the immoral assemblage to disperse and poureth forth upon them his wrath after the manner of the Church.'

OPPOSITE: Antoine, our local sculptor and cabinet-maker, carving a head of a Green Man for my garden.

THIS PAGE, TOP & MIDDLE LEFT: Thirteenth-century Green Men in the Chapter House at Southwell, Nottinghamshire. Are they celebrating man's union with nature or warning us of the wages of sin?
BELOW LEFT: A demonic sixteenth-century misericord in the choir at Beverley Minster, Yorkshire: a Green Man disgorging vine leaves from his mouth. TOP RIGHT: Antoine's original Green Man attached to a dead beech tree in the pleasure ground. Was this to be the start of a dangerous obsession? BELOW RIGHT: One of Antoine's six new Green Men, half-choked by hawthorn leaves.

ABOVE: The Swan River at the end of the Forest Walk: an early eighteenth-century canal transformed.

RIGHT: *Pieris formosa* 'Forest Flame' in the Gingerbread clearing.

OPPOSITE: Clumps of *Primula poissonii* by the pagoda pond in the Forest Walk. I grew them from seed collected in the snow on my trip to Sichuan.

ABOVE: With its coat-of-many-colours, a North American maple (*Acer rubrum*) lights up the Forest Walk in October.

OPPOSITE: What the Chinese call the 'grandfather-grandchild tree': a young ginkgo I grew from seed given to me at Mount Auburn Cemetery outside Boston. Two of them now grow in the arboretum, planted in honour of my grandchildren Anselm and Matilda.

ABOVE: Three young maples (*Acer micranthum*, *Acer cappadocicum* and *Acer davidii*) enjoy a gap by the upper pond, opened up by the death of two large horse chestnuts from bleeding canker.

LEFT: *Sorbus pseudo-hupehensis* in the Forest Walk, grown from seed I collected in Yunnan. Its pearl-white berries attract our local blackbirds and it's spreading naturally.

14

Dancing at Knockeyon

11 September 2013

Two months ago, anxious to identify the source of the fire in the woodland, I climbed the rusty steel ladders up Tullynally's 80-foot-high Gothic tower. From the top I had a spectacular view of 'Knockeyon', the hill sacred to St Eyon. I have never discovered much about the saint. But the 700-foot-high, conical, grassy hill, six miles to the south-east, dominates all our views at Tullynally.

From the arboretum, Knockeyon's the eye-catcher at the end of the main vista leading from the Pumpkin House across the Decoy and the spiky silver firs and beyond. From the pleasure ground, Knockeyon rises like a distant beacon, capping the tallest beech trees. From the lawn, Knockeyon frames the left-hand corner of the heart-stopping view down the Horsepark towards the Swan River. No one has painted it yet, as far as I know. But, if I were a painter, Knockeyon would become my obsession - as the Mont Saint Victoire obsessed Cézanne or Mount Fujiyama obsessed Hokusai.

Strange to say, for nearly two hundred years the hill was masked by a line of beech trees. One of my first acts, when I inherited Tullynally, was to cut a gap in that line of trees in order to see the hill. I still wonder whether I was right to do so. Five huge beech trees, encrusted with silver lichen, were sacrificed to make that romantic gap. And I am still puzzled by the reasons for planting that line of beech trees. You would have thought that a conical hill – sharp-edged and blue-green after summer rain, bisected by bands of mist in autumn, bleary with frost in winter – you would have thought that this delicious cone was perfectly designed to form the focal point of our late-eighteenth-century landscape. It was the age for imitating Claude: a lady took out her 'Claudian' glass to frame the view in its rectangle and assess its picturesque potential. Why ruin the picture with a line of beeches?

I can give you two possible explanations, the first rather pedestrian, the second distinctly macabre.

The pedestrian one is this. The new fashion for 'natural' scenery, popularised in Britain and Ireland by Capability Brown and his followers, involved 'borrowed landscape', meaning that the view was extended to include the fields and woods beyond the wall of the park. But these fields and woods were still part of the landlord's own broad acres, not landscape borrowed from a neighbour. Of course my Pakenham ancestors never claimed to *own* Knockeyon. It was three neighbours away. So, beautiful as it was, it was blocked from view.

The macabre explanation is this. In or about 1760 a shocking crime was committed at the house of a squireen called Nangle at Streamstown, just below Knockeyon. A gang of burglars hacked to death the Nangles and all their children and servants before stealing the contents of the house, including the family silver. The gang divided the loot, then separated. But one of them recklessly tried to sell, in the local town of Mullingar, a piece of silver engraved with the Nangles' family crest. He was arrested, charged with the murders and invited to peach on his friends to save his own skin. So he turned king's evidence. The rest of the gang were then tried, convicted and hanged in chains. But they were not hanged, like most murderers, outside the county gaol. They were paid the compliment of having a special gallows erected for them on the summit of Knockeyon. So there was good reason for planting that line of beech trees to block the view of Knockeyon. The ladies had no wish to see though their Claudian glasses a line of corpses dangling in the wind.

I have no idea which explanation is the right one. But Knockeyon haunts me and tantalises me. From the lawn and arboretum at Tullynally you see its grassy, conventional side. You have to climb the ladders to Tullynally's tower to see its wild, romantic side. The southern flank is bristling with ancient oak trees. And the oaks fall sheer to the shimmering lake below – six-mile-long, lime-rich, ice-begotten Lough Derravaragh, the most beautiful, yet least known of Westmeath's lakes.

In 1682, in the relative calm between the end of the brutal Cromwellian wars and the Battle of the Boyne, a learned Irish baronet called Sir Henry Piers wrote a pioneering essay on County Westmeath. He called it the 'Chorographical Description' of the county – a fancy name for a geographical account. It was dominated by the lakes and rivers which are still today the principal attraction of the county.

For a hundred years Sir Henry Piers' manuscripts collected dust in a few libraries (including our own at Tullynally). Then in 1786 an eccentric antiquarian, Major Charles Vallancey, published Piers' pioneering essay and gave it to the world. Inevitably, the world paid little attention. But Piers, the squire of Baronstown near Mullingar, had a sharp eye and a caustic wit. In his 'Description' he recorded much about local customs and folklore that would otherwise have been lost.

Modern scholars wouldn't pay much attention to his etymology. Instead of the conventional derivation of Lough Derravaragh - 'lake of the oaks' - Piers gives us 'lake of the severe or harsh judgment'. And he has a tall story to go with it:

A poor Fellow . . . in a Frosty Season attempted to drive a Cow he had stolen across the Lake. The ice being strong enough, and he in hast, he drove somewhat hard, and the Cow chanceing to stumble or slide fell, and in the fall, brok one of her Leggs; hereon not knowing how better to dispose of her, he kills her in the place & with the help of his companions he carries off the Hide & Flesh; when safe and at rest he found he had forgotten his Knife, immediately he returns to the Place where the Blood and the Entrails of the Cow yet lay, which by this time has so farr Thaw'd the Ice, as that when he drew near, the Ice broke under his Weight, and falling in the Ice closed again about his Neck, & cut off his head. The Man falling made an hideous outcry (which was heard at a great distance) to this purpose oh, oh, I have received a sad or severe Sentence or Judgement.

A few miles south of Lough Derravaragh, and visible from the hillside, is a companion lake, Lough Owel. Piers thought its name was derived from the Irish for 'lake of the borrowing'. And he had an even taller story to go with it, which the 'Natives blush not to own as a Traditional Truth'.

There lived in I know not what Age of the World two Sisters, one in this country, the other in the County of Roscommon beyond the Shannon; both famous for Skill of inchantments and Sorceries . . . The Sister that lived here on a certain day (be it Tuesday or Wednesday) sent to the Sister in Conacht; to let her know she stood in need of her Lake for some great Design she had then on foot and prayed the Loan thereof promising to restore the Same on Monday to her. The Conacht (good natur'd) Sister immediately grants the Request, and winding up her Lake in a sheete . . . send it to her Sister over Hills and Dales Sailing on the Wings of the Wind into this country. Our Leinster Sister places it here, where now we have it and makes use of it. At last Monday comes but no Lake is returned according to Capitulation; the Conacht Sister hereat storms and becomes as turbulent as the Lake itself on every blast of Wind, sends to the Leinster Sister to demand Restitution of her water . . . but in Vain. She had Possession and likes the Water so well that she resolves not to part with it. Nevertheless because she would not seem to be worse than her word she tells her that she had borrow'd it indeed till Monday; but her meaning was (as the Irish Phrase hath it) till Monday after the Day of Eternity or as we say in English, on Monday come never on a Wheelbarrow.

One of Piers' spiciest passages records the 'Bacchanalian' scenes he had witnessed on the shores of Lough Derravaragh. This was during the annual pilgrimage to the chapel of St Eyon, a rock-cut shrine hidden among the oak woods of St Eyon's sacred hill, Knockeyon.

The ancient forests of Westmeath, according to Piers, had largely vanished from the county - and most other parts of Ireland - by the time he wrote his essay. The county was 'well stored with copses and underwoods'. But these were only the 'small remainders' of the forest trees that had been sacrificed to supply timber for buildings and ships, bark for tanning leather and charcoal for the insatiable ironworks. Now most of the county was bare, and no one bothered to plant new trees for posterity.

But Knockeyon, and its sister hill Knockross, were the exceptions. There were two striking groups of ancient trees - mainly oaks, it appears - clothing the precipitous hillsides. Knockross, according to Piers, was 'well shaded with all sorts of underwood and great store of low spreading oaks'. The hill rose 'to a vast height above the water'. Knockeyon rose higher still, and for more than half its height was 'almost perpendicular with the water'. The hill was indeed 'the tallest of all our hills in Westmeath'. (Piers was mistaken. At 707 feet in height, Knockeyon is 200 feet lower than Mulmaree, near the boundary with County Cavan. But Piers was writing 150 years before the first Ordnance Survey got to work.) The entire hill was 'cloathed with trees that naturally and securely grow here (for no hatchet can come near them) which rising continuously and gradually one above another add no small grace to the landscape'.

Piers ended with a flourish: 'To be in the water, a full view and just distance from these hills, were certainly the most agreeable prospect in nature; if hereunto were added, a noise of trumpets or loud-sounding instruments.'

I couldn't manage the trumpets, as I sailed up Lough Derravaragh to Knockeyon the following day. But I agreed wholeheartedly with Piers. Knockeyon's a stunner seen from the water - even if the ancient oaks are now thinly spread among the hanging thickets of thorn and birch and elder. I landed on the stony shore, now 20 feet higher than in Piers' time. It was hard climbing the muddy path. No sign of any pilgrims these days. But a herd of bullocks had done a fair job keeping the thorns off the path. I stopped several times to examine the oak trees. To my surprise none were of any height or girth. You could call them stunted. There were seven close to the path: gnarled and mossy creatures. Many had forked low down on the trunk. What was Piers' phrase about the oaks of the neighbouring hill, Knockross? 'Low-spreading'. Well, these were low-spreading all right. What age could I make them? I found it hard to guess. Oak trees like this, growing slowly on poor, rocky ground, can be much older than they look. Sometimes you're in for a shock if you count the rings on the trunk after a small oak has been felled by a storm. One hundred, one hundred and fifty, even two hundred can be counted on the stump of a small tree, each closely packed, concentric ring meaning a year's slow growth. Try counting the rings on a much larger tree that has had the luck to find rich soil. The rings are far fewer and far wider apart. In fact the large tree can be twice the size and half the age of the small one.

I looked again at these gnarled, stunted creatures on the stony slopes of Knockeyon. Could they be *three centuries* old - in other words, contemporary with Sir Henry Piers and his oaks? Not very likely. But if I had to guess their age I would put it nearer two centuries than one. Those oak trees could have known the days when the pilgrims staggered up the stony path from the lake - pilgrims that went barefoot for the first stage (according to Piers) and then 'on their bare knees, all along to the chapel, on stone and gravel, intermixt and overgrown with heath and grass'.

But where, I thought, is that chapel today, the rock-cut shrine of the mysterious St Eyon? It's almost as if the gnarled and stunted oaks have swallowed up the chapel. Certainly I had found no trace of it on previous visits. But this time I had brought Piers' text in my knapsack, and Piers had obviously been there himself:

the nearer you approach it, the narrower doth the way become; at last . . . the way appeareth hewn out of the rock side, rendered safe and easy by the trees, which, as aforesaid, rise from the water, and range over one another, and hem up the way so close, that there is no danger either to slip or to fall.

He added a brief description of the chapel. In 1682 it was already without a roof, and a 'curious purling brook of crystal water' flowed out of the rock and across the floor of the building.

Now the current Ordnance Survey of Westmeath shows no trace of a ruined chapel on the slopes of Knockeyon. But when I was halfway up the path I could swear I had found Piers' 'purling brook of crystal water' flowing across the bed of a small clearing. There was a broken wall of loose stones. And just beyond, half buried in leaf mould, a large block of cut stone, perhaps 6 feet long, straddled the east side of the path. I am no archaeologist, but I'd bet my bottom dollar that this block of cut stone is part of the eastern wall of St Eyon's chapel. Who knows what treasures lie below this holy spot? Of course Ireland is full of ruined chapels, some of which are still unexplored. But next time I climb this path I must remember to bring a good metal detector. (I shall not be breaking the law, like the treasure hunters who took the Viking silver from the lake. I shall make sure I have a licence.)

Beyond the chapel, the path winds up through thickets of whitethorn and elder, cherry and ash, until you finally break out into the open below the summit. It was here on 'a green spot' to the east side of Knockeyon that these seventeenth-century Catholic pilgrims gathered for a celebration that scandalised good Sir Henry Piers. (He was a Protestant, like most of his fellow landlords at that date.) Let him tell the story himself:

Their Devotions performed, they return merry and shodd no longer concerned with those Sins, that were the cause of this so severe Pennance. But as if (having now paid off the old Score) they longd to go on in the new again, they return in all hast to a certain green spot of ground . . . and here Men and Women fall a dancing and carousing the rest of the day . . . Thus in Lewd and obscene dancing, and in excess of drinking, the Remainder of the Day is spent, as if they celebrated the Bacchanalia, rather than the memory of a Pious Saint. And oftentimes it falls out that more blood is shedd on the Grass from broken Pates in drunken Quarrells, when the Pilgrimages are ended, than was before on the stones from their bare feet and knees during their Devotions.

Perhaps Sir Henry would have been less shocked – at any rate less surprised – if he'd known more of the significance of what he saw. He tells us nothing of St Eyon or his saint's day. In fact St Eyon seems to have been lost in the mists of antiquity long before Piers went to Knockeyon. At any rate no modern dictionary of saints that I have consulted can trace him. But the reference books say that there was a saint called St Cauragh whose name was associated with the chapel at Knockeyon. According to tradition, St Cauragh was a disciple of the famous St Columbkille (or Columba) in the mid-sixth century, who later founded the monastery at Iona, off the coast of Scotland. But before that period Columbkille had founded a monastery at Kells, thirty miles to the north-east of Knockeyon. Now Cauragh fell out with Columbkille (he was accused of 'indiscipline', whatever that meant) and was expelled from the monastery at Kells. In due course Cauragh came to Knockeyon where he fell ill and was close to death. He prayed that he might have one last drink of water before he died. Then Cauragh touched the rock, so the story goes, and out of the rock flowed a miraculous spring. He drank the water and was healed of his illness. He then built a chapel over the spring and lived there till he died. It was to St Cauragh's chapel and healing spring that people made their pilgrimage.

So much for the Christian tradition which Piers seems to have missed. Still more significant were the *pre*-Christian roots of the pilgrimage. Piers tells us that it took place on the first Sunday in August. This would mean the date coincided with the pre-Christian harvest festival of Lughnasa. In fact modern historians can tell us a good deal about the pagan roots of the Christian pilgrimage described by Piers. And the local Protestant landlords were not the only ones to be scandalised by the 'lewd and obscene dancing', and the 'excess of drinking'. The Catholic authorities, too, recognised that enough was enough. By the mid-nineteenth century the pilgrimage to Knockeyon was in decline – not actually banned, I think, but firmly discouraged. After all there were only the *ruins* of a chapel on the hill, not even a decent shrine dedicated to the little-known saint. Better to make a pilgrimage to one of the officially recognised sites, like St Patrick's Island in County Mayo or the holy mountain of Croagh Patrick. These sites, too, were pre-Christian in origin. But they had been sanitised with new churches and chapels, and the Catholic bishops kept a sharp eye on the goings-on.

I must go back to Knockeyon and the low-spreading oaks around it. When you break into the open and stand on the grassy summit, you can see at least ten counties. Piers claims that the view 'covers the prospect of both seas'; in other words, that it spans Ireland from the Atlantic to the Irish Sea. This isn't strictly true, but I can guess what he means. On a clear day you can see central Ireland from the blue lines of the Mourne Mountains in the north to the Wicklow Mountains in the south, a span of nearly two hundred miles. And it's the absence of trees that strikes me most, an absence that Piers emphasised three hundred years ago.

There are hedgerow trees, of course, and the scrubby little bushes that Piers called 'underwood'. But there are virtually no woods to enrich the view - except for the ancient oaks at our feet, and their younger counterparts at Tullynally and the Millennium Wood six miles away across the waters of the lake.

This afternoon is unusually calm and clear. I can make out our romantic Gothic turrets, rising out of the beech grove at the south side of our house, and the grey cupola of the clock tower in the stable yard. And there's the silver fir with the twisted top. This is the lookout tree for our pair of ravens, and the tallest tree in the arboretum. I shift my gaze to the northern shore of the lake. Is it only my imagination? I swear I can distinguish the two parts of the Millennium Wood although half hidden by the ringfort: the pushy young oaks, raised from our own finest trees, and the poor stunted creatures from Killarney and other parts of the country.

Suddenly something falls into place, something that I should have recognised long ago. The stunted oaks of Knockeyon - gnarled and forked and moss-covered - are hardly a forester's idea of a fine stand. In fact a forester would regard them as barely worth cutting for firewood. But they came of ancient stock, as I knew from Piers. So did the stunted oaks from Killarney, the progeny of which I find so disappointing. Now I have planted the trees, I must bite my lip and embrace their diversity. My Millennium Wood should be a true representative of Ireland: a romantic wilderness as well as a forest of noble oak trees.

* * *

Back from the lake, I must clear my mind for a meeting tomorrow with Antoine, our local cabinet-maker and sculptor. Antoine doesn't plant trees. He takes dead trees and gives them new life.

15

On the Track of the Green Man

12 September 2013

Today I persuaded Antoine to carve six new Green Men for the Grotto Walk.

Antoine is a man of rare talent. He came to the wilds of Ireland from central France some time ago and used to rent one of our flats over the old stables. He had learnt his skills in a French monastery but made good his escape: 'not enough drink', he once confided to me, 'and no girls'. He married a beautiful Irish schoolteacher, and fathered two sons. There's nothing monkish about Antoine now except his shaven head - and his skill with saw and chisel. He has an instinctive rapport with broken furniture and rotting buildings. We owe him more than I can say. Thanks to Antoine, many parts of our crumbling pile at Tullynally have been brought back from the grave. New Gothic doors have been added to keep out the draughts, new lancet windows to bring light into dark corners. He's renewal and rebirth personified.

When some of my favourite trees blew down in the demesne - an ancient oak, an elegant ash, and a squat sweet chestnut - Antoine gave all three trees the gift of new life. He made them into cupboards and cabinets and bookshelves, crowned with intricate carvings of the leaves from each of their species. He also built me wooden follies in various styles: a Gothic pavilion for the Forest Walk, a Buddhist shrine for Tibet, and the Pumpkin House for the arboretum. (Earlier, I had asked him what style he would choose for the folly in the arboretum. I might have guessed his reply:

'I shall not tell you the style. I shall say only one thing. It will be a masterpiece.')

Ten years ago I gave him a commission for a piece of sculpture that might have summoned the ghosts of his monastic past. I asked him to carve me a medieval Green Man to put in the pleasure ground. A rough-and-ready definition of this kind of sculpture would be a face-among-the-leaves. Technically it's a 'foliate head, a face or mask with leaves sprouting from it'. But about seventy years ago an amateur folklorist, Lady Raglan, coined the romantic name 'Green Man', and the name stuck.

All over Europe – in France, Germany, Italy and beyond – there are Green Men in medieval churches if you bother to search for them. Carved in stone or wood, the Green Men look down on us from corbels and capitals and spandrels and roof bosses. But be on your guard: few of them are serene or benevolent. Usually they face you with a blank, enigmatic stare. Sometimes they are as grotesque and demonic as the neighbouring gargoyles. Their tongues stick out, their fangs are bared and their eyes sparkle with malice. Even when they seem most aloof there's an eerie quality to their calm, as if they were only waiting their chance to strike. Yet some are beautiful. And many are certainly victims, tormented creatures, their mouths and nostrils choked with sprouting leaves. Often they cry for help from the thickets in which they have somehow become imprisoned.

I don't know how much of this I told Antoine. But he's very much his own man, and he's French after all. He probably wouldn't have listened if I'd gone into more detail. I gave him a book on the subject and left the rest to Antoine, telling him that I was sure that his Green Man would be a new masterpiece.

A few months later Antoine brought me the Green Man he had carved from the branch of a fallen yew tree. It's carved in low relief, a face hewn out of pink yew-wood. The head emerges boldly from a fan of ivy leaves and its eyes are its strongest feature.

There's a 20-foot-tall beech stump in the pleasure ground, the mutilated stump of a 200-year-old tree that was decapitated some years ago. This is where I asked Antoine to mount the Green Man. Antoine took a ladder and cut a hole for his sculpture. The Green Man's eyes now follow you down the path, deep-set but compelling. The stump used to be a sad relic. Now the Green Man adds nobility, indeed he redeems the place.

In February this year I decided to give Antoine a daring new commission. I would ask him to carve me a *family* of Green Men to keep the first one company. Then I had second thoughts. The hunt for Green Men can become a dangerous obsession. It could happen to any of us. I have known perfectly sensible people who were carried away by the hunt. I have heard it even led them to the doors of the madhouse. They saw Green Men everywhere: not just Green Men mocking them from the walls and roofs of churches, but Green Men leering at them from curtains and the backs of chairs, Green Men poking out behind sofas and tallboys, Green Men waking them in the night with tongues protruding and fangs at the ready. It wasn't fair to Antoine to risk his sanity by proceeding with this new commission.

Then I went back to the pleasure ground, one sunny, icy February day, to look again at Antoine's first Green Man. The ground was crisp with hoar frost. A crust of snow had even encased the upper part of the sculpture. But the eyes were brighter than ever, glowing with light reflected from the snow. And I realised that Antoine was safe after all. His Green Man had a twinkle in the eye. Unlike his medieval counterparts, this was a benevolent and compassionate being. So I went ahead with the commission. Antoine has now promised to carve me a family of six more benevolent Green Men and Green Women to bring new life to the trees of the pleasure ground.

But I cannot escape one historical conundrum, which makes my mind boggle with Green Men. How are we to interpret these enigmatic creatures from the mists of the Middle Ages? It would be hard to find a subject on which there are so many different opinions. Are they celebrations in wood and stone? That is, do they celebrate our one-ness with nature, our delight in renewal, as New Age enthusiasts came to believe? Or are the psychoanalysts right? Do they serve as universal symbols, Jungian archetypes to which our unconscious naturally responds? Or do they on the contrary represent something much darker and more sinister: a glimpse of our pagan past, a whiff of the old gods? Is this a subversive invitation to May Day rites and flower-rich Maypoles and not-so-innocent dancing in the woods, of beliefs hidden but never fully repressed during the centuries of Christian orthodoxy? Or are they the exact opposite: a *warning* to sinners – not subversive but part of the official art of the Middle Ages? Do the Green Men tell us to mend our ways or face hell everlasting? Or is it a mistake to try to *interpret* them at all? Are they simply to be treated as works of art?

The prototypes for the medieval Green Man are to be found scattered about the ruins of the Roman Empire. These faces-in-the-leaves emerge, we are told by art historians, in the second half of the first century AD, and become common a century later. You can spot them, with other pagan motifs of the classical world, like dolphins and horns of plenty and Medusas and satyrs and bacchanals. They are carved on the friezes of temples, on the sides and lids of sarcophagi and on the panels of triumphal arches. Usually they take the form of separate male masks with acanthus spirals sprouting from their faces. But sometimes they are part of a repeating pattern called a 'peopled scroll'. They often share an intimidating family trait which their medieval descendants inherited: a penetrating stare. ('Glare' would often be the right word.) But there is one striking difference between the pre-Christian style and what followed. Pagan heads can look somewhat sinister, half hidden in leaves. But they are never actually repulsive, like many medieval heads, *choked* by greenery sprouting from their mouths. And they are never diabolical.

In fact the tenth century of our era was alive with devils. If you look at a medieval psalter you may be amazed to find the border is thronged with demonic figures. In the centre - somewhat incongruously, you might think - is the saint to whom the church is dedicated, say St Egbert, looking as if butter wouldn't melt in his mouth. Encircling the holy man is a scene of demonic frenzy. Winged monsters chase each other round the page, biting each other's tails. Devils, sprouting new monsters from their heads, complete the horrors.

A century later, the demons have spread from the page and encircled the doorways and windows of Romanesque churches. Sometimes they served a practical function like the gargoyles spouting water from the roof. Usually they were ornaments, but (according to one interpretation) ornaments with a message, however enigmatic. You should pay a visit to that jewel-box of a Romanesque church at Kilpeck in Herefordshire. I have known Kilpeck, and been fascinated by Kilpeck, since childhood. At the centre of the celebrated tympanum - the concentric carvings above the west door - you are confronted with a stylised vine, elegant and heavy with fruit. Perhaps this represents the Tree of Life, or perhaps the Tree of Knowledge which led to the Fall. It must also symbolise the redemptive power of Christ and his church. But immediately to the right is a second vine, disgorged from the mouth of a demonic figure on the capital supporting the tympanum. This is Kilpeck's famous Green Man, choking on the vine, and surrounded with a monstrous semicircle of lesser Green Men. How are we to explain the symbolism?

I must leave this anguished world of the Romanesque, these glimpses of hell carved on the walls of churches and abbeys throughout Europe, and pass to the calmer world of medieval Gothic. By the early twelfth century, a new mood was visible in the work of medieval stonemasons and the abbots and bishops who commissioned it. Something of the spirit of the classics now returned to the Green Man; he was less repulsive at least. The mood seems to have begun in France and spread gradually to Germany, Italy and England. Of course there were still plenty of tormented figures, choking on the foliage spewing out of their mouths. But there were other more fortunate Green Men, the kind called in France by the name of *tête feuillu*. This is the kind that appeals to me most, although still enigmatic: the man wears the leaves like a mask, but his mouth is mercifully free from the tendrils of foliage.

'Enigmatic!' The word's a cliché but inescapable. If only the medieval stonemasons had left an account of their briefs. Yet there are at least some clues to help interpret what these sculptures would have meant to their creators, to their patrons and to their public. Strange to say, one of the best sources is a stern voice from the dark ages of the eighth century. A celebrated theologian, Father Rabanus Maurus, has left us a text explaining that the leaves choking the mouth of the Green Man represent nothing less than the sins of the flesh. So this is a warning to Christians. Follow the rules of the Church or you will be choked by your lusts and condemned to hell everlasting.

If this is correct – and Father Maurus' interpretation can be broadened to include sins of all sorts – the Green Man does not celebrate our one-ness with nature. In fact he has nothing to celebrate. On the contrary he is a spiritual no-go sign to ignore at our peril. He can take numerous forms: by turns menacing or menaced, repulsive or tormented. Sometimes he makes no pretence about his identity. Horns sprout from his head as well as foliage from his mouth, eyes and nostrils. He is the devil incarnate, the three-headed Beelzebub, the root of all evil. But often, according to Fr Maurus, he's the devil's victim, not the devil himself. He confronts us as a wretched sinner beginning to pay the price of his folly, which makes him often a moving and tragic figure.

This year I went to Exeter Cathedral to see its famous Green Man. He is the demonic figure at the foot of the statue of the Virgin and Child. You would expect this to be a scene of joyous incarnation. And in a sense it is. Angels fly overhead, swinging their thuribles. The Virgin, crowned and robed as a queen, dandles her son on her hip. In turn he affectionately strokes his mother under the chin. But what is that face in the undergrowth below her feet? It's Satan of course, and the brute's hoping to wreck the peace of the Holy Family. A loathsome coil of vegetation rises from his mouth. But the Virgin has spotted him, and tramples him underfoot as if this were

Eden and (unlike poor feckless Eve) she were trampling on the serpent himself.

A more subtle and sinister demon is the Green Man in the early Gothic cathedral at Bamberg in northern Bavaria. Tourists flock to see the famous statue of the mounted knight, known as the Rider. Ten years ago I went there myself and marvelled at the lifelike carving of the horse. What I missed at the time – and have only studied later in photographs – is the Green Man *underneath* the Rider, a carving on the bracket supporting the statue. His features are formed entirely from an acanthus leaf. But it's no ordinary acanthus leaf. As one art historian describes it: 'All the darkness and power and mystery of a vast forest seems concentrated in this majestic head of leaves. The Bamberg leaf mask is the Prince of Darkness.'

What of the devil's victims, the Green Men who suffer, if Fr Maurus is to be believed, eternal punishment for their sins? The hunt for Green Men has taken me to at least a dozen churches and cathedrals in England in the last few months. Most of these men were victims: choking on greenery, spewed out of their mouths. This attracted my sympathy – but not, I confess, my admiration for them as works of art. Recently I went to the Chapter House at Southwell in Nottinghamshire, where you can find nine of the most celebrated Green Men in England. The Chapter House is a delicate confection of early Gothic, an incongruous attachment to the ponderous Romanesque minster. It was here, in the rib-vaulted octagon, that the abbot and monks of Southwell first sat in the late thirteenth century to debate the affairs of their community. And the nine Green Men faced them from the forest of Gothic arches. Was it my imagination, or did I see the ghost of Fr Maurus nodding at me grimly from the shadows?

For, with a single exception, the Green Men in Southwell seem to conform to Fr Maurus' interpretation. The first is demonic: his face pudgy, his mouth twisted into a grimace by fronds of some seaweed-like plant. In the adjoining six spandrels you can see what appears to be a sample of sinners taking their punishment. Each face is contorted by the sprouting of a different plant from its mouth. The various leaves – oak, hawthorn, ivy, maple, buttercup and so on – are all carved with astonishing realism. In fact some experts have remarked that the medieval sculptors paid more attention to the leaves than to the rest of the subject. But that's not how I see it. The delicacy of the leaves adds poignancy to the torment of the sinners. So do the elegant crows pecking at the leaves. Saddest of all are two more figures who are struggling to extricate themselves from the plants that will soon choke them. One of them grips the stem of a hawthorn in both hands and appeals to us all to save him.

The ninth Green Man, however, is different in every way from all the others. You could call him the happy Hawthorn Man. Certainly he's at peace with the world. He's not enclosed in a spandrel like his fellows and tormented by sprouting plants. He faces you calmly from the point where two ribs of the vault converge. Below him is a capital decorated with leaves and flowers of hawthorn. His own face is clear except for a stylised mask formed by two pairs of outsize hawthorn leaves. The first pair caps his forehead, the second his chin. Above them is a miniature fleur-de-lys. What does the Hawthorn Man represent? I find it hard to believe that he is there to warn us against the lusts of the flesh and to threaten us with hellfire eternal. He seems far too gentle for that. But if Maurus' interpretation fails for once, what are the alternatives?

Could this really be an example of subversive art, in which the old pagan gods are given a brief airing, half hidden from the official church? One leading art historian says yes, perhaps. She points to the small fleur-de-lys above the Green Man's mask of hawthorn. Is this Green Man, she asks, a May King, a spirit of the greenwood who presides over the pre-Christian rites of May? I suppose anything is possible. But if he really represented the old gods, I doubt if the monks of Southwell would have allowed him such a prominent place in their Chapter House. Why let such a subversive spirit share their secrets?

In fact this line of argument assumes the authorities of the medieval Church knew little and cared little about the meaning of the sculptures they paid for. I can't believe this was generally true. (Although I must admit that St Bernard of Clairvaux, the great Cistercian, once wrote to a fellow bishop complaining about the expense and incongruity of sculpture in medieval churches.) Like other works of art, sculpture in churches was supposed to teach the laity their faith. In a sense history had gone backwards since the fall of the Roman Empire. Few Christians, except the priests and bishops, could read or write in Europe during the Middle Ages. So the decoration of the church was what we would now call a teaching aid. Frescoes and sculptures were lessons in paint and stone. Stonemasons were not allowed much freedom in the subjects they chose, or how they treated them. Like everyone else they had to toe the line.

An ingenious new twist has recently been given to this debate. Albert Radcliffe, a canon of Manchester Cathedral, has written that 'the Green Man could only have got past the ecclesiastical censor if he in some ways served the purposes of the Church'. He could do this in two different ways. Either he represented the sins of the flesh, as Fr Maurus taught us. Or he was a bridge between the pagan world and our own.

He represented 'pagan and natural human nature, witnessing to Christ, and thereby redeemed and brought into the service of the gospel'.

I wish I could believe the good Canon Radcliffe. Better surely to accept that the Hawthorn Man represents a benevolent spirit, with the enigmatic qualities natural to any work of art. Whatever it means, it must have given the stonemason great pleasure to carve it – as much as it has given me to discover it.

10 October 2013

Today Antoine brought me the family of Green Men I had commissioned last month. I'm overwhelmed. He's made me six astonishing sculptures: five men and a woman. All except one are carved from pink yew-wood. (The exception is carved from a pale yellow birch-wood.) The mother tree for three of them was the battered old yew that had been felled because it was believed to have poisoned two of our ten-month-old calves. As I said earlier, it was given the chop at the end of June when I was away in London. (They knew I might plead for its life. After all, it was only a *suspect* in the case of the poisoned calves.) Two others had a happier origin. They were carved from yews that had died in their beds, if you will forgive the pun, a year or two ago.

When I commissioned Antoine, I gave him a vague enough brief for the six sculptures. They were to be Green Men, meaning faces-in-the-leaves, like their medieval counterparts. I showed Antoine several new books on the subject. But I didn't specify whether his new sculptures should represent one type or another. It was up to him to decide whether they should be demons or sinners or benevolent spirits of nature or delightfully enigmatic – like many great works of art.

In the event Antoine has given me a family of enigmas. Each of the six is a face-in-the-leaves of a particular kind of tree. There's a Maple Man, a Vine Man, a Birch Man, an Oak Man, a Chestnut Man and a Hawthorn Woman. None of them are demonic. Only one is actually repulsive: the Birch Man. Half his face is eaten away by decay and his mouth is twisted with pain. Is he, as Fr Rabanus would say, a sinner paying the price of his folly? But look at the Chestnut Man. His mouth, too, is contorted. But is it contorted by pain or by disgust? And why is a small owl perched on his head? What of the Oak Man, who wears a cap of oak leaves squashed down over his forehead? Is he a comic? Or is he another victim? And now look at the Vine Man. Is he a Bacchic reveller? Vine leaves and grapes sprout from his cheeks and nostrils. Somehow I feel he's not enjoying the party. The same could be said about the Maple Man. Red maple leaves threaten to choke him. No wonder he looks under the weather.

By contrast the Hawthorn Woman seems almost too happy. In the Middle Ages she might have been labelled a temptress and ended up burnt as a witch. But I'm captivated by her bold looks and brassy pose and the mysterious smile on her face.

Tomorrow Antoine has promised to come back with a long ladder and mount the six new sculptures high up under the foliage of some of our finest trees. It will certainly spice up the pleasure ground. Perhaps I'll make a May Day Trail for children to follow in the spring, when the gardens reopen to the public. Apart from the Vine Man, I can put them in trees of appropriate species. The Oak Man will be up an oak tree, the Maple Man up a red maple and so on.

But there's one question that will be asked again and again. How are they to be interpreted, these enigmatic new Green People?

Unlike his medieval counterparts, Antoine is alive and well and living near Tullynally. So I could always ask him what was in his head when he carved these people out of the pink yew-wood. But I know what he would reply, and perhaps he would be right. 'Don't ask me what they mean. I shall say only one thing. They are *all* masterpieces.'

16

'But Where Is His Lordship?'

10 October 2013

> But where is his lordship who once in his phaeton
> Drove out twixt his lodges and into the town?
> Oh his tragic misfortunes I will not dilate on;
> His mansion's a ruin, his woods are cut down.
>
> John Betjeman, 'The Small Towns of Ireland'

After Antoine had shown me his six magnificent Green Men, I walked back with him as far as the so-called Grand Lodge, a somewhat battered folly in the shape of a miniature castle. I cast a guilty eye at the adjoining boundary walls of our demesne. (The high-sounding term 'demesne', as I said earlier, is used in Ireland to mean much the same as the Englishman's 'park'.) Even Antoine, a master of the grotesque, was shocked at the deplorable state of our boundary walls.

Of course this is a common sight in Ireland: demesne walls gashed by fallen beech trees, grey stones crumbling under the assault of ash and elder and the insidious plague of bramble and nettle. But those demesne walls are the legacy of a vanished world - the world of Betjeman's poem - where the mansion's a ruin and the woods are cut down.

It *should* be different with us. Our Gothic pile, Tullynally, still stands: battered but unbowed. Every year the roof leads us a merry dance. One year it's a crack in the lead that brings a ring of mushrooms to the ogees of Morrison's tower. The next year it's a puncture in the battlements that deluges the vaults of the dining room. Somehow Tullynally staggers on like a man on crutches. Steel props support the neo-Tudor chimney stacks afflicted by the most alarming lean, and steel bands contain the cracks in the stonework of the chimneys themselves.

But why have I failed to repel the jungle-growth attacking the walls of our demesne? This is a question that Valerie puts to me, and of course she's right.

One answer would be that these crumbling walls, two miles long, belong to a world of top-hatted lodge-keepers and deferential tenants – of private roads and locked gates. Today, thank heavens, the age of deference is over. But we're stuck with our walls. To remove them and replace them with post-and-wire fencing would cost us a fortune. So we must start to think of how to make them look at least moderately decent. After all they enclose and protect some of our most inspiring parkland trees. And I mean not just the individuals like the silver fir in the shape of a giant candelabra – a tree that I would die for (and will describe in due course). The walls protect both the sweeping clumps of beech and lime, and the swooping belts of beech and oak which shelter Tullynally from the icy blast.

And talking of trees, Valerie reminds me that I have failed in a second task. These clumps and shelter belts have been sadly neglected for nearly a century. The towering, 200-year-old beech are magnificent, but some have already died of old age, and many are on their last legs. Even the longer-lived lime and oak are finding life difficult. It will not take much of a storm to bring the majority down. It's high time someone thought about the next generation of parkland trees that will be needed.

To get a better idea of this double task – repairing walls and restoring clumps and shelter belts – I decided to have a look at other demesnes in Ireland. In little more than a month I visited a dozen surviving Irish demesnes, beginning with two celebrated twins, Carton and Castletown, and ending with what I believe is the finest demesne in the whole of Ireland: Mount Stewart in County Down. My tour was delightful, of course. But some of the lessons I learnt were alarming enough.

To begin with the twins, Carton is only a half-hour's stroll from Maynooth, which is itself twenty miles west of Dublin on the main road to Galway. It was here that the young head of the FitzGerald clan, James 20th Earl of Kildare, blazed a trail in the 1750s and 1760s, creating a sumptuous new demesne. His father, the 19th Earl, had bought back the Carton estate from the Ingoldsby family – the estate which had belonged to the FitzGeralds for centuries but then slipped from their grasp. The 19th Earl had hired Richard Castle, the most formidable Palladian architect of the time, who accordingly rebuilt the Ingoldsbys' seventeenth-century house in the latest Palladian style. But the 19th Earl had died before he could remodel the Ingoldsbys' garden and park. Their seventeenth-century garden was a stiff, Dutch-style affair of parterres and grassy *plats*; the park radiated avenues in the shape of a duck's foot or *patte d'oie*. All this geometry was now carefully dug up and removed by James, the 20th Earl.

There's a famous oil painting by Arthur Devis which shows James at work on the Carton landscape in 1753 with his twenty-year-old wife, Emily, one of the four enterprising Lennox sisters, whose father was the Duke of Richmond. I say, 'at work'. Actually, James looks remarkably relaxed, not to say smug, and it's Emily who seems to have the exciting ideas. The pair are sitting beside a table on the lawn at Carton. She shows her husband the architect's plan for what appears to be a new bridge. Behind them the parkland has already been transformed. In place of the Dutch parterres and avenues, there's the kind of rolling landscape of lakes and clumps and belts that came to be called 'Brownian' after the celebrated Capability Brown. (In fact James tried unavailingly to persuade Brown to come to Ireland. Brown is said to have rejected James's offer of £1,000 with the excuse that 'he had not finished England yet'.)

Landscaping on this scale didn't come cheap, even in the eighteenth century when wages for a labourer cost his employer less than a shilling a day. When James died in 1773 he had mortgaged the estate up to the hilt (to more than eleven times his rent-roll of £12,000 a year, according to local gossip). But extravagance was no bar to a leg-up in the peerage. In due course James was promoted to be first a marquess and then a duke – promoted from being 20th Earl of Kildare to being the 1st Duke of Leinster. And who is to say he did not deserve it? The magnificence of this new landscape at Carton was never to be rivalled in eighteenth-century Ireland. (Of course he did not claim it rivalled English parks like the ones at Blenheim or Castle Howard.) At Carton there was a five-mile circuit of demesne walls, and five miles of shelter belts within them. Inside this private world James and Emily had created a new arcadia. A sparkling sheet of water, dotted with islands and crowned with a five-span stone bridge, replaced the muddy stream at the south-west end of the demesne. And trees were planted in tens of thousands: exotic specimens from Europe like larch and spruce and silver fir, as well the Brownian groves of oak and beech.

How does this ducal landscape look 250 years later? Today the five miles of limestone walls are still crisp and clean – a model to all those who own demesnes. But the house is a hotel and the demesne is a golf course. No doubt it's an excellent golf course (in fact several of them) but not the great work of art this demesne once was. The five-span bridge still exists but the lake is half overgrown with reeds. Many of the oak and beech, planted by James and later dukes of Leinster, have grown senile, barely surviving the successive storms from the Atlantic. Many others have succumbed. Where is the next generation of towering beech? I could see no sign of a real programme for replanting the vanishing groves and shelter belts. Much of the parkland is as treeless as a prairie. Gradually the extraordinary landscape of the eighteenth century is becoming the familiar landscape of the twenty-first: of bunkers and fairways and neatly mown greens, with jolly men and women riding the range in golf buggies. Poor James! He would turn in his grave. (By contrast, Emily might be more easily reconciled. After all she had a radical side to her character. It was her son, Lord Edward FitzGerald, who was to be commander-in-chief of the Irish rebels in 1798; he was mortally wounded while resisting arrest.)

Three miles away, across the flat, hedge-lined fields of County Kildare, lies Carton's twin: the great house and demesne of Castletown. It was here that Louisa, Emily's younger sister, presided for more than fifty years. At sixteen she had been married off by Emily to the local squire, Tom Conolly, whose grandfather, Speaker Conolly – inn-keeper's son, land speculator and politician – had built the house in the 1720s. The young couple had little in common, as Conolly was somewhat dim, and interested in not much except dogs and horses. And, sad to say, the marriage was childless. But Louisa had been brought up by Emily at Carton from the age of eleven, when both their parents, the Duke and Duchess of Richmond, died in turn. Like Emily she was bitten by the bug for landscape gardening, and Castletown was a perfect place for it. The house was magnificent, Ireland's first great Palladian palace. Although the demesne was flatter than Carton's, the fields ran down to the River Liffey, a rampaging flood in winter, whose source, the Dublin Mountains, formed a delightful backdrop to the view.

To turn Castletown into a fashionable demesne of the mid-eighteenth century meant, just as it did at Carton, carefully digging up and removing the earlier landscape. Out went the stiff, geometric landscape of lime avenues radiating like a duck's foot. In came the smooth, informal landscape of Brownian clumps and swooping shelter belts. Louisa even turned her back on the most successful of her predecessor's innovations. It was a Baroque eye-catcher, designed by Richard Castle, all of 140 feet high, and it linked, appropriately enough, the two estates of Castletown and Carton. This came to be called, somewhat dismissively, the Conolly Folly, although it had been generously built by Speaker Conolly's widow to give employment to the poor in 1740, a year when the crops failed. At any rate Louisa boldly planted out the avenue that led northwards to the eye-catcher and swung the view southwards to the Liffey. Here she borrowed a leaf (or, should I say, several leaves) from Emily's book.

She widened a stream to make a lake and a cascade that led the eye down to the river. She made an elegant walk alongside the riverbank, decorated with a circular Greek temple dedicated to her friend Mrs Siddons, the celebrated actress. Best of all, in 1780 she built an extraordinary Gothic-Baroque lodge at the gate on the Dublin road. The idea came from a pattern book which the whimsical architect Batty Langley had published forty years before. I wonder if Emily was shocked at the idea of this strange-looking Gothic lodge at the gates of a classical house. It was certainly unconventional to mix the styles in this way. But Emily had left Carton by then, as the Duke had died, and she was now hardly the one to talk about conventions. As a young widow she had married the Scottish tutor of her nineteen children by the Duke, and produced three more children by the tutor.

How does Castletown look today? Fifty years ago the owners, the Conolly-Carew family, found the house and its demesne too heavy a burden. The estate was put up for auction – and disaster loomed. The new owners were land speculators. They sold off the western part of the demesne for building bungalows and Spanish-style villas. Only the great generosity of Desmond Guinness, founder of the new Irish Georgian Society, saved the rest of the demesne from being swallowed by the suburbs, and the house itself from being sold to the knackers. Desmond snapped up the house and the parkland that runs down to the Liffey, then made them over to the Irish Georgian Society, which began the work of restoration with an army of volunteers. In due course the job of restoring them has passed to the Office of Public Works, a slow-moving government department. But its mandarins, fortunately enough, regard Castletown as the jewel in their crown.

It would be hard to exaggerate the contrast which these two great demesnes, Carton and Castletown, present today. While Carton is slipping into the suburbs, Castletown, now rescued from their embrace, is beginning to recapture its former glory. The lake has been dug out and the cascade restored. So has Mrs Siddons' elegant Greek temple and Batty Langley's extraordinary lodge. Everywhere trees are being planted: as individual specimens and in Brownian groves. Only one trick has been missed by the mandarins, and I'm puzzled by the omission. Louisa swung the view towards the Liffey and made the river, foaming over the rocks, the centre of her new landscape. But the Liffey has now vanished behind a line of scrubby thorns and sally-willows. Where are the chainsaws? It would hardly take a week to reopen the view.

The third and greatest demesne I visited, in search of ideas for Tullynally, is the demesne at Mount Stewart, a gilded outpost of the National Trust in County Down, Northern Ireland. History and geography have blessed Mount Stewart like fairy godmothers. In 1818, Charles Stewart – one of Wellington's leading generals in the Peninsula, and younger half-brother of Lord Castlereagh – carried off the greatest prize on offer in the English marriage market. He wooed and won eighteen-year-old Frances Vane-Tempest, heiress to vast coal-rich estates in County Durham. With the Vane-Tempest fortune in the bag, and having unexpectedly inherited his own family's estate and the title of Marquess of Londonderry (after Castlereagh cut his own throat in a fit of depression), Charles was able to double the size of the family's house at Mount Stewart. Two huge porticos were added at the north and west. And the demesne was enriched in proportion. Already it was celebrated for one delightful feature built by his father, the 1st Marquess: an octagonal, two-storey pavilion for banqueting, half hidden in the woods on a ridge east of the main house. This was the Temple of the Winds, based on the famous Greek Tower of the Winds in Athens and commissioned in 1791 from 'Athenian' Stuart, the leading Greek Revival architect of the time. Charles now dammed a stream in order to give the demesne the privilege of a lake. He surrounded it with new shelter belts of beech and sycamore. And a romantic path led to a sham ruin through a ravine overhung with young oaks.

The geography of the estate was exceptional: cradled by low hills, it straddled the narrow peninsula between Strangford Lough and the open sea. This created a climate where sub-tropical plants could flourish even in winter, warmed by the sea, and protected from gales by judicious planting. Yet, strange to say, Mount Stewart had little or no appeal for the next two generations of the family. They lived in London or in their vast estates in County Durham. The house and demesne were left to their own devices. Then in 1915 a new Marchioness, Edith Londonderry, arrived to take over as chatelaine. Edith was a woman of steely will and rare talent.

She had married Charles, the 7th Marquess, then called Lord Stewart, in 1899. Blessed with dazzling good looks and a not inconsiderable fortune, the couple were instant celebrities in the fashionable world. Maharajahs welcomed them to their palaces as if they were old friends. Edith and Charles went pig-sticking on horseback and tiger-hunting from elephants. But there was a dark side to their fairy tale. Charles was a notorious womaniser. His political instincts also led him into trouble. In 1930 he was made Minister of Air in Ramsay MacDonald's government. He was later accused of being a Nazi sympathiser. Certainly he showed extraordinary naïvety in dealing with Hitler, with whom he stayed several times. Edith, by contrast, took a cooler view of the Nazis. Charles invited Ribbentrop, Hitler's oily-tongued ambassador, for a merry weekend at Mount Stewart. Somehow Ribbentrop was persuaded to help crew a boat in a yacht race in Strangford Lough. The yacht gave a sudden lurch. Ribbentrop fell overboard and was nearly drowned. Edith is supposed to have reprimanded the sailor for saving him.

No doubt the garden and demesne at Mount Stewart provided Edith with a refuge from Charles's affairs, amorous as well as political. This was where she could hone her skills as gardener and garden designer. The family's coal mines in County Durham were still turning in a handsome profit. In turn Edith designed and built six new gardens to the south and west of the house: the Spanish garden, the Italian garden, the sunken garden, the fountain pool, the 'Dodo' terrace and the menagerie. In most of these new gardens you sense a whiff of the Mediterranean: the tang of myrtles and Mediterranean cypresses and the fragrance of lavender. For Edith was the first of the family to realise the exceptional advantages for tender trees and other plants offered by the micro-climate of the peninsula. A few of her gardens were outrageously kitsch – like the 'Dodo' terrace, bristling with whimsical sculptures of animals, which were apparently caricatures of her father and her smarter friends. Other gardens were designed in a conventional style, as if laid out by the leading garden designer of the day, Gertrude Jekyll. (In fact Gertrude was invited to stay at Mount Stewart but her visit wasn't a success. She volunteered some advice about the sunken garden, and then sent in a bill for £60. Edith Londonderry replied that she had paid no attention to the advice and was certainly not going to pay the bill.)

My own favourite, which I think is a model of its kind, is the far-flung woodland garden on the north side of the house. The demesne is dominated by an immense lake, a mirror to the sky – doubled in size since Charles's day. A series of mossy paths encircle it, winding in and out of a series of glades. Picturesque groves of small trees and shrubs – Japanese maples, Chinese sorbus, Himalayan rhododendrons – are set against a backdrop of gigantic pines, oaks and cypresses. And a flight of steps, half buried in montbretia and agapanthus, leads you past an amazing New Zealand Christmas tree (*Metrosideros umbellata*) to Edith's masterpiece, an Irish Valhalla for the Stewarts. This is the Tir na nÓg, meaning 'Land of the Young', the family burial ground laid out as if for a powerful chieftain and his family. It's the place where Edith and Charles were united in death. But no Irish chieftain would have aspired to such a bizarre mixture of styles: a Celtic cross cut into the cobbled ground, stone tombs for Norse warriors, a font for Byzantine heroes.

*   *   *

Back at Tullynally, I felt somewhat deflated after my tour of these great demesnes. What were the lessons? There could be no argument about the first lesson. All three demesnes – Carton, Castletown and Mount Stewart – were encircled by miles of well-manicured walls. Our walls at Tullynally are like broken teeth: disfigured by ivy and notched by fallen trees. So my first task is to clean up and restore our demesne walls. This will be difficult and expensive, as it will mean buying local limestone to match the colour and texture of the walls. But it's a task I have shirked for too long. (Valerie's comment: 'You certainly have.')

Equally, I must get a grip on the task of replanting the moth-eaten shelter belts and decayed clumps that make up so much of the eighteenth-century parkland. Every Atlantic storm removes another beech or oak or pine from this once enchanted landscape. The sad fate of Carton should be a warning. Of course golf has exacted a heavy price there. But even if Carton had been spared the ride of the Valkyrie golf buggies, storms would have skittled its great trees. What is needed in all demesnes, great and small, is a systematic plan for replanting the parkland.

Strange to say, Valerie and I are in complete agreement – more or less – about planting these new trees. The blueprint is there in the large-scale estate map of 1835. The map shows the exact locations of all the clumps and shelter belts. It's up to us to choose the most suitable species. And I agree for once to forget the exotic world of China and Tibet. We will dress the demesne in the fashion of 1835. Most of the trees will be the old reliables that revel in the deep, moist clay of Tullynally: big-boned oaks and lichen-encrusted beech, spiky sweet chestnuts and bewhiskered limes. But we will add some adornments: girdles of European larch and silver fir, Scots pine and common spruce. Of course three hundred years ago these would have been called exotic immigrants. But they have got their passports long since. Today they have been Irish for generations.

Do I dare add some of the American trees whose roots go almost as deep into Irish history as their European cousins: red oaks, scarlet oaks, tulip trees? (I'm not sure what Valerie would feel about such flashy trees in the demesne. Perhaps it would be tactless to ask her.) Unfortunately none of these species from the east coast of North America find our summers hot enough to allow them to breed. This is a handicap: self-sown trees add a dash of spontaneity to a plantation. European oaks and beech are particularly good at seeding themselves in the wild, once they are protected from the chomping jaws of cattle. After a good acorn crop you can see regular lines of oak planted in the grass - planted by jays as their winter rations, and then somehow mislaid.

Of course most of the new parkland trees will have to be raised from seed in the nursery, on the far side of the walled garden. Then they will be transplanted to the demesne after two or three years - or as soon as they are tough enough for life in the wild. By a happy coincidence, this year is a bumper year for acorns in the Irish Midlands. I shall collect hundreds of brown and yellow acorns from our finest European oaks - especially from the Squire's Walking Stick and his fellow giants. I shall also collect seeds from various places in County Wicklow, known for the high quality of its oak trees. Most exciting will be the chance of collecting acorns from some of the ancient sessile oaks at Coolattin, near Shillelagh.

But I must go back twenty years to tell the story of myself and the Irish Tree Society and the struggle to save those 2,000 doomed trees which crowned the valley above the River Derry.

17

Coolattin: the Forlorn Hope

15 October 2013

It's twenty years since I first saw the wood at Coolattin, the last beleaguered outpost of Ireland's once celebrated oak woods. That spring, in May 1993, I stood on the narrow road which winds up from the village of Shillelagh and my heart sank. These two thousand ancient sessile oaks, crowning the valley above the River Derry ('oak river'), were apparently doomed. Yet they were the heirs of the great forest of Shillelagh, whose roots stretched far back into history and mythology. Shillelagh was once the Irish equivalent of Sherwood, complete with its own Robin Hoods and Maid Marians. It was not only a magnificent forest. Its oak planks were famous for their muscular strength. Once they had sailed the seven seas in the ships of many navies. And they still roofed some of the most elegant chapels and palaces of Europe, like Henry VIII's chapel at Windsor, Westminster Hall and the Stadt House in Holland. Now their ageing descendants were to be felled and turned into fence posts for motorways or kitchen cabinets or whatever the market demanded.

The struggle to save the ancient oaks at Coolattin had begun in the 1980s when there were still about ten thousand trees in the wood. In 1983 a company called Bridgefarm bought the remains of the Fitzwilliam estate in Wicklow: 1,230 acres of woodland, 570 acres of farmland and the Fitzwilliams' mansion. Two years later Bridgefarm applied to Wicklow County Council for planning permission to fell some of the oaks. Now the council had earlier been persuaded to put preservation orders on these trees. They were marvels of nature, unique in Ireland, a boon for the county. But there was a catch. Under the law, the council would have to pay compensation to the owners if they were denied permission to fell them. Anxious to save their rate-payers any undue expense, the council nimbly revoked the preservation orders. The government confirmed the wisdom of the council by giving Bridgefarm permission to fell the ancient oaks, provided they were replanted with suitable saplings. Soon the chainsaws got to work.

Next year, and the year after, Bridgefarm applied to fell more trees, and the nimble *pas de deux* between council and government was danced once more, to the raucous tune of the chainsaw. Each year the preservation orders were revoked, each year the wisdom of the council confirmed by a felling licence from the government. By 1987 Coolattin looked like a battlefield. Five-sixths of the ancient wood had been devastated, the trees carted off by the loggers, leaving a mere 164 acres untouched. But there at Tomnafinogue, in one small section of the wood, two thousand oaks were still standing.

By this time the raucous sound of the chainsaws at Coolattin had been heard far beyond County Wicklow. In the Dáil (the Irish Parliament) there was a new Fianna Fáil government. Deputies on both sides of the House talked of the Coolattin 'crisis', even of the Coolattin 'tragedy'. A government supporter, Dick Roche, described what he saw on a personal visit:

Anybody with an eye in his head could see that the owners of the wood have behaved in an extraordinarily cynical manner. They have not met their replanting obligations and have put in sceach [scrub] oak here and there. When one gets to the headlands the lines of oak disappear . . . The number of conifers replanted vastly outnumbers the . . . young oak.

But what was to be done? Deputies, shocked by the devastation at Coolattin, seemed numbed by the scale of potential compensation – IR£900,000 it was claimed. And what embarrassed members of both the main parties was that the government inspector had recently reported that Bridgefarm had done an excellent job: replanting was completed 'to a high standard'. So Bridgefarm had every right to a felling licence and the last two thousand trees were doomed.

At this point a saviour appeared, with masterly timing, out of the blue. It was

Charlie Haughey, who had just taken over as Taoiseach (Prime Minister) for the third time. His career had been pungent with scandal. People often talked of the bribes Haughey had taken, the lies he had told in the Dáil, the fashionable women he had seduced. He would brush aside these claims - or fix his enemies with the glare of a Medusa. Politically he seemed to lead a charmed life. On 21 March he landed at Coolattin in a helicopter. He was returning from Wexford, cock-a-hoop after his party's victory in the recent election. Here was the *deus ex machina* to the tune of an election ditty called 'Charlie's Song'. 'I've saved the wood,' he told the cheering crowds. But alas he hadn't done anything of the sort.

In private he told his astonished officials to refuse the felling licence to Bridgefarm. But the company had a right to it, they told their boss. The inspector had said the company had completed the replanting 'to a high standard'. Then get a new inspector, was Haughey's grim reply. (And I assume he gave his officials the Medusa glare to show he was serious.) The officials scuttled about to oblige him. A new inspector was sent to Coolattin whose report contradicted the first inspector's. A felling licence was duly refused. But all Haughey had done was to buy time - a quick fix for a few years' grace - before Bridgefarm put its house in order and reapplied for a felling licence. Accordingly the company reapplied early in 1993.

By now Haughey was powerless to help, even if he had wished to. His charmed life had finally evaporated. Too many ghosts, witnesses of past scandals in which he had played the central part, were pointing their bony fingers in his direction. He was hounded from office in January 1992, caught out at last by his former friends and current rivals. He had been lying all along about his part in the telephone-tapping of two troublesome journalists. (Later a government inquiry reported he had taken IR£8,000,000 in 'unethical payments', that is, in bribes, during his years as Taoiseach.) At any rate by the end of that year Bridgefarm had the licence for felling in their pocket. The first of the two thousand ancient oaks were duly numbered in red on their flanks and made ready for execution. Of course there was a certain amount of wringing of hands inside and outside the Dáil. But what could anyone do - with the shadow of that vast bill for compensation hanging over the ancient trees? To talk of rescuing the oaks was mere folly. There was nothing for it. The oaks were doomed.

It was at this late stage, in May 1993, that I myself, and the fledgling Irish Tree Society, became drawn into the struggle. Three years earlier I and a group of friends had founded the society. Our aim was to educate ourselves - and the Irish public, if we could reach them - about the importance of specimen trees. Our concern was not primarily with woods and forests. Nor did we see ourselves as a campaigning body, like Crann ('People for Trees') or An Taisce, the National Trust for Ireland. Our focus was on identifying individual trees - trees that were remarkable for their size or age or historic associations. Most people thought we were harmless enough (although some of our friends called us TITS). And in our first three years we had achieved something of value. We continued the Ireland-wide hunt for remarkable trees - trees of great size or age or inspiring associations - the hunt begun here many years before by the English tree guru, Alan Mitchell. Discovering and then listing an ancient oak or ash or beech or sycamore doesn't necessarily save it from the chainsaw - especially with a planning system that favours politicians more than trees. But listing a tree is a beginning. (In fact we have now listed over ten thousand specimen trees in 800 different species since we started work at the beginning of the 1990s. And we have saved at least some of those from the chainsaw.)

But back in May 1993 we were faced with those two thousand beleaguered oak trees crowning the valley at Coolattin. How on earth could we save them? This was the question I asked myself as I stood, with a sinking heart, on the narrow road facing the wood. The trees were exceptionally fine examples of sessile oak (*Quercus petraea*), the dominant species of native oak in this part of County Wicklow. The soil, deep sandy loam, was perfect for the species. Even more important, the wood had been carefully managed for at least three centuries. It was part of the far-flung estate of one of Britain's richest country magnates, the Earls Fitzwilliam, who once owned no less than 89,798 acres of County Wicklow, as well as farmland in two other counties in Ireland, and farms and coal mines scattered over half of England.

Were these oaks at Coolattin planted by the foresters employed by the Fitzwilliams? Or were they a last remnant of a vast natural oak forest - the forest at Shillelagh, the Irish Sherwood? No one could say for certain how the trees had originated. Probably many were self-sown and others raised from acorns collected in the wild. The main point was that the trees looked and indeed were magnificent - a unique genetic treasure house. In other parts of the country few oak woods had survived. Those that did survive, for example at Killarney, had gradually deteriorated (as I later found to my cost when planting my Millennium Wood with young oaks from Killarney). This was because, for generations, the best trees had been removed to build carts and houses and ships. The trees that remained were the scrubby ones nobody wanted - except people looking for firewood. At Coolattin and the other meticulously managed Fitzwilliam estates it happened the other way round. The

PREVIOUS PAGE: It may have a name like a Japanese motorbike. But what can beat its scarlet coat in autumn? *Acer palmatum* 'Osakasuki' in the Forest Walk in October.

ABOVE: Pumpkins in the Pumpkin House for a Halloween party. Left to right: my son-in-law, Alex, my grandson, Aidan, and other friends including Octavia. This was in 2012. Next year the party was a wash-out.

Short-lived moment of triumph. I had just struggled 3,500 feet up to the top of Mount Maenam on my second trip to Sikkim. What I didn't realize was that we would have to climb down in the dark through a dense forest – the home of bears and leopards.

LEFT: The gigantic golden Buddha at Ravangala, presented to the people of Sikkim by the government in Delhi. Was it to compensate Sikkim for the forced marriage with India in 1975?

ABOVE: A Himalayan peak in Sikkim photographed by the light of the full moon.

Bleeding canker killed this large horse chestnut by the front door. The rest of our horse chestnuts, like horse chestnuts all over Europe, may now be doomed.

OVERLEAF: Our champion silver fir (*Abies alba*) in the demesne near the Grand Lodge. I believe it lost its head in the Big Wind of 6–7 January 1839.

woods were managed as a long-term investment, producing timber when it was ripe for felling. But the best trees, the tallest and straightest and most vigorous, were kept for breeding. They would produce the tallest and straightest and most vigorous progeny. The poorest, the scrub, were thinned out early in the cycle. So the quality of the woods was progressively improved. And the trees didn't simply look fine. They made a fine amount of money for the Fitzwilliams. True, if you want to make money from planting oak, you must wait at least a century till the trunks are ready to be sawed into planks. But the Fitzwilliams could afford to wait. And they could afford to invest more money in the woods, as each forest plot was harvested, either by replanting with locally raised oaks, or by carefully exploiting the trees' ability to regenerate naturally.

In 1948 the owner of the estate, the 8th Earl Fitzwilliam, was killed in a plane crash. (His companion, who also died, was the recently widowed sister of John Kennedy, the future President of the USA.) For some years his own widow, the Countess, lived quietly at Coolattin. Then she died, and her daughter Juliet had to part with the estate to pay death duties. It was bought by a couple of Dublin speculators who sold it off piecemeal. Eventually they ran into difficulties and the woods at Coolattin were taken over by a Dublin bank – who sold it for a song to an Irish builder in Luton. And it was this man, who controlled Bridgefarm Company Ltd, who was now hell-bent on turning the trees into motorway fence-posts or kitchen cabinets or whatever the market demanded.

'Hell-bent' is strong language. But I was assured that the Irish builder in Luton was a tough customer: quite as hard as the cement in his breeze blocks. Furious at the delays – and the way he thought he had been cheated of his felling licence – he was no more in the mood for compromise than an angry bull. He had waited ten years and now he had the wretched licence. By November the first trees would be carted off by the loggers.

How on earth could anyone persuade this man to change his mind? Hitherto all hopes had been centred on local and national politicians. But both had proved, not for the first time, to be men of straw. When I went down to see the oaks, I talked to the joggers and ramblers and other activists who had led the ten-year campaign. It had been a grim struggle to persuade the Wicklow councillors to put preservation orders on the trees. They felt utterly let down. But what was to be done, now the oaks were already numbered in red paint, meaning they'd be first for the chop? They had no answer - except to talk of further protests. And there was a story that some hot-headed locals would resort to a modern version of the Fenian tactics used two centuries ago in the Land War. They would drive steel spikes into the threatened trees, in order to break the loggers' chainsaws.

When I returned from Wicklow, I admitted to the committee of the Irish Tree Society that I felt a great deal more depressed than when I had set out. To save these oaks was a forlorn hope. Violence was unacceptable. And it was too late for protests. The protesters, heroic as they were, had failed. The angry bull in Luton held all the cards. But there remained one slim chance. The angry bull was passionate about money. So we must somehow raise the huge sum needed to buy the trees off him.

Looking back on it all, twenty years later, I am amazed that no one on the committee said I was mad. How could a fledgling society, with only a couple of hundred members, raise the half a million pounds or so that would be needed? My answer: broaden the campaign and bring in other societies that also felt passionately about the environment. And this is what we did. Desmond FitzGerald, President of the Irish Georgian Society, came riding to the rescue with a sumptuous database of members. So did the committee of An Taisce, the National Trust for Ireland. In fact An Taisce, with delightful eighteenth-century offices, the Tailors Hall, deep in the crumbling heart of Dublin, gave us our launching pad.

It was from here we dispatched our desperate cries for help. Save a tree for a hundred pounds; save a branch for fifty; save a twig for a fiver. Our cries for help found ready ears. The cheques began to accumulate. By May we had raised IR£10,000, by early June IR£25,000. Two hundred fans made merry in our hall at a pop concert which raised IR£5,000. (The extraordinarily generous singer, who took no fee, was the famous Van Morrison, 'Van the Man'. Before I arranged the concert, I am ashamed to say I had never heard of him.) Two big-hearted tycoons contributed over IR£2,000. But most of our cheques came from ordinary people who loved trees. By late June we had raised IR£35,000 and the trees and branches and twigs were still drawing in the cheques. But was there an earthly chance we could raise half a million before November?

Early in July we held a crisis meeting of the friends I had roped in to form an emergency committee for the campaign. There were no passengers on this committee. In fact every one of its members has something absolutely vital to contribute. There was Desmond FitzGerald who had brought in his eager troop of Georgians. There was Liam O'Flanagan, treasurer of the Irish Tree Society and a former general manager of Coiltte, responsible for state forestry. There was John Wilson-Wright, farmer and forester whose wife Hilary came from near Shillelagh. There was John Boorman, the celebrated film director, who lives at Annamoe, among the noblest trees in Wicklow. And, most important of all, because of her contacts in very high places, John's friend and neighbour, Kathy Gilfillan. Our committee was a dream-team.

Our first aim was to buy time. We needed a few extra months to show we were serious fund-raisers. Message from the angry bull in Luton, by way of one of his henchmen: not a day's reprieve, not one. In fact it was worse than that. The angry bull was a master of PR. His henchmen leaked stories into the press warning people not to throw away their money contributing to our fund. The matter was closed: it was a 'done deal'. In desperation I flew over to Luton myself to try to calm the angry bull and explain he would make *more* money if he listened to us than he would if he chopped down the oaks. My visit was more thrilling than I expected. I found myself on a large building site with giant bulldozers weaving about among pools of congealing concrete. My guide told me his boss had refused to see me. The fellow added: 'You're not wanted here. If I were you, I'd scram. You know, there *could* be an accident . . .' I liked that Mafia touch. A concrete shroud and all that. But I suppose he was only joking.

Back in Dublin there was at last some good news. Liam O'Flanagan, our forestry expert, had been down to Coolattin to value the oaks. He discovered that the *net* value of the oaks was much less than we had believed. This was because of an odd twist in the planning laws. If you want to fell a tree (or trees) you have to agree to replant it, and normally there's a subsidy for the replanting. But if the tree has been subject to a preservation order, even one that failed to stick, the subsidy is refused. Oaks are notoriously expensive to replant and keep clean from weeds. Replanting the two thousand oaks at Coolattin could cost as much as IR£200,000. So Liam valued the trees at little more than half our previous estimate. The net value was a quarter of a million pounds.

The second bit of good news was that John Wilson-Wright happened to know someone who had leverage where we needed it most. This man, an estate agent, had once done a favour for the angry bull. He was now prepared to negotiate on our behalf. He would explain that we had already raised enough for a deposit on the deal. He would then put it bluntly to the fellow. Sell the trees to them. It will pay you much better than cutting them down. A few days later we got the angry bull's reply: yes, he would sell the trees – for a million. Of course this was only the first round. But the best deal we could extract from him was still double the new value Liam had put on the wood. We were back to our original estimate of half a million pounds.

July passed to August. I was beginning to panic. I heard the loggers were planning to hire extra men with chainsaws and tractors. Local opinion in Shillelagh and

Coolattin was bitterly divided. Many men were out of work and angry. Here was their chance of a job. And for God's sake, weren't these old trees long overdue for felling? The local action group did their best with peaceful protests, but had no new ideas for saving the trees. Still others waited in the shadows, Fenian-style, planning to spike the tractor tyres and impale the oaks themselves.

*   *   *

In desperation I turned to Kathy Gilfillan. I knew it was a tall order. But there was only one chance of raising the enormous sum needed. We would have to take our begging bowl to Irish industry. First we needed an assurance from the government that they were now on our side – and the side of the trees. After ten years of feeding the angry bull with felling licences, the government must turn its policy on its head. They must support our campaign by offering to double the money, pound for pound, that we raised from industry. Perhaps I was somewhat hysterical. Kathy remained calm. She would put it to Padraig O'hUiginn, Secretary to the Department of the Taoiseach and the most powerful civil servant in the country – a man who could work miracles.

She rang me a couple of days later with two questions. Would the owner sell? If so, what was his price? I gave her the answers. She seemed pleased. She rang me again next day. Padraig wanted me to write on a single sheet of paper the case for saving the oaks. Two days later she rang me again.

'Padraig says that's fine.'

I gasped at the news. 'You mean they're going to double the money we raise from industry?'

'Oh no. They're going to buy the wood. They'll take our money as a deposit.'

Sometimes victory is as hard to digest as defeat. I felt as dazed as someone who has won a Nobel Prize. Of course the feeling was wonderful. Saving the oaks was no longer a forlorn hope. Against all the odds we had won, thanks to Kathy and all our team. And most of all it was thanks to Padraig.

Somehow he had persuaded the new Taoiseach, Albert Reynolds, to upend his government's policy and make a special case for Coolattin. I can imagine the arguments. The Green Party candidate for the European election was exploiting the issue. Wouldn't it be sensible to give his rival, the Fianna Fail candidate, a bit of a leg-up? Anyway what was half a million pounds to a government that spent fifteen *billion* a year? But I'm talking rubbish. I know that Padraig had worked a miracle.

18

Fireworks

31 October 2013

Tonight is the night of the wandering spirits and the Lost Souls, the night of Halloween. My teenage grandchildren - Aidan and Ciaran and Gabriel - will cover their faces with demonic masks, according to the sensible Irish custom, to hide their identity from evil spirits. As for myself, I'll do my best to defend myself from the undead with turnips and pumpkins. In fact this is the night when Antoine's masterpiece, the oak-hewn hut in the arboretum, deserves to be called the Pumpkin House rather than the Womb with a View. Six pairs of pumpkin eyes, lit by candles, will glare into the darkness in front of us: quite hideous enough, I'll assure my grandchildren, to scare away any normal wandering spirits.

Originally I had planned a short ceremony to precede the party in the Pumpkin House. I would take my guests to see the glories of the arboretum before darkness fell. This was to be the climax of my Year of the Trees: flaming maples - scarlet and orange and crimson - girdling the grass in the clearing like a ring of fire. But this year the ring of fire looks more like a damp squib.

Part of the trouble is that last Sunday we were attacked by the first storm of the season: a vicious, rain-sodden blast from the north-west. Even the young trees in my arboretum, sheltered by ancient beeches and by the rambling walls of the East

Wing, are not immune to an attack of this kind. Young trees, still a hearty green, were stripped naked by the storm. They had no chance of slowly changing colour, while the green pigment was progressively withdrawn from their leaves, exposing the red and yellow pigments.

Normally the leaves would have plenty of time to perform this theatrical change of costumes. Chlorophyll, the green pigment, dominates the leaf throughout the growing season. This is the leaf's outer dress. It feeds the plant with sugars, by mixing sunlight with water and carbon dioxide, and feeds us with the oxygen we breathe. (The vital process, which keeps us all ticking, has the unromantic name of photosynthesis.) But inside the leaf, hidden by the chlorophyll during spring and summer, are more exotic pigments: orange-yellow carotenoid and red and purple anthocyanin. As the days shorten and the earth cools, the supply of chlorophyll begins to fail. At the same time, bright days and cool nights intensify the production of anthocyanin. And now the inner dress is slowly revealed, giving us who live in the temperate world our dramatic autumn colours.

*   *   *

To return to last Sunday's storm, some of the more fragile trees lost whole branches. But I mustn't grumble. We needed the rain. The upper pond, fed by hidden springs, was begging to be topped up. Soon the pump could air-lock, and our five hundred dairy cows start to bellow for water.

Anyway, storm or no storm, I don't think this would have been a dazzling year of autumn colour here at Tullynally - at least in the arboretum. I had thought it would be easy enough to create these pyrotechnics. All I need do was to choose the species of trees which the experts tell us will turn orange or red or purple before their leaves fell. I was only too naïve. Ornamental trees are not like a gas ring that you can turn on and off. You have got to discover which particular species or variety of tree colours best in your own soil and climate - and it may take half a lifetime to find the answers.

In the arboretum I've had a patchy kind of success this year: a series of flickering flames rather than a ring of fire. The richest flame - the orange-red of a steel furnace - is provided by a pushy, new American hybrid (*Acer x freemanii*), which I planted six years ago. It's a stunning tree, a hybrid maple with the best qualities of both its parents without any of the bad ones. (How many of us can claim that for ourselves?) It has the athletic vigour of its mother, the silver maple (*Acer saccharinum*), and the Red Indian-like colours of its father, the red maple (*Acer rubrum*). Mine rose like a firework, exploding in orange and magenta and gold. But I had no idea of how magnificent it would look. So I planted it absurdly far from the main clearing, half hidden by some scrawny sycamores. I made the same mistake with a pair of liquidambars which glow with all the colours of the rainbow, including scarlet, green and blue. They are glowing away more or less invisibly, buried behind a patch of self-sown beech.

The maples that I chose to be centre stage in that clearing are largely Japanese maples. They squat in a semicircle: green and yellow and orange against the dark green of different kinds of holly. I think the contrast works rather well. About half of the hollies are fast-growing hybrids, mongrels if you like, called *Ilex x altaclerensis* as they were originally bred at Highclere (the home of the Lord Carnarvon who discovered the tomb of Tutankhamun). These are hybrids of the European holly crossed with the Madeira holly, a happy combination if you want Brobdingnag leaves and berries. The native hollies (*Ilex aquifolium* varieties) are also fairly exotic, some as spiky as hedgehogs; others look as if splashed with custard or something worse. (These are not Valerie's favourites.) Most of them are female and very fertile, it appears, as they are already producing sumptuous crops of red and yellow berries.

But in choosing my Japanese maples from the hundreds of varieties now available in the market, I made a beginner's mistake. What I wanted was trees that would turn scarlet and orange - in effect burst into flame in October. But I only chose two Japanese maples of this kind out of the dozen I planted: one orange-red called 'Osakasuki'(the one with a name like a Japanese motorbike), the other tomato-red, called 'Bloodgood'. Both will be magnificent, I'm sure, in days to come. Meanwhile they have remained rather small - in fact no larger than a decent-sized cabbage. The Japanese maples that have grown best have turned butter-yellow, not red or orange this autumn. Very beautiful they look, as the delicate five-lobed or seven-lobed leaves fade to an elegant bronze. But why didn't I plant two of these and ten of a more vigorous scarlet kind? I suppose I was fumbling and groping when I designed the arboretum. And now I must pay the price of my fumbling - unless other species of scarlet and orange maples can fill the gap.

What I need is bigger tree-maples to fill the gap. By October next year I shall need to plant half a dozen more Freeman hybrids and half a dozen red maples - that is, *Acer rubrum*, the rainbow-coloured mother tree of the Freeman. Both these maples will grow much faster than any of the Japanese maples, although it will be a year or two before they are big enough to set the arboretum ablaze.

1 November 2013

I was wrong about the Halloween party being a damp squib. It was much worse – a washout. The rain poured down and put out the candles inside the turnips and pumpkins. So it was not just the wandering spirits and the souls of the dead that were lost. My guests, too, were lost. Eventually the more fortunate members of the party fought their way out of the mud and the darkness and spotted the prosecco in the conservatory. Luckily the teenagers, wearing the demonic masks, had vanished before the party began. They were off to Dublin, heading for what they said, no doubt correctly, if somewhat tactlessly, would be 'a much better party'.

2 November 2013

The rain has stopped at last and I have been able to make a tour of the other parts of the garden, especially the pleasure ground. I must say I'm surprised and delighted. Although there's no set piece designed for the autumn, there are some stunning autumn colours after all.

The upper pond in the pleasure ground is champagne-clear after the rain. On one side of its waters is the pair of Boston-Chinese ginkgos which I grew from seed a decade ago. (They're brothers or sisters to the pair planted for my older twin grandchildren in the arboretum.) Caught in the low sun at ten in the morning, they make a dazzling picture, their butterfly-winged leaves the yellow of a mandarin's coat. Crucial to the effect is their background. Behind them, on the other side of the pond, I planted two trees with an astonishing autumn colour: an American swamp cypress (*Taxodium distichum*) and a Chinese dawn redwood (*Metasequoia glyptostroboides*). Both go as red as a fox's brush before the leaves fall. I planted them thirty years ago, knowing little or nothing about them. (Although I remember going to Kew Gardens in October and being stunned by the hundred-year-old swamp cypresses on the island.) Behind them is a tulip tree going up like a rocket, and now its strangely sculpted leaves are coloured green and gold. The combination – and contrast – of these three makes a dramatic setting for the pair of ginkgos. I wish I could pretend that was my intention all along.

In the rest of the pleasure ground there are splashes of yellow and gold supplied mainly by young oak and a large copper beech. But I don't think I gave any thought to autumn colour when I planted these trees. At best it might be a bonus. That's what I would have said. But I expect I was thinking more of spring and summer when I chose their places – with one exception.

Thirty years ago I planted three Japanese maples, of the variety called 'Osakasuki', which I was told would turn a brilliant scarlet in autumn even if they never saw the sun. (It was these three maples that later inspired me to plant the 'Osakasuki' up in the arboretum.) They were my first love in the world of trees. They grew fast and sturdy although the soil was stony. Their scarlet dress in autumn defied description. They were brighter than a pillar-box or a huntsman's coat. All I can say is that I went to Kyoto in central Japan to savour the sight of the famous maples in autumn. None of them seemed to me to be a patch on my three 'Osakasuki'. And when two of them were accidentally poisoned – sprayed with a lethal herbicide – it made the survivor even more precious to me. Today this magnificent tree glows like a scarlet lantern under the ancient yew tree at the eastern end of the pleasure ground.

But tomorrow I'm off to Gloucestershire to see the English equivalent of Kyoto in autumn: the arboretum created by the Holfords at Westonbirt and now in the care of the Forestry Commission. How do they create and manage their own ring of fire? By next week I should have the answer to that secret.

Westonbirt, 4 November 2013

'Why these enormous crowds?' I asked the man at the gate. 'Is there a pop concert?' He seemed to think it a silly question. 'Like *you*, they're here to see the colours.' I should have guessed. He told me that every autumn, alerted by the local TV station, people flock from all over the Cotswolds and beyond to see Westonbirt's maples. I told him I was afraid I would be a bit late for the performance, which normally hits its peak in mid-October. Fortunately it turned out that the maples had been in no hurry to perform this year. They were now running a fortnight late. I set off eagerly along the main trail through the arboretum, following the muddy tracks of hundreds of maple addicts. And there, centre stage, was the famous 'Maple Glade' – or rather two maple glades, the original one planted by the founding father, Robert Holford, in about 1870, the second planted about ninety years later by the Forestry Commission.

As the heir to a million-pound fortune, Robert Holford could indulge his taste for anything that caught his fancy. He could fill his picture gallery with Old Masters like Rembrandt and Titian and Tintoretto. He could also afford to create a picture gallery of new trees planted at Westonbirt. Over the years his collection came to include hundreds of exotic maples from all over the world. But for his original maple glade he concentrated on one particular species: the Japanese maple, *Acer palmatum*, and its numerous varieties. The species was still fairly new to England, although the first record of its introduction dates from 1820. To combine these Japanese maples in a theatrical composition he chose a long, irregular clearing in a shelter belt he had planted thirty years earlier. This shelter belt was (and still is) a subtle mixture of deciduous and evergreen trees: in autumn the russet-coloured larch contrast with the inky-green of the Douglas firs and the old-gold of the common oaks. Beneath them was a solemn evergreen tapestry of yews and hollies. And against this background was the set piece, the grand firework display of a hundred dazzling Japanese maples.

Sad to say, few of those originals survive. A hundred and forty years is two lifetimes for most small trees, even those that have had every advantage. I think I saw about twenty survivors that afternoon, twisting and coiling their limbs like giant green pythons. Most of their flaming leaves had fallen, and their labels have long gone. But I thought I could recognise some of my favourites, including *Acer palmatum atropurpureum*, a variety that must have delighted the Victorians. Its sumptuous purple would have been a good match for a cardinal's vestments in Holy Week.

Next door I found the new maple glade and here a hundred trees were trying to upstage their neighbours. In forty years some had grown to a prodigious size: at least 40 feet high. Others were content to swagger like peacocks. There was a tree the colour of honey, and another like a marmalade cat. The number of reds astonished me: from sealing-wax scarlet to the colour of molten lava. The yellows were also stunning: chrome-yellow, straw-yellow, canary-yellow, banana-yellow, jaundice-yellow. The list was endless, like the menu at a great banquet. It was all a bit too rich for my stomach. Of course I am talking nonsense. I was green with envy.

Royal Botanic Gardens, Kew, 5 November 2013

Back in London in time for the night of the bonfires, I couldn't resist a snatched visit to Kew Gardens that afternoon. It was at Kew that I had first seen the rainbow of autumn colours on the island in the lake, the rainbow created by a grove of American swamp cypresses planted in the nineteenth century. Now, thirty years after my first visit, they had reached perfection: leaping, orange, green and red, into the pale blue sky, as their reflection dived into the dark blue waters of the lake below. Nearby, a tree like a torch illuminated the white pillars of the Greek temple built by Sir William Chambers. This was another astonishing American species, *Cotinus obovatus*, the Chittamwood or American smoke tree. In Britain it's rare to find it growing as a tree, rather than an ungainly bush, and I suspect this is the finest example in western Europe. It gave us a dazzling performance that afternoon, a Catherine wheel of canary-coloured carotenoids, and purple anthocyanins, as it was caught and held by the November sun.

That night I watched the rockets arch across London, to celebrate the hanging of the unfortunate Guy Fawkes and the defeat of the Gunpowder Plot. But it was all a bit of an anti-climax after the autumn fireworks at Westonbirt and Kew – and my own flickering flames at Tullynally.

19

The Trees That Lost Their Heads

8 November 2013

'Awe-inspiring,' said my beautiful, grey-eyed garden consultant, Octavia, as we carried our long tape measure across the spongy grass of the upper demesne. 'You could almost call it Jurassic.' Octavia was right, as she usually is. In the harsh November sunshine the bloated silver trunk and branches of our tallest tree, a champion silver fir (*Abies alba*), seemed strangely menacing. About 170 years ago it lost its head, torn from its body 60 feet from the ground. The head re-grew. This is a trick that a silver fir finds easy to perform. It turns the upper branches into trunks. But our tree was now the shape of a gigantic, six-trunked candelabra dominating the landscape by the north-east wall of the demesne.

I say, 'about 170 years ago'. In fact I think I know the exact date the silver fir was decapitated: the night of 6–7 January 1839. This was the famous (or infamous) Night of the Big Wind, the most ferocious hurricane in modern Irish history. Forty-two ships foundered at sea that night, drowning most of their crews. All over Ireland the wretched mud-and-thatch cabins were blown down or torn to pieces, and hundreds of poor people were killed by fires or falling debris. Lord Castlemaine, owner of

Moydrum Castle, shared the fate of some of his tenants. In attempting to close a window he was blown off his feet and (according to the local press) 'instantly expired'.

Next morning Dublin looked like a city sacked by the enemy; a quarter of the houses in north Dublin were in ruins. Trees were uprooted by the million and some demesnes were swept clean, as if they had never been planted. Other demesnes looked like battlefields. And the market for timber had gone, gone with the wind. Here at Tullynally, as we know from James Fraser's report on our woodlands in 1862, smashed trees were still lying where they had fallen on that terrible night twenty-three years earlier.

Miraculously, what James Fraser called 'the great silver fir' was still standing upright in the north-east part of the demesne. This must be the menacing, six-trunked champion standing there today. At a height of 137 feet (42 metres) from the ground, its six spiky pinnacles make it by far our tallest tree – and the second tallest common silver fir in the Republic. It's also a champion for girth. When it was last measured, back in 2007, it was only a whisker short of 20 feet round the belly, measured at 5 feet from the ground. Today, as Octavia and I were delighted to confirm with our tape measure, its girth is 20 feet, 4.5 inches. And with so many bloated trunks its volume must be prodigious.

No one knows when silver firs were first introduced into Ireland. I expect that packets of seeds of this European species were brought over via Britain sometime early in the seventeenth century. By nature it's a tree of the mountains, of the icy crags and canyons of the Alps and Pyrenees. But it took to the pastures and woodlands of western Europe like a duck to water. You can imagine the gusto with which the local country gentlemen received the pushy new immigrant. Britain and Ireland had only an odd trio of native conifers: the pink-barked Scots pine (by nature confined to the Highlands of Scotland), the blue-berried juniper (but rarely more than a bush) and the bushy, slow-growing, red-berried yew. Suddenly British and Irish planters had a choice of three dazzling new European conifers: deciduous larch, common spruce, and silver fir. All three would soon outstrip the Scots pine in height and girth, and growing good timber for planking became money for jam. But the giant of the athletic newcomers was the silver fir. By the end of the eighteenth century the European silver fir had overtaken its rivals and its spiky silhouette had begun to dominate the skyline. It was not, I must admit, as beautiful as the Scots pine, although the bloated silver bark gave it a certain brutal charm. What gave it a supreme advantage was its ability to survive exposed to the wind and rain above the canopy of other trees - even in the wettest and windiest parts of our islands. However its supremacy was to be short-lived

In 1823 a young gardener, originally an apprentice at Scone Palace, Lord Mansfield's country house near Perth, was commissioned to set sail for America to hunt for exotic new trees. He was David Douglas, who became, in his short life, the most daring and successful of all British plant hunters. It was Douglas whose discoveries changed for ever the composition - and appearance - of our commercial woodlands. Among the hundreds of North American trees and shrubs he introduced were a pair of gigantic conifers that he found on the Pacific side of the Rockies: the Douglas fir that bears his name, and the Sitka spruce. Together these two astonishingly fast-growing species now provide Britain and Ireland with most of its home-grown timber. A third introduction by Douglas, the American silver fir or grand fir (*Abies grandis*), rivalled the other two as a species for ornamental planting, but its timber was too soft to make good planks.

The eclipse of the European silver firs (*Abies alba*), trees like the giant in my demesne, was now accelerated by a malevolent greenfly, *Adelges nuslinii*, which attacked the young plants. By the early 1900s the unfortunate tree had passed out of fashion, even in Scotland and Ireland where it had been most welcomed. Other trees now dominated the skyline, all from the Pacific side of the Rockies in North America: Douglas's three giants, and two redwoods that emerged after his untimely death (see Chapter 9), the coast redwood and the giant sequoia (alias the Sierra redwood or Wellingtonia). These five new species tend to grow taller than any hardwood or softwood, native or introduced, growing in Britain. They also present a more striking silhouette than the spiky European silver fir when they puncture the canopy of smaller trees. At its best a giant sequoia can make a perfect green cone, turning up its nose at the wind. By contrast a European silver fir, emerging from the canopy, looks as tattered as an old lavatory brush.

Which of these five new species has won the race to be tallest tree in Britain or Ireland? You would expect the coast redwood (*Sequoia sempervirens*) to be the easy winner. Back in north-west California, in the fog-bound Coastal range, there are whole forests of trees more than 300 feet high. The tallest tree in the world, a hidden giant 374 feet tall, comes from this Brobdingnag zone. But over in Europe, even in the rain-battered hills of Scotland which suit it best, the species cannot keep up with its four compatriots. Once it breaks out of the canopy it begins to struggle, its leading shoots fighting the wind. In fact the tallest coast redwood in Britain, as far as we know, is a tree at Bodnant in Wales - a mere 160 feet tall, still 10 feet short of the tallest known European silver fir. No doubt it will overtake this older tree in due course. Meanwhile the giant sequoia has also dropped behind in the race. The tallest known, at Blair Castle in Scotland, is a mere 174 feet high. Compare its height with that of the three other contenders, the gigantic fruit of David Douglas's discoveries. They are all over 190 feet and the race is still wide open.

Twenty years ago I criss-crossed Britain and Ireland on the trail of trees that would feature in my book, *Meetings with Remarkable Trees*. At that time I read in Alan Mitchell's own pioneering book, *Trees of Britain and Northern Europe* (reprinted in 1988) that our three tallest trees yet discovered were all in Scotland. In a February snowstorm I set off to inspect them. Two were elegant Douglas firs - one a most delightful tree overlooking the folly at the Hermitage near Dunkeld, the other hidden in a wood further north at Moniack near Inverness - and the third was a spiky grand fir at Ardkinglas near Lough Fyne. All three were then uncannily equal in height, that is, 61 metres, which is a whisker more than 200 feet.

To which goddess of a tree should I award the prize of being illustrated in my book? I knew what Paris must have felt when he was given the apple and told to choose between Athena, Juno and Venus. But I need not have worried. New information reached me about two of these contenders. The Douglas fir at Moniack was two feet less than its supporters claimed. And when I reached the grand fir at Ardkinglas I found a hostile blast from Lough Fyne had stripped the top six feet from its spiky top. So it was the elegant Douglas fir at the Hermitage that received my apple, so to speak - and was illustrated twice in my book.

Twenty years have passed and once again one has to make a choice. But now, strange to relate, the roles are reversed. With that mysterious gift for reinventing itself (displayed by my own silver fir at Tullynally) the grand fir at Ardkinglas had apparently regrown its head after two separate storms. In April 2010 a team of intrepid tree surgeons climbed to its new summit and reported its height to be 64.5 metres - 211 feet and 7 inches. The Douglas fir at the Hermitage was re-measured and relegated to third place. It was found to be 61.3 metres - a mere 201 feet and 1 inch. (But I believe that one of the reasons for its humiliation was the way it was now penalised for growing on sloping ground. Under American rules it would be reckoned to be about 206 feet tall.) The Douglas fir at Moniack was judged to have grown to 62 metres - 203 feet 5 inches. So the Moniack fir pipped the Hermitage fir for second place. Finally, the third of Douglas's new introductions, the Sitka spruce, had reached fourth place. The tree at Blair Castle, north of Perth, was reckoned to be 59 metres tall – 193 feet 7 inches.

Did the bloated brute of a grand fir deserve to be judged the winner – instead of one of the elegant Douglas firs? I couldn't make up my mind. So last April I decided to go back to Ardkinglas to see the brute for myself. Perhaps it had already been decapitated once again. I would soon know.

In the event I realised I had misjudged the grand fir at Ardkinglas. It could hardly be called handsome. Old silver firs are too grotesque, too primeval for that. But I warmed to its courage and stoicism. Most trees would have succumbed long before to that punishing wind from Lough Fyne. The great-hearted grand fir had proved irrepressible. It was a worthy winner.

Nearby, in a more sheltered part of the same garden, was another famous silver fir – a European silver fir planted at least a century earlier. I had proudly illustrated it in my first tree book. At one time it must have been the tallest tree in the garden, and was then overtaken by what seemed like an upstart, the young grand fir. But its shape is extraordinary. Like my own silver fir in the demesne, it lost its head – and then grew another. There's a local tradition that the beheading was no accident: during the 1745 rebellion – the second abortive Jacobite rising in Scotland – 'Butcher' Cumberland's troops are supposed to have cut off its head as a warning to traitors. Unlike my own silver fir, decapitated 60 feet up (or the grand fir decapitated 200 feet up), the tree lost its head only a few feet from the ground. The result is a vast candelabra rising from a stumpy bole, a Jurassic monster indeed. But, like the grand fir, it has proved irrepressible. According to the Tree Register, it's a national champion for girth. In fact no other silver fir has ever dared to challenge the size of its belly – now over 30 feet in circumference, measured just below its six monstrous trunks. It's possible this is Britain's biggest conifer, calculated by volume. But no one has yet been able to do the sums.

To return to the national champions for height, I consulted Owen Johnson to see how he views the race. Owen is the man who succeeded Alan Mitchell as the collector and adjudicator of national champions – now numbering about 6,000 trees, in 3,100 species and varieties, scattered over hill and dale. In his inspiring new book, *Champion Trees in Britain and Ireland: The Tree Register Handbook* (2011), Owen tells us that the race to be the tallest tree is by no means over, and Scotland may soon lose it.

He explains that *c.*1919 the Forestry Commission planted several remarkable stands of Douglas fir and grand fir in the rain-soaked hills of Snowdonia, in north

Wales. By 2005 the best trees of both species in these plantations had topped 60 metres (197 feet) and are still at full gallop, so to speak. These late-starting Welsh contenders 'seem likely within a few more years', according to Owen, 'to provide all of our tallest trees'.

*   *   *

'Enough of national champions,' I said to Octavia as we carried our tape measure back through the grass from the bloated silver fir to the road. 'There are more interesting kinds of trees.'

'Do I detect a touch of sour grapes?' Octavia was winding me up: our silver fir is our *only* Irish champion, and none of our trees feature in Owen's rolls of honour, the lists of champions in both islands. But I'm sure Octavia knew what I meant. Sheer size, by itself, can be dull enough. Bigger is not always better or more inspiring, let alone more elegant. What excites me most of all about trees are their personalities and their personal histories. It was this that I tried to make the main theme of my last four books, starting with *Meetings*.

'Let's look at some of your smaller silver firs,' said Octavia soothingly. We turned down through the pleasure ground, past the loud-mouthed family of mallards, into the broken shade of the Forest Walk. Beyond the pagoda garden, where the soil's too thin and limy for comfort, conditions begin to improve. You can see there's a healthier green to the canopy of the Norway spruce on the right of the path. Like most conifers, they resent lime at their feet – at least if it's near the surface. But down here there's a deep seam of acid peat which must be the remains of an ancient lake. It's here that my great-grandfather very sensibly planted his line of Caucasian silver firs.

Alan Mitchell once pointed out that, oddly enough, if Europe produced a good tree, the Caucasus could produce a better one. I know Alan's rule doesn't work for every species. But it certainly works for half a dozen, like ash, lime, beech and spruce – and above all the silver fir. Although it may not ever rival the European silver fir in size, the Caucasian fir (*Abies nordmanniana*) appears to have every other advantage. For a start, the saplings don't attract the dreaded aphid, *Adelges nuslinii*, which munches up their European cousins. The foliage is also much more decorative, as the needles are thicker and less like a comb; underneath they are more richly embossed with silver. (In fact the species is now overtaking the European spruce as the most popular kind of Christmas tree. This is not only because the foliage is more sumptuous. It also holds its needles longer in over-heated rooms.) Best of all, the tree keeps its looks longer and is generally more shapely in old age (as we all should like to be). To the best of my knowledge its head is never blown off – or reduced to the shape of a lavatory brush.

My great-grandfather's line of five Caucasian silver firs begins where the soil is deep, acid peat and most welcoming. I believe the trees were planted soon after 1860, when he inherited the family estate. This would make him one of the first people to introduce the species to Ireland; it had only reached Britain in 1848. William Lygon Pakenham, the 4th Earl, had found the estate 'much overgrown' when he succeeded his elder brother, the 3rd Earl. But it was not only the legacy of the Night of the Big Wind whose wreckage still needed removing from the demesne. His elder brother, 'Fluffy', was a black sheep, sacked from Winchester, apparently after an affair with one of the boys; he then fell into bad company in London, caught venereal disease and died unmarried in a hotel in Charing Cross, leaving £500 to his mistress and an unpaid bill for £2,000 owing to his London doctor.

Poor Fluffy. He had no time (or capacity) for planting trees. But William Lygon was a soldier by profession, more than anxious to do what the family expected of him. He had already fought in two major wars: against the sepoys in the Indian Mutiny of 1857, and against the Russians in the Crimean War of 1853-6. (He was promoted Deputy Adjutant-General on Lord Raglan's staff.) Now he planted trees with both good taste and military efficiency. We have his planting list for the 1860s, which includes many recent introductions, like the tender Himalayan cypress (*C. torulosa*) and the tough North American red cedar (*Chamaecyparis lawsoniana*). But the Caucasian firs are the most prominent feature. I'm sure the irony didn't escape him: that his best trees were Russians.

These Caucasian firs now dominate the clearing by the Gothic hut, the 'Gingerbread House' built by Antoine. Pushy young Sitka spruce, and even pushier grand firs, are waiting their chance. But the Caucasian firs are still in their prime and could boss them around for another hundred years. Octavia was lyrical in her praises of the tallest of them, which I'm sure is over 100 feet high. Its sparkling foliage, stamped with twin silver bars under the needles, encloses its trunk like a cloak. Its manly head defies the gales of winter. And every spring its male cones, proof of its potency, illuminate its ivy-green foliage with scarlet flowers.

Octavia, you're right as usual. It's far too elegant to be a champion.

* * *

Tomorrow I shall be setting off for a new expedition.

Below the line of the Caucasian firs and the pushy young Sitka spruce and grand firs, the peaty soil is perfect for rhododendrons. This was once an outlier of Lough Derravaragh, but in the twelve thousand years since the end of the last ice age, rushes and alders invaded the lake. So lake became marsh and marsh became peat-bog. All my happiest rhododendrons grow here. But this peaty hollow is a natural frost pocket – and a death-trap for the more delicate species.

One tree rhododendron, however, that can brave the iciest winter is a species that Joseph Hooker discovered in Sikkim and named after his friend, Dr Hugh Falconer. This was a plant whose seeds I hoped to collect last year when I explored Sikkim in Hooker's footsteps. I found the plant but not its seeds. Tomorrow I return to Sikkim for a second attempt.

20

Hunting for Dr Falconer's Rhodo

25 November 2013

A fortnight ago I found myself in Sikkim for the second time.

Almost exactly a year before I had stood panting on the stony crescent of Mount Tonglu, on the south-west side of the Sikkim Himalaya, 10,000 feet above sea level. Far below us – more than 4,000 feet, I think – unfolded a skein of green, wooded valleys leading up to the blue ridge splattered with the tin roofs of Darjeeling. Ten thousand feet above sea level! And the air so thin that the lethal profile of my obsession, the killer-goddess, 28,000-foot Kanchenjunga, seemed hardly further than the next hill (she was actually more than 45 miles to the north). And even 29,000-foot Everest poked up his nose, a small, smudgy triangle of snow 120 miles to the north-west, where the southern rim of the great Tibetan plateau meets the central flanks of the Himalayas.

My quest, as I explained in Chapter 1, was only partly successful. I had gathered about a dozen packets of seeds, representing about twenty species of trees and other plants. Most exciting were the three hundred scarlet seeds from the giant white magnolia, *M. campbellii alba*, which Joseph Hooker had named after his long-suffering companion, Archibald Campbell – the British agent arrested with Hooker in 1849 after Hooker had ridden recklessly (and illegally) into Tibet.

I had found Dr Falconer's rhodo near the summit of Tonglu. It was a grizzly bear of a tree. You couldn't miss the authentic cinnamon-coloured bark and the enormous, bright green leaves, shiny and deep-veined above, rusty and felted below. But the bear had no cubs - I mean, there were no seed-pods on the tree. At the time I thought it would be easy to find other examples of Dr Falconer's rhodo in northern or eastern Sikkim. The species is supposed to be common enough at high altitudes. But in the event I failed to collect seeds last year from any of the grizzly specimens we saw. There was only one solution to the search for Dr Falconer's rhodo. I must return to Sikkim.

Valerie was unenthusiastic, to say the least. Of course she would not dream of going herself. But why would a second visit succeed when the first had failed? Anyway, I would miss her seventy-fourth birthday.

I promised to bring her back something wonderful from the wilds - a silk sari or even a Tibetan god. And this is how I found myself, less than a fortnight ago, back in Sikkim, back in my old Himalayan hunting grounds.

*　*　*

At first I felt rather dazed. Was this all a delightful dream: to be retracing my steps, with many of the same companions, in search of the same mysterious giants which had eluded me a year earlier? Or was it something that I believe is common among octogenarians (I was eighty in August): a harmless delusion about one's whereabouts that would evaporate soon enough? My friends told me I had nothing to worry about. The second Sikkim expedition would break exciting new ground. I was a devoted fan of Joseph Hooker. And I still had plenty of mountains to climb in the footsteps of the great man. One of my main targets was Mount Maenam, near Ravangala in central Sikkim. Hooker climbed it shortly before his ill-omened foray into Tibet. The summit was a little higher than Tonglu's: about 10,500 feet. We would find the climb easy enough, a mere three or four hours' easy walk - so Tashi, our soft-spoken Nepalese guide, assured me. The rewards should be spectacular: huge magnolias and maples, both named by Hooker after Archibald Campbell, and (for me the ultimate prize) that elusive giant, Dr Falconer's rhodo.

We reached Ravangala, in the valley below Mount Maenam, early on the morning of 12 November. (I could hardly forget the date. It was the day before Valerie's seventy-fourth birthday.) There were a dozen in the party - four muscular gardeners, several tree hunters (like me) and other enthusiasts. At eighty, I was much the oldest -

fifteen years older than the next oldest. (The thirteenth member of the team, only six years my junior, had prudently decided to spend the day in the valley.) The weather remained calm, the sky blue. we wore trekking boots, but it was too hot for anoraks, and most of us had stripped to our shirtsleeves. The air was champagne-clear all the way to the horizon, dominated, as usual, by the jagged profile of Kanchenjunga.

Seen through field glasses from Ravangala, the climb didn't look too alarming. True, it would not be as straightforward as the ascent of Mount Tonglu the previous year. Tonglu is the airy magnet for thousands of Buddhist pilgrims who come every year at festival time to worship on the summit. A broad stony path, marked with red, white and green prayer flags and a series of small whitewashed shrines, leads you up the whole way. Most of the mountain is open to the sky, with flights of granite steps cut into the steepest parts. By contrast, Mount Maenam looked almost trackless. What happened to the pilgrims, I wondered. They'd certainly have to fight their way through that dense green forest which clothed the mountain almost to the summit. Our guides explained that recently the path has become overgrown as the mountain has been designated a wildlife sanctuary by the government, a sort of Noah's ark for trees and other plants – with black bears and snow leopards to go with them. Bears and leopards? I didn't like the sound of that. 'Don't give it another thought,' said Tashi. 'The bears and leopards are not aggressive. Anyway, they only come out in the dark.' And we would be safely home, of course, long before darkness fell.

Ravangala is no more beautiful than most Sikkimese towns in these green, Alpine-like valleys below the Himalayas. It's a jumble of tin roofs and wooden shacks and half-built concrete shops and offices. Many buildings look as if they will hardly survive the next earthquake and its accompanying landsides. (In September 2011, an earthquake measuring 6.9 on the Richter scale struck North Sikkim. The main roads were blocked for days and hundreds were injured, and about sixty died before help could reach them.) But Ravangala escaped that earthquake and has become a place with one very remarkable jewel in its crown. Ten years ago the central government in Delhi was eager to be generous to Sikkim. They had snuffed out Sikkim's independence in a controversial referendum in 1975. Now they decided to give the state a giant new statue of Buddha. The statue, 100 feet high and weighing at least 5,000 tons, is entirely encased in gold plate. It straddles a vast amphitheatre just outside Ravangala. And this, I assume, is another reason (apart from the bears and the leopards) why the path to Mount Maenam is now overgrown. Pilgrims have no need these days to make the ascent to the small shrine on the mountain. Easier to pray to the giant new golden Buddha in the valley.

Our own ascent was not easy, not by any reckoning. There was only one footpath, steep and slippery, through the dense forest of oaks and laurels and maples. Fortunately the others climbed slowly, intent on searching for botanical rarities, like orchids and other epiphytes. Otherwise I could never have kept up with them. In my own search for Dr Falconer's rhodo, I relied entirely on the generosity of our accomplished Nepalese guide, Tashi. He had promised me the first seed-pod from the first good specimen of Dr Falconer's rhodo. But on we struggled, meeting occasional rhododendrons fat with seed, but never rhodos of the species I coveted. After two and a half hours I was near the end of my tether. 'Are we close to the top?' I asked, panting like a gun dog. 'Is that the final hut?' I pointed to a disused tin-and-concrete hut which must once have been a place where pilgrims could take a breather. 'That's the halfway hut,' came the gentle answer from Tashi, framed like an apology. 'You'll find it much flatter very soon,' he added. Of course it wasn't true. The path was just as steep and slippery as before. But sometimes you need a white lie to carry you to the summit of a mountain.

After four and a half hours we broke out of the forest at last. We were now in an Alpine paradise of gold-flowering hypericums *(H. hookerianum)*, silver everlasting flowers (*Anaphalis nepalensis*) and auburn-leaved maples (*Acer sikkimensis*). Ahead was the summit itself, crowned with a ragged grove of ancient silver firs and a fillet of colourful prayer flags. Somehow, I was going to make it after all.

The view from the summit of Mount Maenam made even the view from Mount Tonglu seem rather parochial. We were now only sixty miles from my obsession, the killer-goddess Kanchenjunga. I saw new details of her lethal profile: the long, elegant neck, the snow-flecked jaws, the snarling lips, the imperious nose, the queenly forehead. But there are other dangerous goddesses. The horizon is walled in with snow mountains, rising like battlements to defend the wastes of Tibet beyond. There must have been at least fifty of them, covering a span of more than two hundred miles from Nepal to China. Many were unknown and unmapped until very recently. (Even Kanchenjunga, so close to civilisation, was unconquered until 1955. And technically she remains a virgin. By request of the Maharajah of Sikkim, then the ruler of the country, the first climbers agreed to leave a few feet of the summit inviolate.)

It was three o'clock in the afternoon, and still warm enough for shirtsleeves even at that airy height. I collected hypericum seeds, ate a picnic lunch of pasties and took jolly photographs of each other against a backdrop of pearly mountains. (We must have looked like Japanese tourists at the Taj Mahal.) Then I was seized by a thought impossible to ignore, a thought like a sharp pain in the stomach. What time was sunset? Wasn't it *pitch*-dark by 5 p.m.? We had taken five hours to make the ascent. Could we be down in two hours? Or were we doomed to be overtaken by darkness as we struggled down that steep, slippery path through the forest? Yes, darkness would certainly find us there - not to speak of the bears and the leopards. I shouted to my friends. Down, we must start down immediately. And, strange to say, this was an occasion when they all agreed with me. So down we went - slithering over the mud and rocks as fast as we could go.

There are times when it would be a great blessing to be able to detach oneself from the grim reality of life and let the spirit roam. I believe some Buddhists - the holiest at any rate - have mastered the trick. I wish I could say I had even a moment's escape from reality as we descended Mount Maenam. It was one of the most unnerving experiences of my life: an afternoon assailed by demons. Daylight faded with brutal speed. By 5 p.m. we were in the land of the blind: tripping over roots in the darkness, ambushed by fallen trees, sliding off the path into gullies. A broken leg - even a twisted ankle - would have earned a night in this forest, a night not to be imagined. But we had the best spiritual protection. At 6 p.m., three hours after we had started down, we saw an extraordinary sight below us: the giant new Buddha of Ravangula exploding with golden light. We were safely down.

Looking back on the ordeal, there were two things which kept me going. The first was that one of the most accomplished gardeners in our group has the strength and agility of a bear. With great generosity he led me down the steepest and most slippery part of the descent, pirouetting over the rocks, alternating his arms in a strange, unearthly bear-dance. The second was that, shortly before daylight deserted us, Tashi came to greet me. Tashi looks very much the Tibetan and normally his face is impassive, but now he was smiling. There was a pair of large brown seed-pods in his hand. Yes, they were the fruit of Dr Falconer's rhodo. And at long last that prize was mine.

Later that evening I telephoned Valerie from our hotel outside Ravangula. Perhaps I was a little incoherent. I think I wanted to tell her I was safe, that I had found at long last the rhodo seed missing from my collection, that I had slithered down a mountain in the dark, that I had been saved from death by a bear - a human bear. But I must confess I had forgotten the date, and that it was the eve of her seventy-fourth birthday.

'*Why* did you ring me?' she asked, somewhat sharply. 'Oh yes, darling. You remembered it was my birthday tomorrow. You wanted to know what I would like for a present. Well, I don't really want *anything* from India . . . No, I don't want a sari – nor a Tibetan god. But I'll tell you what I'd like. Bring me a small packet of Sikkimese tea.'

20 December 2013

Just over a year ago I invited some close friends to the conservatory to celebrate the sowing of my first crop of seeds from Sikkim. We drank the health of these newcomers in prosecco that evening – Aidan, Charles, Octavia, Valerie and I – raising our glasses to the invisible seeds, snug in their green plastic trays of compost. Tonight will be a double celebration worthy of champagne.

First, we will salute the pushy youngsters, some already more than a foot high, who have graduated from the greenhouse and are ready to face the perils of the world outside, the murderous assaults of slugs, snails and grey mould. Some of these pushy youngsters were already stirring eleven months ago, less than a month after they were sown. The list of new arrivals now totals over thirty trees and other plants. It includes the willow-leaved Asiatic buckthorn (*Hippophae salicifolia*), some gorgeous purple-flowering primulas (*Primula capitata*), the tree rhododendrons named after Hooker's friends, Thomson and Hodgson, and the Himalayan birch with bark like brown parchment (*Betula utilis*).

Sadly, there's one Himalayan tree conspicuous by its absence: Hooker's White Goddess, and, first of the Big Five, the white-flowering form of *Magnolia campbellii*. I cannot imagine why this beautiful creature has rejected me. I planted more than a hundred of its scarlet seeds in tray number 17. Not a single one of those hundred deigned to germinate. Fortunately I gave another hundred seeds to Bill, one of my friends who has often given me treasures from his collection. Who knows, he may be feeling generous this Christmas.

We will also welcome the new generation of newcomers: the seeds brought back from Sikkim only three weeks ago. They are now tucked up in their green plastic trays and look quite as snug as their predecessors did a year ago. I wonder how many of these will deign to germinate. I have ten more species of rhododendron, including many that I failed to collect last year - or failed to grow in this one. Of course the seeds which are nearest my heart are the seeds of the giant tree rhododendron, Dr Falconer's rhodo, from the wilds of Mount Maenam. These came from the seed-pod given me by our guide Tashi- a generous reward after that terrifying descent in the darkness through the lairs of brown bears and snow leopards.

The second reason to make it a champagne evening is even more exciting than the first. We have to toast two new grandchildren, Lyra and Sasha, twin girls born ten days ago, the children of our son Fred and his partner, Claire. I'm sure these two newcomers will be crazy about trees, especially about the two that I shall plant in their honour - when I can think of a suitable species.

Christmas Day 2013

Wonderful news. My friend Bill has grown *thirty* of my magnolia plants. He has given me two as Christmas presents. And what better tree to plant for Lyra and Sasha than a pair of White Goddesses?

Epilogue

15 February 2014

Yesterday a February storm raided the garden and demesne. I had watched it on my computer screen as it gathered strength out in the Atlantic. As the isobars narrowed (meaning the depression was deepening) the forecasters warned of storm-winds gusting, that afternoon, to nearly one hundred miles an hour. Usually these storms last several hours. But this one, like an earlier tornado, was freakishly short-lived. It arrived at tea-time and left us, hell-bent on attacking Dublin, after half an hour. But in that short time it had smashed six ancient trees to the ground, including two of my particular favourites.

Today I summoned courage to view the corpses. In the pleasure ground I found a hundred-year-old Monterey cypress lying on its haunches among the snowberry bushes. This tree had never been one of my close friends - it was too spiky to be responsive - but I shall miss it all the same. Two of these fast-growing cypresses had been planted by the bridge over the upper pond. Later they had served as a sober green backdrop for the jolly pink and white oriental magnolias I had planted higher up the slope. Now the sober green backdrop has a large hole in it, which will take years to fill - too long, I expect, for me.

Worse was the loss of a large, gnarled copper beech which had shared the corner of the main garden path with a pair of London planes. It had also shared many happy days with me. I knew it was nearing the end of its two hundred years of life.

Bracket fungi, the colour and shape of pie-crust, were sprouting from its feet, and this meant that much of the lower trunk was hollow. Pustules of honey fungus emerged every autumn. But old trees, like old people, can live for years with terminal decay. (I remember showing this copper beech to the celebrated tree guru Alan Mitchell, when he visited us in 1990. It was already ailing then. I knew Alan could not abide copper beeches. He looked at the tree with disgust and told me he was 'afraid it may live for years'.) Now the poor old creature lay bottom upwards in the rhododendrons, waiting for the chainsaw. In its fall it had sheared off the head of one of the London planes beside it.

Worse still was the loss of a 110-foot-high beech tree in the arboretum, one of our tallest and most magnificent trees. This was one of the fifteen giants (the Tolkienian 'Ents') which had dominated that grove when I started to plant exotic trees there eleven years ago. It was part of the original shelter belt planted about 1780 - a dense belt of beech and oak and sycamore designed to shelter our house from the north-east wind. In those last eleven years, six of its fellow Ents had already been smashed to the ground by storms. Now it lay prone, a huge corpse among a forest of young companions: oak I had planted there myself and beech which were the progeny of its own beech nuts, scattered in thousands from its branches.

And this week a prodigiously large horse chestnut, fifty yards from the front door, has gone to the knackers. For more than a century it had shielded the house from westerly gales. Now it has to be felled, as it had died of bleeding canker.

I retreated to the house, sickened by these disasters. *Disasters?* Yes, of course. But opportunities, too. When the shriek of the chainsaw has finally faded from the garden, I shall have to decide how to fill these interesting new voids.

In the pleasure ground I shall indulge my appetite for maples: *Acer*, the most poetical of genera, with as many colours as a chameleon or Joseph's famous coat. It was one of my first loves. Recklessly, in the last thirty years, I have planted more than forty species and varieties of maple in the pleasure ground alone. Half a dozen have died mysterious deaths - mainly victims, I imagine, of honey fungus. I have lost two of my best snake-bark maples, including the grey-budded one with red and white stripes on its bark, *Acer rufinerve*. I have also lost my only paper-bark maple, *Acer griseum*, the maple discovered by Ernest 'Chinese' Wilson in 1901 when he was dispatched by the firm of Veitch to ransack the East for novelties. Even a young plant can dazzle you with its flaking orange bark. Mine was everyone's favourite - till it sickened and died in its teens. Now I shall replace these lost generations before the winter is over. And I shall plant some more Japanese maples that will be irresistible next autumn. I shall plant the flaming 'Osakasuki', as well as my fire-breathing new hybrid, *Acer x freemanii*, the tree that has proved heaven-sent for the arboretum. Whatever I do, I shall keep my new plants well away from the roots of the fallen copper beech. It is there, I believe, hidden beneath the snowdrops and Siberian bluebells, that my enemy lies in wait: honey fungus in its subterranean lair.

In the arboretum I shall be more adventurous. There will be a large gap where that towering beech, the giant 'Ent', used to stand. Part of the gap will be closed naturally by its own crop of youngsters, born from the nuts in its branches. My contribution will be to plant a monkey puzzle in the sheltered part of the site. This is to celebrate the birth, a year ago, of my youngest male grandchild, Tom Pakenham, the son of Ned and Sarah. The choice of tree may seem a little odd. Monkey puzzles are spiky, Jurassic-looking creatures which many people find repellent. They're native to rocky canyons in the Andes, as I described in Chapter 4. I have already planted several at Tullynally in the wildest terrain I could find, the rocky bank in the garden below the grotto. Ned and Sarah seem happy about my choice. At least I shall make sure the monkey puzzle's female (they'll have to be grafted from nut-bearing mother trees). But I don't expect to hear that Tom enjoys climbing it – any more than the eponymous monkeys.

On the sunny side of the arboretum, I shall finish my exotic new planting by borrowing a leaf (in fact a lot of leaves) from my favourite author, Homer.

You'll find the passage in the final, climactic pages of the *Odyssey*, the epic which Homer composed about 700 BC. After nineteen years (ten years besieging Troy, then nine years wandering) the hero Odysseus, alias Ulysses, returns to Ithaca, his island kingdom, disguised as a beggar. At a banquet he strings his famous bow and shoots dead the rascally suitors who have been plaguing his wife Penelope and his son Telemachus. He then goes to meet his father, Laertes, who has abdicated years before and is living in misery on an orchard far away from the palace, mourning his lost son. At first Odysseus assumes the identity of a rich visitor from the mainland. Then he takes pity on his father and tells him he is the lost son who has at last returned and killed the suitors. But Laertes cannot accept he is really Odysseus. 'Give me some proof,' says the old man. So Odysseus explains: 'I can tell you all the trees you gave me one day on this garden terrace. I was only a little boy at the time, trotting after you through the orchard, begging for this and that, and as we wound our way through these very trees you told me all their names. You gave me thirteen pear-trees, ten apple-trees, forty fig-trees . . .' And Laertes, convinced at last, flings his arms around the neck of his beloved son.

So this is my plan for the sunny side of the arboretum. Using the shelter of an ancient stone wall I shall plant the same trees that Odysseus treasured in his memory for all those years. *Thirteen pear-trees, ten apple-trees* . . . Well, one or two fig-trees. It will be a Homeric planting and my homage to the author of one of the first good tree stories ever written.

List of chapter illustrations

Title page

Oak with a deer behind. From Samuel Hayes *Practical Treatise on Planting etc* (Dublin 1794). Original drawings by Samuel Hayes engraved by William Esdall

Chapter

1. Golden Buddha at Ravangala, Sikkim, from a photograph
2. The Cowthorpe Oak, near Wetherby, Yorkshire, from an engraving *c*.1840
3. Stumps of oak trees showing dos and don'ts for forestry, from Hayes (ibid)
4. Giant monkey puzzle in Patagonia, west Argentina, from a photograph
5. Ancient ash tree, from Hayes (ibid)
6. Flower of *Magnolia campbellii*, from a photograph
7. Pagoda in Yunnan at Tullynally, from a photograph
8. Ten-year-old ginkgo in the pleasure ground at Tullynally, from a photograph
9. The great sycamore at Bishopton, Renfrewshire, from Jacob Strutt, *Sylva Britannica* (privately printed 1822-6), drawn and engraved by Strutt
10. Hut in Tibet at Tullynally, from a photograph
11. The yew at Ankerwycke, Berkshire, from Strutt (ibid)
12. Scots pines at Dunmore, Stirlingshire, from Strutt (ibid)
13. 'Majesty', the great oak at Fredville, Kent, from Strutt (ibid)
14. The Salcey Oak, Northamptonshire, from H.S. Rooke (ed.) *c*.1794
15. Misericord of a Green Man in the choir at Beverley Minster, Yorkshire, from a photograph
16 Man moving a tree, from Hayes (ibid)
17. 'The Twelve Apostles', ancient oaks in the New Forest from Strutt (ibid)
18. Maple at Boldre, Hampshire, from Strutt (ibid)
19. Siver fir at Roseneath, from Strutt (ibid)
20. *Rhododendron decorum subsp. diaprepes* by L. Snelling (1938)
21. Gothic hut at Avondale, Co. Wicklow, from Hayes (ibid)

Bibliography

Addison, J. and others, *The Spectator*, no. 477 September 1712 (London, 1776)

Allen, M., *The Hookers of Kew 1785-1911* (London, 1967)

Altman, N., *Sacred Trees* (San Francisco, 1994)

Anderson, W., *Green Man: The Archetype of our Oneness with the Earth* (London, 1990)

Barnard, T., *Making the Grand Figure: Lives and Possessions in Ireland 1641-1770* (London, 2004)

Basford, K., *The Green Man* (London, 2004)

Bean, W. J., *Trees and Shrubs Hardy in the British Isles*, 8th edition revised 4 vols, supplementary volume 1988 (London, 1976)

Beaulieu, A. le H. de, *An Illustrated Guide to Maples* (Cambridge, 2003)

Bretschneider, E., *History of European Botanical Discoveries in China*, 2 vols (St Petersburg, 1898)

Candolle, A. de and Sprengel, K., *Elements of the Philosophy of Plants etc* (Edinburgh, 1821)

Candolle, A. de, *Prodromus Systematicus Naturalis Regni Vegetabilis*, 7 vols (Paris, 1824-41)

Chambers, Sir W., *Dissertation on Oriental Gardening* (London, 1772)

Costello, V., *Irish Demesne Landscapes, 1660-1740* (Dublin, 2015)

Cox, E., *Plant Hunting in China* (London, 1987)

Crane, P.R., *Ginkgo* (London, 2013)

Desmond, R., *Sir Joseph Dalton Hooker: Traveller and Plant Collector* (London, 1999)

Desmond, R., *The History of the Royal Botanic Gardens, Kew* (London, 2007)

Dezallier d'Argenville, A. J., *The Theory and Practice of Gardening*, translated by John James, illustrations by A. Le Blond (2nd edition London, 1728)

Dillon, H., *On Gardening* (Dublin, 2010)

Elliott, C. (ed.), *The Treasury of Trees* (London, 2007)

Elwes, H.J. and Henry, A., *Trees of Great Britain and Ireland*, 7 vols (Edinburgh, 1906-13)

Evelyn, J., *Silva: or a Discourse of Forest-Trees etc, with notes by Dr A. Hunter* (York, 1776; 1st edition 1664)

Farjon, A., *A Handbook of the World's Conifers* (Leiden, 2010)

Farjon, A., *A Natural History of Conifers* (London, 2010)

Feehan, J. and O'Donovan, G., *The Bogs of Ireland: An Introduction to the Natural, Cultural and Industrial Heritage of Irish Peatlands* (Dublin, 1996)

Fennell, A., *Heritage Trees of Ireland* (Cork, 2013)

FitzGerald, R., *A Gardener's Guide to Native Plants of Britain and Ireland* (Ramsbury, 2012)

Flanagan, M. and Kirkham, T., *Wilson's China: A Century On* (Kew, 2009)

Forrest, M., *Trees and Shrubs Cultivated in Ireland* (Kilkenny, 1985)

Gardiner, J.M., *Magnolias* (Chester, Connecticut, 1989)

Giraldus Cambrensis, *The Historical Works*, ed. R. C. Hoare (modern edition) (London, 2012)

Griffiths, M., *Index of Garden Plants* (London, 1994)

Grimshaw, J. and Bayton, R., *New Trees: Recent Introductions to Cultivation* (Kew, 2009)

Hageneder, F., *Yew: A History* (Stroud, 2007)

Harris, J. G. S., *The Gardener's Guide to Growing Maples* (Newton Abbot, 2000)

Hicks, C., *The Green Man: A Field Guide* (Hellhoughton, 2000)

Hillier, Sir H., *The Hillier Manual of Trees and Shrubs* (London, 1971)

Hooker, J. D., *Himalayan Journals, etc,* 2 vols (London, 1854)

Hooker, J. D., *The Rhododendrons of Sikkim-Himalaya*, 3 vols (London, 1849-51)

Hunt, D. R. (ed.), *Magnolias and Their Allies: Proceedings of an International Symposium* (London, 1998)

Johnson, H., *The International Book of Trees* (1st edition 1974), revised as *The World of Trees* (Berkeley, California, 2010)

Johnson, O., *Champion Trees of Britain and Ireland: The Tree Register Handbook* (London, 2011)

Lamb, K. and Bowe, P., *A History of Gardening in Ireland* (Dublin, 1995)

Lancaster, R., *Plantsman's Paradise: Travels in China* (Woodbridge, 1989)

Leighton, C., *The Wood That Came Back* (London, 1935)

Lloyd Praeger, R., *Natural History of Ireland etc* (London, 1950)

Loudon, J. C., *An Encyclopaedia of Gardening etc* (London, 1822)

Loudon, J.C., *Arboretum et Fruticetum Britannicum etc*, 8 vols (London, 1838)

Lowe, J., *The Yew-Trees of Great Britain and Ireland* (London, 1897)

Mabberley, D.J., *Mabberley's Plant Book: A portable dictionary of plants, their classification and uses* (Cambridge, 2000)

Mabey, R., *Flora Britannica* (London, 1996)

MacQueen Cowan, J. (ed.), *The Journeys and Plant Introductions of George Forrest* (London, 1952)

Malins, E. and FitzGerald, D., *Lost Demesnes: Irish Landscape Gardening 1660-1845* (London, 1976)

McAllister, H., *The Genus Sorbus: Mountain Ash and Other Rowans* (Kew, 2005)

Merrill, E. D., 'Metasequoia, another "living fossil"', *Arnoldia* 8: 1-8 (1948)

Mitchell, A., *A Field Guide to the Trees of Britain and Northern Europe* (London, 1974)

Mitchell, A., *The Gardener's Book of Trees etc* (London, 1981)

Mitchell, A., *The Trees of Britain and Northern Europe* (London, 1982)

Moir, A. K., 'The dendrochronological potential of modern yew etc', *New Phytol.* 144, 479-88 (1999)

Musgrave, W. and Gardner, C., *The Plant Hunters* (London, 1999)

Nelson, E. C., 'Augustine Henry and the exploration of the Chinese flora', *Arnoldia* 43: 21-38 (1983)

Nelson, E. C., *A Heritage of Beauty: An Illustrated Encyclopaedia* (Dublin, 2000)

Nelson, E. C., 'Magnolia campbellii in County Cork', *The Garden* 104: 495-6 (1979)

Nelson, E.C. and Walsh, W., *The Wild & Garden Plants of Ireland* (London, 2009)

Nelson, E.C. and Walsh, W., *Trees of Ireland: Native and Naturalised* (Dublin, 1993)

O'Brien, S., *In the Footsteps of Augustine Henry* (London, 2011)

O'Kane, F., *Ireland and the Picturesque: Design, Landscape Painting and Tourism* (London, 2013)

O'Sullivan, A. and Kelly, D., 'A recent history of sessile oak ... dominated woodland in Killarney etc', *Proceedings of the Royal Irish Academy* 106B, No. 3, 355-70 (November 2006)

Pakenham, T., *In Search of Remarkable Trees: On Safari in Southern Africa* (London, 2007)

Pakenham, T., *Meetings with Remarkable Trees* (London, 1996)

Pakenham, T., *Remarkable Trees of the World* (London, 2002)

Phillips, R., *Trees in Britain, Europe and North America* (London, 1978)

Pim, S., *The Wood and the Trees: Augustine Henry* (Kilkenny, 1984)

Polunin, O. and Stainton, A., *Flowers of the Himalayas* (Oxford, 1984)

Pradhan, U. C. and Lachungpa, S. T., *Sikkim-Himalayan Rhododendrons* (Kalimpong, 1990)

Primack, R. B., 'Ancient and notable trees of Japan', *Arnoldia* 65: 10-21 (2008)

Rackham, O., *Trees and Woodland in the British Landscape* (London, 1990)

Raglan, Lady, 'The Green Man in Church Architecture', *Folklore* 50, 45-57 (1939)

Raphael, S., *An Oak Spring Sylva etc* (Upperville, Virginia, 1989)

Reeves-Smyth, T., 'The Natural History of Demesnes' in Foster, J. W. and Chesney, H. C. G. (eds), *Nature in Ireland: A Cultural History* (Dublin, 1997)

Reeves-Smyth, T., *Gardens of Ireland. A Touring Guide to over 100 of the Best Gardens* (London, 2001)

Rich, T. C. G., Houston, L., Robertson, A., Proctor, M. C. F., *Whitebeams, Rowans and Service Trees of Britain and Ireland. A Monograph of British and Irish Sorbus* (London, 2010)

Robinson, W. and Darke, R., *The Wild Garden* (London, 2009; 1st edition 1870)

Rushforth, K., *Conifers* (London, 1987)

Rushforth, K., *Trees of Britain and Europe* (London, 1999)

Sargent, C. S. *Plantae Wilsonianae etc* (Cambridge, 1913)

Sitwell, Sir G., *On the Making of Gardens* (London, 1949)

Spongberg, S., *A Reunion of Trees* (Cambridge, Massachusetts, 1990)

Stearn, W. T., *Botanical Latin* (London, 1966)

Strutt, J. G., *Sylva Britannica or Portraits of Forest Trees etc* (London, 1830)

Temple, Sir W., *Upon the Garden of Epicurus* (London, 1685)

Treseder, N., *Magnolias* (London, 1978)

Vallancey, C., *Collectanea de Rebus Hibernicis*, 6 vols (Dublin, 1770-1804)

Veitch, J. H., *Hortus Veitchii*, (reprinted Exeter, 2006)

Walpole, H., *Essay on Modern Gardening* (London, 1770)

Ward, F.K., *Land of the Blue Poppy* (Cambridge, 1913)

Ward, F. K. and Cox, C. (eds) *Riddle of the Tsangpo Gorges* (London, 1926)

Webb, D. A., *An Irish Flora* (1st edition 1943; reissued as *Webb's An Irish Flora*, eds Parnell, J. and Curtis, T. (Dublin, 2012)

Williamson, P., *Gothic Sculpture 1140-1300* (London, 1995)

Williamson, R., *The Great Yew Forest: The Natural History of Kingley Vale* (London, 1978)

Wilson, E. H., *A Naturalist in Western China with Vasculum, Camera and Gun* (London, 1913)

Young, A., *A Tour in Ireland etc* (Dublin, 1780)

Young, P., *Oak* (London, 2013)

Manuscripts
Pakenham, G. E., Ms diary 1737-8. Pakenham Archives at Tullynally

Piers, Sir H., Chorographical History of Westmeath (1682), Pakenham Archives at Tullynally

Periodicals
Garden History
Gardener's Magazine
IDS Yearbook 1966-2014
The Garden (RHS) 1983-2015
The Plantsman

Online
Debates.oireachtas.ie/dail/1987/06/03/00020.asp

Index

Abies delavayi 69
Abies fordei 101-2
Abominable Snowman (yeti) 97
Acer cappadocicum sinicum 89
Acer davidii 69-70, 89
Acer forrestii 70, 89
Acer giraldii 98
Acer griseum 198
Acer palmatum 'Osakasuki' 177, 179, 198
Acer pictum (mono) 89, 117
Acer pseudoplatanus (European sycamore) 85-7
Acer rufinerve 198
Acer sikkimensis 192
Aceraceae 86, 198
acorns 22, 163
Acute Oak Death 4
Acute Oak Decline (AOD), 45-6
Addison, Joseph 65
Agent Orange 120
Agincourt, Battle 106
Aidan Chisholm, author's grandchild 127, 175
Alex Chisholm, author's son-in-law 8
alien invaders 126
American garden 103
An Taisce (National Trust for Ireland) 168, 170
Anaphalis nepalensis 194
Andes 14-15, 32-9, 199
Anhui 60
Anselm Winner, author's grandchild 8

Antoine Pierson, cabinet-maker and sculptor 30, 155, 187
Antrim oak 129-32
apparitions, unexplained 123-4

apple-trees (*Malus sp.*) 199-200
Araucano Indians 34
Araucaria genus 33, 34, 199
Arboretum 86-7, 91, 117, 174-6, 200-1
arboretum, planning 22-30
archaeophytes 86
Ardkinglas 184-5
Argentine 14-15
Argyll, 3rd Duke 80
Arnold Arboretum 54-5, 83
ash die-back (*Chalara fraxinea*) 41-2, 46
ash, common (*Fraxinus excelsior*) 4, 41, 46, 68, 90
ash, uses of 42
Asiatic buckthorn (*Hippophae salicifolia*) 196
Assam 96
Attiret, Fr Jean-Denis 65
Australia, loggers 37
Australian botanists 84
autumn colours 175-81
Avenue at Tullynally 20

badgers 118
Bailey, Colonel 98
balloonists 127
Bamberg, Bavaria 150
Banks, Sir Joseph 51
Bariloche 36
bark beetles 42
Baronstown, Co. Westmeath 139
Bartram, John 81
Bean, W.J. 111, 116
bear-dance, unearthly 193
bears, black 191, 193, 195
Beauchamp, Earl 110

beech, age 24

beech, common (*Fagus sylvatica*) 2, 4, 23-6, 35-6, 38, 44, 91, 137

beech, southern, from South America (*Nothofagus spp.*) 26

Beethoven 8

Belfast 59

Berberis temolaica 101, 104

Bernard, St of Clairvaux 151

Betjeman, John 155-6

Betula pendula (Silver birch) 76

Betula pubescens (Downy birch) 76

Betula utilis (Himalayan birch) 68, 118, 194

Bhutan 9

Big Wind 181, 187

big-leaf maple (*Acer macrophyllum*) 88

bilberries, or *frochain* (*Vaccinium sp.*) 121, 124

Bill, nurseryman 194-5

Billington, Rachel, author's sister, 125

Birch Man 152

birch *see Betula pubescens, Betula pendula*

Birr Castle 59

Blair Castle, Perthshire 184

Bligh, Capt. of *Bounty* 51

Blumhardt, Oswald, plant breeder 60

Boer War, The 3

Bog Meadow field 120

Boorman, John 170-1

Boston, 81

Boyne, Battle 139

Brahmaputra, River 95

Bridgefarm Company 167, 167-172

Bristlecone pine (*Pinus longaeva*) 112

Bronze Age sword 133-4

Brown, Lancelot ('Capability') 21, 65, 140, 157

Buddha, giant statue 191-3

Buddhist monks in China 82, 84

Buddhist shrines 13, 19

Buddhists, sacred mountains 12-13

Buddleia colvilei 15

Buenos Aires 36

Bulley, Arthur 54

Caerhays Castle 54, 57-8, 61

Calcutta, 8-10

Caledonian forest 100, 106, 111, 116

Campbell, Archibald 9-14, 53, 191-192

Campbell's magnolia (*see Magnolia campbellii*)

Canal at Tullynally 19, 21

Candolle, Prof. Augustin de 110, 114, 116

Cape Town 92

Carnarvon, Lord 175

Carricknamaddow Mt 109

Carton house and estate, Co. Kildare 156-8

Cascade at Castletown 159-60

Cascade at Tullynally 19, 21

Castle, Richard, architect 157, 159

Castlemaine, Lord 181

Castlereagh, Lord 160

Castletown house and estate, Co. Kildare 158

Castletown, missed trick 160

Caucasian fir (*Abies nordmanniana*) 28, 185-7

Caucasus, superior trees 186

Cauragh, St of Knockeyon 143

cedar, Japanese (*Cryptomeria japonica*) 12

Celtic chief 133, 135

Celts reverence for yews 106

Cerro Tronador 35, 37

Cézanne, Paul 139

Chalara fraxinea (Ash die-back) 41, 46, 90

Chambers, Sir William 65-6, 179

Champion tree at Ardkinglas 185

Champion Trees in Britain and Ireland 185

Chapel of St Eyon 141-3

chemical warfare 120

Cherry, Bob 100

Chestnut Man 154

chestnut, horse (*Aesculus hippocastanum*) 4

chestnut, sweet (*Castanea sativa*) 4

Children of Lir 17, 44

Chile 34, 37, 39

China 10, 47, 51-2, 192

China border war with India 11, 94

China, exploring 28-9, 53-6, 94

Chinese gardens 64-6

Chinese mountains, miniature 71

Chinese porcelain 64, 71

chinoiserie 64-6

chlorophyll 176

Chorographical Description of Westmeath 139-44

Christian, Early 132

churchyards, Irish 107

Chusquea spp. (bamboo) 37-8
Ciaran Chisholm, author's grandchild 175, 127
Claire Halligan, my son Fred's partner 8
Claudian glass 140
Clear, Professor Tom, UCD 3
climate, 74, 84-5, 115, 117-18
clumps and shelter belts, restoring 156
cluster pine (*Pinus pinaster*) 92
coast redwood (*Sequoia sempervirens*) 183
Columbkille, St of Kells and Iona 143
common oak (*Quercus robur*) 127
Comyns, Kevin, farm manager 105, 120
Congreve, Ambrose 49-50, 53, 56
Congreve, Marjorie 50
Conolly-Carew family 159
Conolly, Lady Louisa 158-9
Conolly, Tom, Speaker, 158-9
Conolly, Tom, squire of Castletown 158
Cook, Capt. James 33, 51
Coolattin acorns 163
Coolattin ancient oaks 163, 165-72
Coolattin oaks, superiority 168-9
Coolattin oaks, value 168,173
Coolure House 127
copper beech (*Fagus sylvatica purpurea*) 197-8
Crane, Sir Peter 73-80
Crann 167
crannog (man-made island) 134-5
Crawford, William 53
Crimean War 187
Cruckawn, field at Tullynally 41
Cultural Revolution 104

Dail speeches on Coolattin crisis 168
dairy farm at Tullynally 3, 86, 119
Dalhousie, Lord 9
Dali 66
Darjeeling 8-12, 189
Darwin, Charles 9-10, 108, 130
David, Père Armand 69, 89, 98
dawn redwood (*Metasequoia glyptostroboides*) 176
Dawson, Jackson T. 54
death duties 2, 24, 119, 169
decoy at Tullynally 137
Delavay, Père Jean-Marie 69, 71
demesne 3, 86

demesne at Carton 157-9
demesne at Castletown 158-60
demesne at Mount Stewart 160-2
demesne at Tullynally 17-22, 155-6
demesne replanting 162
demesnes destroyed by Big Wind 182
demesnes in Ireland 155-63
dendrochronology 111, 135
Derravaragh, Lough 17, 44, 120-35, 139-44
Derry, River at Coolattin 165
Deshima Island 64-78, 80
Deutzia purpurascens 68
Devis, Arthur, painter 157
Dewan (Sikkim Rajah's vizier) 10-14
Discovery, Cook's ship 33-4
disease immunity 47
disease, tree 26, 41
Disraeli, Benjamin 25
Doshong La pass 94, 96-8, 100, 103
Douglas fir (*Pseudotsuga menziesii*) 88, 90, 178,
    183-5
Douglas fir, champions 184
Douglas, David, plant hunter 88, 183-4
Douglas, Gerry 46
downy Japanese maple (*Acer palmatum*) 89
Durham coal mines 161-2
Dutch East India Company 80
Dutch elm disease 42
Dutch merchants 64

Edgeworth (Pakenham), Michael, half-brother
    of Maria 13
Edgeworth, Maria 103
Edgeworthia gardneri 13
Edinburgh Royal Botanic Garden 39
Edo (modern Tokyo) 78
Eliza, Chisholm, author's second daughter 1, 8
elm disease, Dutch 4
Endeavour, Cook's ship 51
Enniskillen, Lord 109-110
Ents (ancient beech) 23-4, 26, 28, 200
Erebus, HMS 9
Eucalyptus, giant 37
European climate 65
excavations by archaeologists 135
Exeter Cathedral 149

eye-catcher (Conolly Folly) 159
Eyon, Saint 137

Fagan, Michael, builder 71
Falconer, Dr Hugh 10, 188-90
felling licences 165-6, 169, 172
Fenian tactics 169-70
Fianna Fail party 166, 172
Finbosch, South African 92
Fire Brigade 120-1
fire in the bog 1, 121-3
FitzGerald, Desmond, Knight of Glin 170
FitzGerald, Lord Edward, rebel leader 158
Fitzroya cupressoides (Alerce) 36-9
Fitzwilliam estate, Co. Wicklow 165, 168
Fitzwilliam, 8th Countess 169
Fitzwilliam, 8th Earl 168-9
Fitzwilliam, Lady Juliet 169
Flora Japonica by Siebold 79
Flora Japonica by Thunberg 79
Florence Court estate 109-10
Flower garden at Tullynally 88
Forde, Patrick 101-2
Forest Walk at Tullynally 17-18, 41-2, 60-1, 67-8,
    72, 83, 93, 107, 118-20, 186-7
Forestry Commission 177
Forestry subsidies 127
Fort de Soignes 100
Forêt de Soignes, Brussels 91, 100
Forrest, George 53-6, 70, 89
Franklin, Benjamin 81
Fraser, Antonia, author's eldest sister 1-2, 125
Fraser, James, landscape designer and author
    182
Freeman's maple (*Acer x freemanii*) 174-5, 198
fund-raising 170-2

Gabriel Chisholm, author's grandchild 125, 173
Gardener's Magazine 52
Gardens of Epicurus, 63
Gate Theatre, Dublin 2
Getty Museum, California 134
giant hogweed (*Heracleum mantegazzium*) 91
giant sequoias (*Sequoiadendron giganteum*) 36-7,
    90, 183-4
Gilfillan, Kathy 171-3

Gingerbread House at Tullynally *see* Gothic Hut
ginkgo 90, 176
Ginkgo biloba 20, 29, 66, 72
ginkgo nuts 76, 79
ginkgo refuges 77
gignkgo seeds from Mount Auburn 81-2
ginkgo, 'Old Lion' at Kew 80
ginkgo, origin of name 79
ginkgophilia 73
ginkgos from Japan 81
ginkgos in Arctic 75
ginkgos in Buddhist temples 77
ginkgos in China 76-7, 80
ginkgos in Chinese poetry 77
ginkgos in Europe 75
ginkgos in Japan 77-80
ginkgos in Korea 77
ginkgos in Tasmania 75
ginkgos in USA 81
ginkgos, decline and death 74
ginkgos, pavement 74
ginkgos, planting at Tullynally 82
ginkgos, seed distribution 76
Giraldus Cambrensis (Gerald de Barry) 106
global warming 1, 4
golf course at Carton 158
Gordon, James, nurseryman 80
gospels 7-8
Gothic hut ('Gingerbread House') at Tullynally
    187
Gothic tower at Tullynally 120
Gothick lodge at Castletown 159
Greek Temple at Castletown 159-61
grand fir (*Abies grandis*) 88, 183, 187-9
grand fir, champion 184-5
Grand Lodge at Tullynally 155
Greece, northern 43
Greek Temple at Castletown 159-61
Green Men 145-53
Green Men family 146-8, 152-3
Green Men, diabolical 148
Green Men, enigma 147-52
Green Men, European 146, 149
Green Men, Gothic 148-52
Green Men, medieval sculptures 146
Green Men, obsession with 146
Green Men, pre-Christian 147-8

Green Men, Romanesque 148
Green Party 172
greenfly, malignant (*Adelges nuslinii*) 183, 186
greenhouse 7-8, 25, 66, 102-3, 110
Grimm, Friedrich Baron von 33
Groote Schuur, Cape Town 92
Grotto Hill at Tullynally 74-5
Guinness, Desmond 159
Gyala Peri 95, 98, 100-1, 103-4

Halloween party 173, 176
Hamilton, William 81
Harvard University 54
Haughey, Charles, Taoiseach 166-7
Hawthorn Man 151
Hawthorn Woman 152-3
heather, pink 120-1
Henry, Augustine 29, 53
Henry's lime (*Tilia henryana*) 29
Henry's viburnum (*Viburnum henryi*) 29
Hermitage, Dunkeld 184
Himalayan birch (*Betula utilis*) 168, 118, 194
Himalayan cypress (*Cupressus torulosa*) 187
Himalayan Journals 13
Himalayas 7-14, 53-6, 93-102
Hippophae salicifolia (willow-leaved buckthorn) 15
Hiroshima 20
Hokusai 137
Holford family 177
Holford, Robert 27-8
Holford, Sir George 27-8
Holland 41
Holly (*Ilex spp.*) 28, 106, 178
Homer 200-2
honey fungus 197-9
Hooker, Sir Joseph 8-14, 27, 53, 54-55, 57, 60, 94, 197-8
Hooker, Sir William 9
horse chestnut (*Aesculus hippocastanum*) 42-3, 68, 91
horse chestnut bleeding canker (*Pseudomonas syringae aesculi*) 4-5, 43
Horsepark at Tullynally 137
Horton, Charles 8, 49, 196
Hupeh 55

hurricanes 44, 115, 181
hybrid oak 127
Hypericum hookerianum 192-3

Ilex aquifolium 175
Ilex x altaclarensis 175
In Search of Remarkable Trees: On Safari in Southern Africa 4
India 47
Indian mutiny 187
Ingoldsby family of Carton 157
Inny drainage 133
Inny River 132
Iris chrysofrages 102
Irish Georgian Society 159-70
Irish Tree Society 3, 163, 167-72
Irish Yew (*Taxus baccata* 'Fastigiata') 107-8

James, John 18
Japan 47
Japan 51-2
Japanese gardens 64
Japanese knotweed (*Fallopia japonica*) 91
Japanese maple (*Acer palmatum* 'Osakasuki') 30
Japanese maples (*Acer palmatum*) 89, 119, 177, 180, 200
Jefferson, Thomas 81
Jekyll, Gertrude 161
Jinfo Mt refuge for ginkgos 77
Johnson, Owen 185
Julia Pakenham, author's grandchild, 29, 39, 72, 82
juniper (*Juniper communis*) 106

Kaempfer, Engelbert 78-9, 89
Kan, T., Chinese forester 83
Kanchenjunga, Mt (first White Goddess) 8, 12-13, 189, 191-2
kauris, giant 37
Kent, William 65
Kew Gardens (RBG) 8-9, 51, 53, 65, 73, 80, 94
Kildare, Emily 20th Countess, later 1st Duchess of Leinster 157, 159
Kildare, James Fitz-Gerald 20th Earl, later 1st Duke of Leinster 157-9
Killarney oak 129-32, 144, 168

Kilpeck, Herefordshire 148
Kingdon-Ward, Frank 94-6, 98, 104
kingfishers 72
Kingley Vale, Sussex 115-16
Knockeyon 30, 127, 135, 137-42
Kunming 66, 70
Kyoto 179

Laertes 199
Lago Futalaufquen 36
Lago Menendez 36, 38
Lago Nahuel Huapi 36
Lago Prias 37-8
Lakelands, Co. Cork 53
Laline Mt 35
lamas, murderous 69
Land of the Blue Poppy 98
landscape English, 42
landscape, 'natural' 21, 65, 157-9
landscape, borrowed 138
landscape, formal 18, 21, 64, 157-9
Langley, Batty, architect 159-60
larch, European (*Larix europaea*) 25, 91
Larch, European, introduction 182
Larix potaninii 101
Latham, James, artist 19
Lawson cedar (*Chamaecyparis lawsoniana*) 189
Le Blond, Alexandre 18
Lear, Edward 116
leaves of Southwell 150
leaves, carved from wood 145
Lee of Hammersmith, nurseryman 110
Leiden botanic garden 80
Leighton, Clare 1
Leinster, James Fitz-Gerald, 1st Duke 157-8
leopards, snow 191, 193, 195
Lhasa 95
lichen, white 120-1, 124
Liffey, River at Castletown 158-60
Lime, common (*Tilia x europea*) 20, 44
Lindera obtusiloba 101, 104
Linnaeus, Carl 79
Liquidambar styraciflua 29, 175
Lissu tribesmen 53
listing specimen trees 168
Lithuania 41

living fossils 82-4
Lobb, William 34
Loebner, Max 53
loggers 36-7, 66, 166
London plane (*Platanus x hispanica*) 91, 197
Londonderry, Charles Stewart 3rd Marquess 160
Londonderry, Charles Stewart 7th Marquess 161
Londonderry, Edith 7th Marchioness 160-2
longbow 106
Longford heiress, Elizabeth Cuffe, later 1st
    Countess of Longford 19, 21
Longford, 'Fluffy' Pakenham, 3rd Earl 43, 187
Longford, 2nd Countess 103
Longford, 2nd Earl 110
Longford, Edward 6th Earl, author's uncle (died
    1961) 2, 24
Longford, Elizabeth 7th Countess, author's
    mother (died 2002) 1, 32
Longford, Francis Aungier Earl of 21
Longford, Frank 7th Earl, author's father (died
    2001) 2
Longford, William Lygon Pakenham, 4th Earl
    187
Lorrain, Claude 3, 21, 138
lost in woods 122
Loudon, J.C. 22, 81, 89
Lough Neagh, Northern Ireland 89
Loughcrew, County Meath 112-13
Lowe, John 111-12, 113, 116
Lower Horsepark at Tullynally 60-1
Lughnasa 145
Luton builder 169-72
Lygon, Georgiana (later 2nd Countess of
    Longford) 110
Lyra Pakenham, author's grandchild 195
MacDonald, Ramsay, Prime Minister 161
Madam Butterfly 78-80
magnolia 'Charles Raffill' 57
magnolia 'Star Wars' 60
magnolia addiction 51
Magnolia campbellii alba (Hooker's White
    Goddess) 8, 12, 13, 15, 55, 57-8, 61, 189, 194-5
Magnolia campbellii mollicomata 55, 57
Magnolia cylindrica 60
Magnolia dawsoniana 54
Magnolia delavayi 69

Magnolia kobus 52
Magnolia salicifolia 'Wada's Memory' 58
Magnolia sargentiana 54
Magnolia sargentiana robusta 56
Magnolia sprengeri 'Diva' 54, 57, 60
Magnolia sprengeri 54
Magnolia stellata (Star magnolia) 52
Magnolia Walk at Tullynally 59-61
Magnolia x loebneri 53, 58-9
Magnolia x soulangeana 52
Magnolia x veitchii 60
magnolia, Japanese hybrids 59
magnolia, Mulan (*Magnolia liliiflora*) 51-2
magnolia, Yulan (*Magnolia denudata*) 51-2, 60
magnolias, American species 52
magnolias, Big Five 53-9, 61
magnolias, giant 47, 50
magnolias, New Zealand 60
magnolias, reigning champion 57
Mansfield, Lord 183
maoris, 37
maple glades at Westonbirt 177
Maple Man 152-3
maple syrup 86
Maples from Japan 89
Maples, Kyoto 89
Matilda Winner, author's grandchild 82
Maurus, Fr Rabanus 149-51
May Day trail 153
May King rites 151
Meconopsis baileyi (Bailey's blue poppy) 102, 104
Mediterranean Cypress (*Cupressus sempervirens*)
Meetings with Remarkable Trees 3, 22, 57, 61, 112,
    184
Mekong 53, 66
Menzies, Archibald 33-4, 36
Metasequoia glyptostroboides (Dawn redwood) 83
Miki, Shigeru, Japanese palaeobotanist 83
Millenium Wood 127-32, 144
missionaries, persecution of 78
Mitchell, Alan 108-9, 168, 184, 186, 198
Mo-tao-chi, source of Metasequoia 83
mobile phone left behind 121, 125
Moniack, Inverness 184
Monkey puzzle (*Araucaria araucana*) 31-6, 199
Monkey puzzle, biggest 33

Monterey cypress (*Cupressus macrocarpa*) 197
Montpellier botanic garden 80
Moor Park, Herts. 64
Morrison, Sir Richard at Tullynally 43,
Morrison, Van 170
Mount Auburn Cemetery 81
Mount Congreve, 49-56
Mount Maenam, Sikkim 190-3, 195
Mount Stewart estate, Co. Down 160-2
Mount Stewart, Edith's new Mediterranean
    gardens 161
Mount Stewart, micro-climate for plants 160-1
Mount Tonglu 12
Mount Tonglu, Sikkim/Nepal border 12,
    189-90
Moydrum Castle, Co. Westmeath 181
Much Marcle, Herefordshire 112
Mullingar assizes 138
Mulvey, Martin 23-4
Musee d'Histoire Naturelle, Paris 69
Mutisia spp. 34

Nagasaki 64, 78-9
Namche Barwa 95, 98, 100-1, 103-4
Nangle family murdered 138
Naper family of Loughcrew 113
Naper, Emily 113-114
National Museum, Dublin 133-5
National Trust 160
Nepal 9-10, 13, 192
Ness Gardens 54
New Zealand loggers 37
Newlands Corner, Surrey 114
Nicolson, Harold 32
Noble, David, Australian ranger 84
Normans 105-7
North Oxford garden 43
Norway maple (*Acer platanoides*) 86-8
Norway spruce (*Picea abies*) 45, 118-19, 121
Nothofagus alpina 38
Nothofagus antarctica 38
Nothofagus dombeyi (coihue) 36, 39
Nothofagus obliqua 38
Nothofagus spp. (southern beech) 35
nursery trade 90
Nyima La pass 98-100

O'Flanagan, Liam 171-2
O'hUiginn, Padraig, Secretary of the Dept. of the Taoiseach 172
oak 90-1
oak at Tullynally 129-30
oak dug-outs 132
Oak Man 152-3
oak natural selection 130-2
oak wood, modern 127
oak, common 178
oak, provenance 127-8
oak, red, from North America (*Quercus rubra* etc) 26
oak, sessile 165, 167-9
oaks at Knockeyon 138-41, 143-4
oaks in arboretum 117
oaks, ancient 45
Odysseus (Ulysses) 199-201
Odyssey 199-201
Office of Public Works (government department) 160
Oine, daughter of Sonogi 79-80
Old Masters collected by Holford 178
Owel, Lough 139

Paeonia delavayi 71
Pagoda garden *see* Yunnan at Tullynally
painted maple (*Acer pictum*) 117
Pakenham Hall (*see* Tullynally)
Pakenham, Fred, author's brother 123
Pakenham, George Edward, diarist 19
Pakenham, Sir Francis, ambassador to Chile 39
Pakenham, Kevin, author's brother 125
Pakenham, Michael, author's brother 125
Pakenham, Thomas, 1st Baron Longford 18-21
Pakenham, Valerie, author's wife 8, 26, 73-4, 105, 110, 123, 127, 156, 175, 190, 193-4
pampas 36
Paris 81
Paris Jardin de Plantes 80
parliament, Dublin 21
Patagonia 17, 23, 30-5
Pe 96-9
pear-trees (*Pyrus sp.*) 199-201
peat-bog, wild 119
Pemako 94-7

Père David 53
Père Delavay 53
Perry, Commodore 80
Persian ironwood (*Parrotia persica*) 30
Petigny, Paris gardening enthusiast 81
Philadelphus delavayi 68
photosynthesis 174
Phytophora ramorum, cause of SOD 45
Piers, Sir Henry 139-44
Pierson, Antoine 145-7, 152-3
pilgrimage opposed by Catholic authorities 143
pilgrimage sites 143
pine marten 91
pine, lodgepole (*Pinus contorta*) 24
Pinus armandii 69, 98, 101
Pinus ponderosa (western yellow pine) 34
Piptanthus nepalensis 14
Pisa botanic garden 80
plant explorers, French 69
plant-hunting 66-7, 88
pleasure ground at Tullynally 3, 88, 197-9
Plunkett, Oliver, Archbishop of Armagh 113
podocarps (*Podocarpus totara*) 37
pollards, beech 44
ponymen 100-1
Pope, Alexander 65
prayer flags 191
predecessors, 19th century 3
preservation orders 165-6, 169
Primula capitata 15, 19
Primula secundiflora 71-2
Prince Consort, Albert 9
Pumpkin House at Tullynally 86, 117, 137, 173
purple primula (*Primula poissonii*) 118

Quercus aliena 68
Quercus semecarpifolia (golden oak of Himalayas) 99, 104
Quercus variabilis 68

Rackham, Arthur 33
Radcliffe, Canon Albert 151
Rafferty, Dr, archaeologist 133-4
Raglan, Lady, folklorist 146
Ravangala, Sikkim 190-3
red maple (*Acer rubrum*) 87-8, 174-6

Reilly's Field 128, 129
Remarkable Trees of the World 4
Reynolds, Albert, Taoiseach 172
Rhodes, Cecil 92
Rhododendron falconeri 192-3, 195
Rhododendron hodgsonii 14, 194
Rhododendron niveum 14
Rhododendron ponticum 91
rhododendron sowing 7-8
Rhododendron thomsonii 8, 14, 194
rhododendron, green wall 121-2
rhododendrons, dwarf 100
rhododendrons, peaty soil 188
rhubarb, giant 100
Ribbentrop, German ambassador 161
Riddle of the Tsangpo Gorges 95-6
ringfort 144
ringfort at Reilly's Field 132-3
River Sham (upper pond) at Tullynally 93, 103
Rix, Martyn 70
Roberto, chauffeur 31
Roca, Gen., Argentine dictator 38
Roche, Dick 166
rockies, giant conifers 183
Rodgersia aesculifolia 102
Romanian painter (Mikael) 104
Rongchu valley 98, 101-2
Rosa macrophylla 14, 101, 104
Rosa sericea pterocantha 101
Rosa soulieana 71
Rose Hill, Oxford (Singletree) 1
Ross, Capt. James 9
Rosse, Michael, Earl of 59
Rouen botanic garden 80
Rowan, white berried (*Sorbus arachnoides*) 120
Rushforth, Keith 66-7, 70, 72, 94-102
Russian larch (*Larix potaninii*) 29

Sackville-West, Vita 32, 39
Salix 'Chrysocoma' 72
Salix babylonica 72
Salween 66
Sargent, Prof. Charles 54-5
Sasha Pakenham, author's grandchild 195
Satan 151-152
Schulman, Dr. E., dendrochronologist 111-12, 116

Scone Palace, Perth 185
Scots pine (*Pinus sylvestris*) 25, 91, 106, 112, 116
    120-1, 125
Scramble for Africa, The 3
seed sowing 7-8
sessile oak (*Quercus petraea*) 128
Shangri-La 97, 107
Shannon River 132
Sharawadgi 63-6, 71
shelter belts, 24
sherpas 96-8
Sherwood, Irish 167-9
Shillelagh ancient forest 165, 167-9
Shogunate 78, 80
Sichuan 53-6, 66, 70
Siddons, Mrs 159-60
Siebold, Philipp von 79-80
Sierra Nevada loggers 37
Sikkim 7-14, 55
Sikkim, 2nd expedition 188-95
Sikkim, dense forest 192
Sikkim, earthquake 191
Sikkim, independence 191
Sikkim, Maharajah 192
Sikkim, Rajah 9-14
Sikkim, seeds 194
Sikkimese asters (*Aster sikkimensis*) 13
silver fir (*Abies alba*) 45, 91, 101, 182, 185
silver fir, champion 181
silver maple (*Acer saccharinum*) 87, 174
Silvestri, Fr 55, 60
Singletree, Oxford 1
Sitka spruce (*Picea sitchensis*) 3, 24, 88, 118-19,
    121, 183-4, 187-8
Smoke tree, American (*Cotinus obovatus*) 179
Sonogi, mistress of Siebold 79-8
Soulange-Bodin, Chevalier Etienne 52, 60
Soulié, Père 70-1
South Africa 4
Southwell Chapter House, Notts. 150-1
sowing seeds 103
Spanish yew 106
Spectator 65
Spode china 71
Spoelberch, Adolf de (husband of Ghislaine) 32
Spoelberch, Ghislaine de 31-2

Sprenger, Carl, 55
spruce 90, 120, 182
Squire's Walking Stick (*Quercus robur*) 22, 129-31, 163
squirrel, grey 25, 91, 119
St Paul's School, Darjeeling 11
Stadt House 165
storm, most violent 181
storms 1, 4, 44, 173-4, 197
Strangford Lough 161-2
Streamstown, Nangle house 138
Stuart, James 'Athenian', architect 160
Sudden Oak Death, caused by *Phytophora ramorum* 4, 45-6
sugar maple (*Acer saccharum*) 87
Sunday Telegraph 2
Surrey Wildlife Trust 114-115
swamp cypress (*Taxodium distichum*) 176, 179
Swan River (lower lake) at Tullynally 17, 19, 44, 68, 137
swans 17-18, 45
Swift, Jonathan 6
sycamore, European (*Acer pseudoplatanus*) 68, 85-7, 89-91
Sydney, Australia 84

Talibans 90-2
Tandridge, Surrey 112
Tashi, Nepalese guide 190-3
Taxodium distichum (Swamp cypress) 83
Teesta River 13
Telemachus 199
Temple of the Winds at Mount Stewart 160
Temple, Sir W. 63-5, 71
Tengchong 66
Tennyson, Alfred 116
Tennyson, Hallam 116
Tesco walnuts 29
Thalictrum delavayi 71-2
Theroux, Paul 36
Thunberg, Carl 79
Thuya (*Thuya plicata*) 24
Tianmu Mt. refuge for ginkgos 77
Tibet 192
Tibet 9-14, 28, 53, 92-102
'Tibet' at Tullynally 88, 93, 117

Tibetan bridges 99
Tibetan cowslip (*Primula florindae*) 93-4, 98, 104, 118
Tibetan dragons 104
Tibetan forest 100
Tibetan rats 70-1
Tibetan seeds 102-3
Tibetan shrines 70
Tibetan temple, miniature 104
Tibetan thin air 99
Tiffney, Bruce 76
Tilia x europaea (common lime)
timber dealers 86
Tir na nog at Mount Stewart 162
Tolkien, John 33
Tom Pakenham, author's grandchild 29, 199
Tomnafinogue at Coolattin 166
Topographica Hibernica 106
traders, Dutch 78
traders, Portuguese 78
treasure hunters, illegal 134-5
Tree Register of the British Isles (TROBI) 108-9, 185
tree rings, counting 112, 114, 115-16
Trees and Shrubs (W.J. Bean) 111
trees at Carton 157-8
trees from Europe 162
trees from Himalayas 163
trees from North America 163
Trees of Britain and Northern Europe 184
trees, absence 144
trees, bark colour 68-9, 86
trees, breeding champion 22
trees, champions in Britain and Ireland 183-6
trees, disease 35
trees, long-lived species 111
trees, murdering 30
trees, native 90-1
trees, naturalized 89-92
trees, new diseases 1, 4-5, 43
trees, nurses 22
trees, parkland 2-3
trees, passion for 2-3
trees, planting 3, 21-2
trees, re-planting 160, 162-3
trees, threats to 4

trees, world's tallest 183
Troy 199
Tsangpo cypress (*Cupressus gigantea*) 104
Tsangpo, River 94-6, 100-2
Tulloch, Octavia, garden adviser 8, 181, 186-7, 194
Tullynally (formerly Pakenham Hall) 1-2, 7-8,
    21, 39 57, 82
Tullynally Buddhist shrine 145
Tullynally Gothic pavilion 145
Tullynally Gothic tower 137-8
Tullynally Gothicised 110
Tullynally oaks 144
Tullynally Pumpkin House 145
Tullynally re-planting 162-3
Tullynally restoration 145
Tullynally roof decay 156
Tullynally yews 107-10
turkey oak (*Quercus cerris*) 29
two Sisters, story 139-40

umbrella pine (Pinus pinea) 92
upper pond (River Sham) at Tullynally 83, 176-7
Utrecht botanic garden 80

Vallancey, Major Charles 139
Valparaiso 34
Vancouver, Capt. 33
Vane-Tempest, Francis later 3rd Marchioness of
    Londonderry 160
Versailles 1
Viking silver 134-5
Villa Angustura 36
Vine Man 153-4
vine maple (*Acer circinatum*) 88
Virgin and Child 149-50

walls, repairing 155-6
walnut, common (*Juglans regia*) 91
Walpole, Horace 65
Walsh, Aidan 8, 49, 194
Washington, George 81
wavy grain sycamore 86
Westmeath climate 49, 67, 70
Westmeath oak 129
Westmeath Tsangpo 103
Westminster Hall 165

Westonbirt arboretum 27-8, 89, 177
Westonbirt tree planting 178
Westport oak 129
White Mts, California 112
White, Michael 50, 56
Wicklow ancient trees 165, 167-9
Wicklow County Coucil 166
Wicklow oak 129-30
wild bog cleaned by flames 124
Williams, J.C. 54
Williams, Julian 57-8
Willis, Lord Enniskillen's tenant 109-110
willow pattern plate 71
Wilson-Wright, John 170-1
Wilson, Ernest, plant-hunter 53-6, 198
Wilson, Richard 3
Windsor, Henry VIII's chapel 165
Wisley 57
Wollemi National Park, NSW 84
Wollemia nobilis 84
Wood That Came Back, The 1
woodland garden at Mount Stewart 161-2
woodlands, Philadelphia 81

Yangtse 66, 70
Year of Liberty, The 3
yew, common (*Taxus baccata*) 105-7
yew, counting annual rings 108
yew, Spanish 106
yews 178
yews at Druids Grove, Surrey 115
yews for longbows 106
yews, champion 108
yews, Christian symbol 106
yews, churchyard 106
yews, fantastic shapes at Newlands Corner 115
yews, longevity, 108, 111-17
yews, Loughcrew 113-14
yews, Newlands Corner 114
Yews, poetic at Kingley Vale 116
Yews, poisonous 105
yews, solemn at Druids Grove 115
Yunnan 53-6, 66-72, 92-3
'Yunnan' at Tullynally (Pagoda garden) 66-72,
    88, 93
'Yunnan', design flaws 67-8, 70